The Animal Lover's Guide to Changing the World

Practical Advice and Everyday Actions for a More Sustainable, Humane, and Compassionate Planet

STEPHANIE FELDSTEIN

St. Martin's Griffin ☒ New York

www.stmartins.com

Text stock contains 10% pre-consumer and 10% post-consumer waste recycled fiber.

Library of Congress Cataloging-in-Publication Data

Names: Feldstein, Stephanie.
Title: The animal lover's guide to changing the world : practical
    advice and everyday actions for a more sustainable, humane,
    and compassionate planet / Stephanie Feldstein.
Description: First Edition. | New York : St. Martin's Griffin,
    [2018] | Includes bibliographical references.
Identifiers: LCCN 2017060761| ISBN 9781250153258 (trade pbk.) |
    ISBN 9781250153265 (ebook)
Subjects: LCSH: Animal rights.
Classification: LCC HV4708 .F345 2018 | DDC 179/.3—dc23
LC record available at https://lccn.loc.gov/2017060761

Our books may be purchased in bulk for promotional, educational, or business use. Please contact your local bookseller or the Macmillan Corporate and Premium Sales Department at 1-800-221-7945, extension 5442, or by email at MacmillanSpecialMarkets@macmillan.com.

First Edition: June 2018

10   9   8   7   6   5   4   3   2   1

For Juno, who changed my world

CONTENTS

ACKNOWLEDGMENTS

I'm fortunate to be surrounded by a herd of incredible, supportive animal lovers who made this book possible. This stray idea never would've found a home without my agent, Rachel Ekstrom, who never gave up on the animals. Thanks to Daniela Rapp for adopting it—I knew it was in good hands from the moment I saw the picture of Rika—and to the entire animal-loving pack at St. Martin's Press for nurturing it into the world.

Thanks to Corinne Ball, Mike Stark, and Pulin Modi for helping make this a better book and making me a better advocate for animals over the years. I've learned so much from each of you. Also, thanks to Hannah Connor for your expertise, insight, and excellent taste in YouTube videos. And to Eliot Schrefer for your early encouragement for this book and for writing wonderful animal stories.

Thanks to Bethany Neal for basically being my emotional support animal during the publication process, and Robyn Ford for giving the kind of enthusiastic, unconditional encouragement that only an animal lover can appreciate. And to Karen Simpson for the years of wisdom, sanity, and helping me become a rabbit-real writer (and for being almost as excited as I was when I adopted Moby). To Michelle Hodkin for always answering my texts about animal emergencies (or writing, food, and horror movies) at 3:00 A.M. And to Amy, Deanna, and Lisa for taking such good care of my animals (and me) for so many years.

I'm lucky to have the Three Bares in my life—thank you for always believing in me and always asking about my animals. To Zibby, Scott, Andy, and Liane for keeping things wild and making me who I am today. To my dad for giving me his obsession with his dogs and love for nature documentaries, and my mom, who said that it felt right for me to dedicate this book to my first rescue dog instead of to her.

I'm especially fortunate to work with an incredible group of passionate, creative, and effective organizers, lawyers, scientists, and wildlife advocates at the Center for Biological Diversity. Many of the wild animals mentioned throughout this book are still here because of your dedication to saving them.

And to all the animal lovers who work tirelessly to protect all creatures great and small—thank you for making the world a better, more compassionate place.

INTRODUCTION

It can be a struggle to get out of bed in the morning. Literally. On the most difficult days, I'm pinned in place by the dogs and cats who let me live in this house with them, stiff from sleeping in awkward positions so they could slumber undisturbed. On the best days, there's nothing cozier than snuggling with an adorable, warm bundle of fur and devotion. Eventually, I do get up—these bundles have to eat. Once they're taken care of, I scrounge together my own breakfast and start scrolling social media, where my feeds are full of animal news, animal photos, animal videos, animal gifs, and petitions to save animals.

My morning routine might sound familiar. After all, this is a book for animal lovers, so it's a safe guess that a number of readers share their homes with animals, too. Perhaps you don't have any four-legged bed hogs in your family, but you're not entirely comfortable with the idea of eating animals, or you worry about wildlife being evicted from their homes and not having anywhere safe to sleep at all.

Maybe your love of animals started with your childhood dog or the neighborhood cat who adopted you as an adult. Maybe, not so deep down, you're still the little kid who dreams of horses or who could watch an anthill for hours. Or maybe you haven't really given it much thought, but the video of a wombat riding a tortoise crossed your feed on a day when that was exactly what you needed, and you're just happy that we live in a world with wombats and tortoises so videos like that can exist.

I've loved animals as long as I can remember—even longer, from what I've been told. I still remember when I figured out where the fur in fur coats came from and refused to let anyone in my family leave the house wearing anything too hairy. I was five years old and protested the hall closet until the suspect coats were banished. I remember when I picked up a book about how farmed animals were treated and understood for the first time how much animals suffered to put food on my plate. I was sixteen years old and stopped eating meat, much to the chagrin of my parents, my friends' parents, servers in restaurants, and anyone else faced with helping me figure out what I could make into a meal (veggie burgers weren't as easy to find back then). As I learned what animals went through for our food, clothes, comfort, and entertainment, I realized there was a lot I could do—even as a kid—to make the world a better place for them. And that mattered, because their existence made the world a better place for me, too.

The more I learned about animals as I grew up, the more I adored them. That's still true today. Also true: The more I learn about the ways animals are in trouble, the more I want to protect them. I know I'm not alone in this. If you've ever shared the latest kitten video, tried to convince your friends to choose beans instead of beef, attended a protest, or even just looked at your dog and wondered what you could do to make her life happier and safer, this guide is for you.

Animal lovers come in all shapes, sizes, and personalities. You may worship your dog, but you can't imagine life without bacon. Or you may feel compelled to speak out, but not if it means fake blood or naked protests. That's okay. Humans are constantly interacting with animals, whether we're aware of it or not, from the eighty million or so households with companion animals[1] to the wildlife who live outside our doorsteps to the decisions we make every time we sit down to eat. There's no shortage of ways to help them, and they need us to help in any way we can.

There's No Us Versus Them

All kids have that moment in life when they learn for the first time that humans are mammals, just like their Labrador retriever or guinea pig, or their favorite stuffed lion. For many kids, this bit of knowledge is mindblowing. Because by the time we learn this, we've been functional humans for a while—getting food at the grocery store, using electronics, and putting our shoes on the right feet before we tie them. Human society has come a long way in severing our connection with other animals. And that's a huge problem.

Not only do animals make our lives richer in countless ways, but the way we treat animals—and the environment that animals (including humans) rely on—comes back to bite us. I don't mean karmic retribution, though I wouldn't discount the possibility. I mean that our actions boomerang at us in very direct ways. When we pump greenhouse gases into the atmosphere, polar bears aren't the only ones seeing their homes and food disappear—climate change has already forced human communities to move and is changing the face of agriculture. When we destroy habitat, we destroy the natural systems that filter water, create oxygen, provide food, and give us medicines derived from plants, like quinine, morphine, codeine, and anti-cancer drugs. When we subject animals to cruelty, we begin to accept being cruel to each other.

Most importantly, we'd never want to replace the happiness of someone we love with suffering. There's no question that animals experience both pain and pleasure. Maybe it's not exactly the way humans do, but different species naturally have different ways they prefer to live their lives. Rolling around on dead things isn't my cup of tea, but the joy it gives my dog is undeniable. Other animals deserve to live their lives with as much pleasure and as little pain as we strive for in our own.

There is one very significant way that we're different from other animals: We've caused more devastation to the planet and other species, wild and domestic, than any other animal in history. We're also more capable than most other species of helping other animals live happily ever after, whether it's stopping animal abuse or simply getting out of the way.

We created this mess, and it's up to us to clean it up for their sake and ours.

Technology: A Love Story

It's inevitable that animals and technology—two of the most ubiquitous things in our lives—regularly cross paths. That intersection is not inherently good or bad; even when it comes to animals, it's how we use technology that matters. Sometimes amazing things happen. Microchips have reunited dogs and cats with their families after many years and hundreds of miles traveled. 3-D printed prosthetic legs, joints, beaks, and turtle shells are giving injured animals a second chance. Drones are being used to monitor imperiled species and expose cruel mistreatment of animals. Scientists are creating hamburgers—both plant-based and meat-based—that don't require a butcher.

But sometimes terrible things happen. Technological advances have allowed us to destroy previously untouchable wildlife habitat in our search for fossil fuels and other nonrenewable resources. Broiler chickens (the ones who become nuggets, breasts, and wings) are now growing three hundred times faster than they did fifty years ago to get them to slaughter as quickly as possible, and as a result, their organs and legs can't keep up with the weight gain.[2] The internet has opened up new markets that make it harder to stop the abusive pet trade. People can now hunt and kill animals confined on game ranches with a few clicks from the comfort of their living room.

Technology has not only changed the way we interact with animals, it's also revolutionized the ways in which we can speak up for them. Animal lovers no longer have to rely on phone trees, snail mail, door-to-door canvassing, and community events scheduled far in advance to connect with each other or with decision-makers. Old-school communication still plays an important role in advocacy, but we can respond a lot faster and reach much farther than we could have imagined before the internet and smartphones took over. Thanks to Google, social media, and twenty-four-hour news networks, it no longer takes stumbling across the right book at a used book sale to get a glimpse into how animals are treated in food production or waiting for the next ASPCA mailing to learn about puppy mills or dogfighting. Local stories of animal abuse no longer stay local. Graphic images of cruelty show up in news feeds alongside family photos and articles on politics. Unrestricted access to information like this is both empowering and overwhelming. But here's the good news: Our ability to protest abuse, stop animal cruelty, and create a more compassionate world is also unrestricted.

"Clicktivism" has gotten a bad rap and is all too often used disparagingly and unfairly to describe people who are perceived to limit their activism to signing online petitions or sharing status updates. Clicktivism really refers, more broadly, to using the internet or social media to advance a cause. The internet can't replace offline action any more than it can fully replace your IRL (in real life) relationships, but just as social media has become a big part of staying in touch, deepening friendships, and finding new friends, online activism plays a big role in creating real-world change. Technology has become a core part of how we communicate, and it should be a part of how we advocate for the causes we care about.

Videos allow people to connect with animals they'll never meet in person, to hear the stories of other animal lovers, and get information in visually engaging, shareable clips. Email, texts, communication apps, and social media boost the organization of meetings, protests, briefings, and other events. And not only can online petitions be effective in drawing attention to a problem and influencing decision-makers, but the fact that all this technology has made it easier for animal lovers to learn more about issues they might not otherwise know about and engage in campaigns to protect animals is a beautiful thing.

If sharing videos and news or signing petitions is all someone has the time, energy, or knowledge to do, they don't deserve criticism. They deserve a warm welcome, support for the actions they've taken, and friendly encouragement to keep going. You never know when clicking "like" might be the beginning of a life-changing relationship with animals.

The Myth of Perfection

When it comes to helping animals, there are few sayings as apt as this one: Don't let the perfect be the enemy of the good. Every animal-friendly step you take is a step toward saving lives. So put away that halo-shining kit and get out your work gloves. Because when you spend time beating yourself up for every imperfection—or worse, criticizing others for not doing enough—that's time that could've been spent helping people newer to the cause get more involved or making your voice heard to protect animals. Expecting perfection from yourself is a recipe for failure, and expecting it from others is far more likely to alienate than inspire. After all, we're only human.

An even bigger barrier to perfection than our flawed humanity is that we're all entrenched in a system that's designed to use and abuse other species. Even when we know better, it's nearly impossible to function in society without causing any distress to any animal somewhere along the way. Even if you don't eat animal products, you're probably cooking your veggies in a house powered by fossil fuels. Even if you have solar panels on your home, you're probably taking medication that was tested on animals. I could go on for pages about all the ways animal mistreatment is built into our society in virtually unavoidable ways, thus making this the most depressing book you'll read this year. But that's not the point of this guide.

There are all kinds of ways that you can buck the system by making changes to how you live your life and demanding changes to how things are run around here—and that's what you'll find in these pages. The worst thing that can happen for animals is for us to stop paying attention or to give up trying to live a more compassionate life because we don't know where to start or the scale of animal suffering becomes too much.

What you do matters. And your actions are part of changing the system. Don't let every small setback distract you from the work that needs to be done to create a more animal-friendly world. If you're feeling angry or disheartened or just generally having a rough day, play with your cat or take your dog for a walk. It'll make his day better, and you can get back into action tomorrow.

Changing the World, One Chapter at a Time

There are three key ways that your everyday actions can change the world for animals:

1. **Building momentum.** Every day, you make choices that influence how animals are treated in the world. With each one, you get to decide whether you want to be part of the movement that will change the system of cruelty or keep the status quo.

2. **Inspiring others.** When you decide to live more compassionately, people notice. They notice your adorable, unique shelter dog. They notice that the vegetarian option at the banquet looks better than whatever they're eating. They notice that you're passion-

ate enough and brave enough to speak up when you see cruelty and injustice. And noticing has a way of empowering people to follow your lead and be bolder about the things they care about, too.

3. **Being the change.** Your actions are powerful, not only in aligning your lifestyle with your values as an animal lover, but in leading by example. Nothing convinces people that change is possible like seeing someone who has already done it.

What you choose to snack on during late-night binge-watching sessions or which shampoo you buy may not seem like revolutionary acts, but they're part of the countless decisions we make in the course of our day-to-day lives that affect animals. By becoming more conscientious about our choices, we can start making those decisions count toward a better world for them—and us.

Fair warning: There are some inconvenient and uncomfortable truths ahead. It's easier to look away, hide under a blanket, and not change a thing about ourselves or the world. But the animals need us to care enough to face how the world treats them so we know how to make things better. They need our courage and our actions. Some of those actions may even be easier than you think.

From personal choices, such as shifting what you eat or where you get your next dog to changing local laws and influencing the market, this book will guide you through dozens of actions you can take to help animals, starting wherever you are and using tools you already have. Part 1 will discuss the big picture of how animals fit into the human world and how to use your political, economic, and social power to create a more animal-friendly society. Part 2 is all about how we fit into their world, with an in-depth look at the ways human activity affects wildlife and how we can become better at sharing nature's limited resources. In part 3, things get personal with the individual choices we make in our homes and communities that directly impact animals. And in the final chapter, I'll share tips on how to avoid burnout, because the animals need you in this for the long haul. If we're going to change the world, we need to take care of ourselves and each other. The action continues in the appendix with detailed resources for each chapter, including apps, product recommendations, links, and nonprofit organizations working on the animal issues you care about most.

You choose where you want to start. All I ask is that you start somewhere. Let's go save some animals.

Get Political

Some people talk to animals. Not many
listen though. That's the problem.

—A. A. MILNE, *Winnie-the-Pooh*

The Animals Need You   1

Pigs are some of the smartest animals out there. They've figured out how to use mirrors—not in a Miss Piggy checking-out-her-hair kind of way, but to check out their surroundings (which already makes them smarter than the majority of horror film victims). Pigs can figure out who knows where the good food is and trail them to the stash. The pigs who know where the stash is will try to lose their followers to keep it for themselves. They can complete puzzles, learn tricks, and play video games.[1] The point isn't that you should invite a pig over for the next big Xbox release, but we should recognize that they're a whole lot more than future ham sandwiches. Yet despite their intelligence and empathy (and their political leadership in Animal Farm), pigs can't form a union to protest abusive factory farm conditions. If we value pigs at least a fraction of how much Miss Piggy values herself, we need to be their voice.

It's not just pigs in this position. Birds can use tools, but they can't testify at city council meetings when their nesting grounds are threatened by a new strip mall. Bottlenose dolphins have been observed following recipe-like meal prep prior to eating cuttlefish,[2] but they can't lobby to end the use of fishing gear that threatens them with deadly entanglement. Your dog may be part of the family, but he doesn't get a vote on Election Day if his favorite park or even his right to exist in your town is under attack by local officials. The animals need you to speak up for them and to live your life with them in mind.

Change happens in a number of ways. Laws and policies can directly influence how animals are treated, such as factory farm regulations that require minimum standards of care, or they can indirectly provide incentives or disincentives that influence animals' lives, such as reduced license fees for spayed or neutered dogs or fines for pollution that puts wildlife at risk. The political system plays a huge role in creating change—both good and bad. A single policy that's passed or overturned can have sweeping consequences. Learning how to use your voice to defend and protect animals at the local, state, and national level can change the world.

But these policies aren't created in a vacuum. Not only do elected representatives have to listen to their constituents, but they spend a lot of time gauging which way the wind is blowing to try to anticipate what will make them popular with voters and donors. (In other words, what will keep them in office when the next election rolls around.) Shifting cultural expectations and demands to reflect our love for animals and pressuring companies to be more humane can generate hurricane-level winds that can uproot animal suffering in our day-to-day lives, our communities, and the market, forcing politicians to pay attention to the issues you care about while making the world a better place in the process. Each time you choose to act on behalf of animals, you're helping create that storm.

The Chicken and the Egg

Consider the egg and the chickens who lay them: Two decades ago, no one was talking about cage-free eggs. But today, there's widespread concern about hens' living conditions after dedicated animal lovers and activists spent years exposing how much egg-laying hens suffer crammed in battery cages in dark, dirty warehouses, unable even to spread their wings. iPads have more personal space than your average commercial egg-laying hen. Maybe some people were just grossed out by their eggs coming from a place like that and worried about the safety of their scrambles. But a lot of people recognized chickens as living, feeling creatures and decided no omelet was worth that much misery. Even as awareness grew, egg producers were sure people would ultimately want to stick with the cheapest option. Ultimately, they were wrong.

Thanks to the cultural shift driven by education campaigns, outcry against these practices, pressure from animal protection groups, and rising demand for eggs from humanely raised chickens (i.e., regular people going into stores and happily paying a few cents more per egg), corporate giants from Costco to McDonald's have made commitments to shift their supplies to cage-free eggs, and several states, such as California, Massachusetts, Michigan, and Washington, passed laws to ban the use of battery cages.

Cage-free facilities aren't perfect, but they're a flap in the right direction. The demand for better, more humane conditions for farm animals has had a ripple effect. Companies are not only making cage-free commitments, they're also reporting on the steps they're taking to source more humanely across their supply chain, because they know people care about animals. Restaurants and food service providers are expanding animal-free options on their menus. There's been a rise of egg-free alternatives and vegan bakeries. People across the country are raising and spoiling backyard chickens, so if they do eat eggs, they know the names of the hens who laid them and exactly how they were treated.

Public outcry, behind-the-scenes efforts from animal protection groups, and individual actions and choices all work together to change the outlook for animals.

Every [Insert-Motivational-Cliché-Here] Makes a Difference

From laws that turn a blind eye to animal suffering to the challenge of finding cruelty-free products at your local store, our impact on animals is woven into the fabric of society's customs, markets, and legal system. The odds are stacked against the animals, and unfortunately, that's not going to change overnight. That can feel pretty daunting when you're trying to change the world, but every person's actions matter. Every thread of cruelty that's tugged apart helps weaken the tapestry so we can patch it with a more compassionate design. Every avalanche is made of individual snowflakes. Tiny drops of water band together to make tsunamis. Whichever metaphor you prefer, there's an underlying truth to it.

If you and everyone you know, and everyone they know, adopt their next pet, your local shelter would have a lot more empty kennels. If you and everyone you know, and everyone they know, cut down their meat and dairy consumption, the industry would be forced to decrease production, saving millions of farmed animals and wild animals harmed in the process of producing animal products. If you and everyone you know, and everyone they know, demanded cruelty-free cosmetics, eye shadow tested on animals would be relegated to listicles of bizarre old beauty routines, like using arsenic and cocaine in skin and hair treatments.

You get the idea. Change has to ignite somewhere, and you can be the spark.

How to Know You're Helping

If you rescue a starving cat from the streets, you know you've made a difference in that cat's life. Maybe you even feel like you've helped the fight against animal cruelty and pet homelessness. (Spoiler alert: You have.) If you and all your friends use social media and Yelp reviews to convince your favorite restaurant to offer more veggie options, you can see the results when those tasty, cruelty-free dishes show up on the menu. If you ask your city council to pass an ordinance against breed discrimination or stop lethal wildlife trapping, you know when you've scored a victory. But what about all the animal-friendly things you do where you don't actually see the animals you're saving or how you're having an impact?

Sometimes doing the right thing takes a leap of faith. When you make animal-friendly choices, you have to believe that somewhere out there is a chicken flapping her wings or a pig digging into his cache of food or a wolf pack safely raising their pups thanks to your actions. You won't get a thank-you bouquet from the animals. Even when you know you're doing the right thing, sometimes you still need a little reassurance. Something to show for your efforts. It's hard to keep going on faith alone. Luckily, you don't have to.

Let's begin with the first level of action: changes in your own life. Start keeping track of what you're doing differently. If you're changing your diet, write down what you're eating and how many meals, days, or weeks you've gone meat-free. Vegetarian calculator apps and websites can tell you how many farmed animals you've saved with each week that you've chosen the veggie options. Some sites will tell you how you've shrunken your environmental footprint so you can get a sense of how you're also helping wild animals threatened by meat and dairy production. If you're changing your shopping habits to avoid plastic or products tested on animals, keep track of what the Old You would've bought and what the New You did instead. If you volunteer to walk dogs at your local shelter or join a stream cleanup day, mark the occasion. If you're signing petitions, writing letters to the editor, calling your representatives, or making donations to an animal charity, keep track of it.

Make note of your new favorite cruelty-free products, animal activism apps, and plant-based recipes. Start a Changing the World journal, put a cute little turtle sticker in your calendar, give yourself a gold star, jot it on a scrap of colorful paper to put in a jar, add pictures of the animals your actions helped to your photo journal app. However you do it and wherever you start, mark the changes you're making and what's helped you along the way. At the end of each month, you can see the progress you've made. Whether you have one entry or thirty entries, that's one or thirty more actions for animals than you used to take and one or thirty more steps building toward change. Not only can this inspire you to keep going—and to go further—but it can also be handy in showing your friends what change can look like in their lives.

Which brings us to the next level of action: getting others involved. It's tempting to think, *If only people knew how horrible things were, they'd do things differently.* Sadly, most people don't work that way. Humans have an incredible capacity for compartmentalizing, so simply "raising awareness" about animal suffering doesn't necessarily make a difference unless you pair it with opportunities for action. Let your friends know what you're doing to change the world and ask them to give it a shot, too. When you see people around you taking up the causes that matter to you because you've asked them to get involved or shown them the way, you're helping build the movement. When you write a letter to the editor, it might not get published, but someone read it. And that someone is now aware that people in the community care about animal issues, and you might just start to see more animal-related coverage in the news. When you go out with your friends and order an animal-friendly meal, it may start a conversation about why you've chosen to change the way you eat and how it makes you feel. After a while, you might notice a few more people flipping to the veggie section of the menu. If you share articles and opportunities to take action on social media, you may start to notice your friends sharing more animal news and campaigns, too.

Last, but not least: how to know you're changing the system. When it comes to having a larger impact, it can take years for your efforts to bear fruit. But even before the moment when you know Things Have Changed—whether that's a new animal protection law or a shift in market trends—there are a few key ways that you can make sure you're being an effective voice for animals. First, always aim for meaningful change that will make it easier or, even better, inevitable for others to make the animal-friendly choice. For example, you can try to convince people to stop buying bottled water by educating them about the perils of plastic bottles for wildlife. But you'll get rid of a lot more plastic bottles if the places that sell bottled water start selling reusable bottles instead and have accessible water fountains so that becomes the easier (not to mention cheaper) option.

Your personal actions, your calls to action, and your demands for action from decision-makers are all important parts of creating change, even if you don't get the instant gratification type of results. Pay attention to the conversations and trends happening around you in your circle of friends and in your community. You can help normalize animal-friendly living, creating the space for companies and policy-makers to make positive changes. Person by person, week by week, you'll start to see a ripple effect if you watch for it. As larger change takes place in your community, look back at your journal or your jar or your sticker collection and know that you helped make it happen.

Start Now

We all start somewhere. Every vegetarian or vegan (except those raised as veggie babies) ate meat or dairy once upon a time, and many struggled with giving up burgers or bacon or cheese until the day that they did. SeaWorld was once a popular attraction until word got out, most recently thanks to the documentary *Blackfish*, about how miserable the orcas were in their tiny tanks, performing tricks for treats. Animal lovers who used to go to SeaWorld for the thrill of seeing marine mammals up close stopped buying tickets. Most of us have taken medication and received vaccines that were developed through animal testing—and we have no choice but to continue to do so if we want to remain healthy enough to keep helping animals and working toward changing animal testing laws.

I've been obsessed with animals since infancy, yet this entire book is a diary of mistakes I've made, things I've learned, and ongoing struggles to keep doing better. I grapple with the knowledge that I've inadvertently contributed to animal suffering over the years. I know I'm not alone in this. But if we're going to change the world for animals, we need to accept that there are things we can't control so we can focus on the things that we can. Whatever you did in the past is in the past. The animals don't need our guilt—they need our action.

Comment and Share

Don't be shy about sharing the actions you're taking or the ways you're changing your life. The internet loves photos of food, so show off your meat-free meals. Let people know what animal organizations you support or the latest cool action you found to help save endangered species. And everyone definitely wants to see pics of the kittens you're fostering or the dog you just adopted. Show people how easy—and adorable—it is to make the world a better place for animals. And never be embarrassed about how much you care about animals and how they're treated.

Always remember that you're the animals' voice. Write letters, sign petitions, comment on social media pages, make calls, make art . . . whatever it is that you can do to speak up for animals, do it.

Don't forget to celebrate good news and victories, and share them with your networks. Success is a great way to motivate people to get or stay involved. Also, show your support for people trying to do the right thing, including you—don't be hard on yourself or others for not being able to do everything at once.

Start living your animal-loving values today, as best you can, and pledge to keep doing better tomorrow and the next day and the day after that. Promise yourself and the animals that you'll keep fighting for a more humane world. Starting now, decide what kind of life you want to live. You won't be perfect. It won't always be pretty. But you'll be doing something, and that's how change begins.

! Action Alert

THREE THINGS YOU CAN DO TODAY

1 • Choose your first animal-saving project and decide what steps you'll take this week to be the change.

2 • Start tracking your activism and adding up your actions so you can see the difference you've made by the end of the month.

3 • Embrace patience. Changing the world takes time.

 ANIMALS YOU'LL HELP SAVE
Take your pick—who will you take action for?

Animal Advocacy 101

Octopuses have been documented snatching up coconut shells and hoarding them to use later on as shelter. If they manage to get ahold of two halves, they'll reassemble them into a closed hideaway.[1] In captivity, they have a reputation for thwarting researchers and causing mischief. Otto the octopus in Germany's Sea Star Aquarium figured out how to short-circuit the aquarium's electrical system by shooting water at a spotlight over his tank.[2] Others decide they've had enough of tank life, like Inky the octopus, who made his famous escape from New Zealand's National Aquarium by slipping out of his tank under the cover of night and squeezing through a pipe back to the ocean.[3] It's hard to know exactly what these crafty cephalopods are thinking, but they seem to have a clear goal, the ability to envision a series of actions to achieve it, and a lot of patience. We should all strive to be like octopuses—when we see a problem in the world around us, we need to create a plan and put that plan into action.

Some days, scrolling through your newsfeed can be an exercise in anger management. Between the stories of people doing unthinkable acts of cruelty to innocent animals and reports of wildlife pushed to the edge of extinction by poachers or pollution, it can feel like dark times for someone who cares about animals. (The news isn't exactly sunshine and rainbows if you care about people, too; many of the tools and tactics in this chapter can be applied to help our own species.) On the brighter side, there's a lot we can do to take action in our own lives and demand that policy-makers, corporations, and other influencers do their part to help animals.

We can't change the world through lifestyle changes alone. There are society-wide problems that are bigger than any choices you or I can make at the dinner table, the store, the office, our homes, classrooms, the yoga studio, the local sports bar, or wherever we hang out. With a few basic tools, every animal lover can spot opportunities to take on those bigger problems and craft effective animal-saving campaigns, whether you're trying to influence the local bodega or your governor, and whether you're doing it from the comfort of your couch or out in the streets.

You may not have the time to start and run your own campaign right now. The idea of protesting, speaking in front of your city council, or even putting your name at the top of an online petition may cause you to break out into hives. There are many reasons why leading campaigns can feel uncomfortable or intimidating. That's completely understandable. Even if you're not ready to take the lead, there are lots of important things you can do for animals, including joining campaigns started by others. And if you do decide to jump into your own campaign or hold a protest, this chapter will be here for you when you need it.

Turning Anger into Action

The first step to creating a campaign to help animals is to know what you're campaigning about. In other words: What is the specific thing that you want to change in the world? That may seem obvious, but in this era of fake news, we need to be extra careful about knee-jerk reactions to partial information that we may pick up via screenshots and hashtags. Social media has made it all too easy for anyone, including people in power, to post half-truths and even outright fabrications posing as fact.

Read between the headlines, check your sources, and try to get the full story before getting up in arms. And always check the date—shocking animal stories have a tendency to resurface online every few years. Nothing destroys your credibility faster with a decision-maker than attacking them for something they didn't actually do or that was resolved years ago. If you go after Big Jim's Puppy Emporium (a fictional example of a typical real-life, puppy-peddling pet store) based on rumors that they sell puppies to research labs and that turns out to have no basis in reality, it's going to be a lot harder to get Jim to listen to your reasonable request to switch from puppy mill sales to adoption events.

Here's one more reminder from Captain Obvious: In order to create a campaign, you need to choose a place to start. You may feel the urge to solve all the things, but it's going to be a challenge to do that effectively if you try to do them all at once. You can take action on every issue that comes across your feed—sign petitions, make calls, write letters, and change your own behavior. But if you're going to create a campaign from scratch and see it through, it's going to need special attention. It doesn't take too long to create an online petition against Big Jim's Puppy Emporium. However, if you also decide to lobby for Meatless Mondays at your high school and rally to stop wildlife poisoning in your city and kick off a letter-writing campaign to get your favorite moisturizer to stop testing on animals and educate your neighbors on why they should urge your utility company to support wildlife-friendly renewable energy, and then tomorrow you start another dozen projects, you'll have a lot of balls in the air and no time to keep juggling.

Every one of these causes deserves to get the attention it needs to succeed. If you have to choose between being strategic or being prolific, always go the strategic route.

Five Things You Need to Know Before You Launch Your Campaign

1 · What problem do you want to solve? The first thing to identify in any campaign is what you want to change. Be as specific as possible. It's hard to build a campaign around solving huge, multifaceted problems like ending all animal cruelty. That may be the ultimate goal, but you need to break it into bite-sized pieces so you can achieve the smaller-but-important victories that build momentum along the way. If, for example, you narrow your focus to ending puppy mill cruelty, you can map out the steps that will make it harder for puppy mills to keep doing business as usual, like getting Big Jim's Puppy Emporium to stop selling their puppies.

2 · What's the solution? Once you know the problem, identify what it would take to solve it. There are usually several possible answers, so it's helpful to think about where you can have the most influence. As an individual building a campaign from scratch, you're likely to be more successful in changing a local ordinance than an international treaty. But at the same time, think about what's really needed to create positive change for animals. If you only ask Big Jim to put signs up about where his puppies came from, he'll happily slap up claims that they're "family-raised in Pennsylvania" (a common code for puppy mill) and everyone in the commercial puppy industry keeps on raking in the cash. However, if you can get Big Jim to stop selling puppies and support rescue group adoption days instead, it would take a bite out of puppy mill profits, making the whole operation less lucrative (with the added bonus of helping homeless animals).

Not sure what's the best way to solve the problem? You don't earn any bonus points for figuring everything out by yourself—talk to other activists and organizations who have been working on these issues for a while to get ideas and feedback on your campaign.

3 • **Who are the decision-makers who can make it happen?** It may be tempting to go straight to the top, but the president of the United States is not going to intervene in Big Jim's business. You need to approach the people who can actually make the decision you're asking for. In this case, Big Jim himself is your primary target since he's in charge of the business. But Jim doesn't make his decisions in a bubble. Think about who else has influence over him. If the Puppy Emporium is in a mall, the management company can change their policy to stop allowing pet sales, forcing Jim to stop stocking puppies or find a new location (and if he does move, your campaign can follow him to his new spot). You can ask the places where Jim advertises his business to stop accepting unethical ads. You can talk to your city council about passing an ordinance to ban pet sales as cities from Chicago to Los Angeles have done.

4 • **Who else cares about it?** Your campaign is going to need support from others. Big Jim has to see that he's got more than a lone disgruntled customer on his hands. Think about who has been affected by the Puppy Emporium and who is likely to support ending puppy mill sales. There are people in the community who have bought sick dogs from Big Jim and veterinarians who have treated them. There are rescuers who have taken in former puppy mill dogs and dog lovers who simply want to stop cruelty.

You may be able to get animal-loving business owners and city council members on board who share your goal of building a more compassionate community. Once you've launched your campaign, don't be shy about it. Ask your friends to join your online and offline actions. Post about it on social media. Talk to people who have a similar interest. Hand out flyers at the dog park. Keep in touch with your fellow puppy mill protestors through email, Facebook groups, meetups, or whatever mode of communication works for you to update them on any developments and engage them in each step of your campaign.

5 · **How will you convince the decision-makers?** There's no one-size-fits-all set of tactics for a successful campaign. If Big Jim's Puppy Emporium does most of its sales online, holding a protest outside of a warehouse with no foot traffic probably won't have much of an effect, but posting negative reviews and pressuring websites to refuse his advertisements could get his attention. If Big Jim isn't on social media, you'll need to plan more offline actions. But before you launch your campaign, try approaching the main decision-maker to give him a chance to respond before you go public. If Big Jim refuses to talk to you or turns down your request, have a campaign plan ready with a series of steps that continue to increase pressure. You can't count on Jim to stumble upon a petition or blog post or to change his ways if he only hears about it once or twice. Make sure he knows about your campaign and that you're not going away.

An online petition can be a useful way to think through your campaign and recruit people to the cause, but it often won't get results without additional action. Deliver your petition signatures in person. If Jim won't meet with you, show up with a protest. Coordinate other dog lovers to flood his in-box and phone line. Talk to Big Jim's neighboring businesses—they may be willing to talk to him business owner to business owner to avoid a protest in front of their stores. Call the local media. Whether your online petition is gaining steam or you've gathered letters of support from community leaders or heartfelt crayon drawings from your kid's kindergarten class, Jim needs to see that your campaign keeps getting bigger and louder. And be ready to get big and loud.

The idea is to keep escalating pressure until your target can no longer ignore you. Campaigns take creativity and patience, but it's a small price for changing the world.

Protesting from Your Couch

An effective campaign will meet people where they are—and a lot of people are online. We're more connected than ever before. Email and social media make it easy to reach a large audience very quickly, engage new supporters, and contact decision-makers. And a lot can be done without ever leaving your house. Post updates in your pajamas. Make calls from your couch. Create digital media from your dining room.

It's so easy to post things online that sometimes it's too easy for our own good. Grammar still counts. Whether you're starting a petition, creating protest signs, writing letters, or preparing notes to speak at a community meeting, reread what you've written. Ask a friend to review it for typos and to see if your message is as straightforward to others as it was inside your head. It's worth investing the time to craft clear, compelling language. Specificity helps: "Stop supporting puppy mill cruelty" will likely be more effective than "Stop being mean to puppies." And if you want to be taken seriously, especially when approaching decision-makers and recruiting people to your cause who aren't already on your side, represent your campaign professionally and respectfully in all your communications. You don't need to be a polished public relations pro, but the wrong tone, a misspelled word, or misplaced apostrophe can kill a meme and won't do your campaign any favors.

When writing an online petition, succinctly explain what the problem is, why it matters, what the solution is, and how the petition will help the cause to entice people to sign on. If you're creating memes, posters, or ads, spend a little extra time to come up with smart messages and catchy one-liners. It can take more brainpower to choose the five perfect words arranged in the perfect order for a meme than to write a whole blog post. But the right graphic or the right mix of informative and provocative in your petition headline can launch your campaign far beyond your circle of friends. Just make sure you don't get so creative that people have no idea what you're trying to say. (Again, this is where running your materials by a friend can come in handy.)

Think about all the ways that you use the internet and how those can help ramp up public pressure on your target. In addition to sending emails and sharing online petitions, Big Jim's Puppy Emporium probably has a Facebook page, a Twitter account, and an Instagram profile. Create social media protests with you and everyone you can recruit posting on Big Jim's page, leaving comments about your campaign, and tweeting at him. Leave negative reviews on Yelp and similar sites. Urge websites where the Puppy Emporium advertises to refuse their business. Buy your own ads promoting adoption on the same sites where the emporium is trying to reach customers.

Protesting in the Streets

Demonstrations have played a key role in the decline of animal circuses, fur sales, and puppy mill retailers. Showing up in person is a powerful tool, especially when your other campaign efforts have stalled, such as if Big Jim at the Puppy Emporium has stopped answering your emails and calls, has turned off comments on his Facebook page, and is blowing off your petition. Protests can also come in handy when there's an event, political decision, or other development that you want to speak out against, even if you haven't been actively planning a bigger campaign around the issue. An animal circus or rodeo coming to town has often provided a good excuse for animal lovers to get a crowd together with signs outside the arena or fairgrounds to make ticket buyers think twice about their afternoon plans.

There are several things to know ahead of time to plan a successful protest:

- **Know where you're going.** Is there a nice, wide public sidewalk? Will your protest be visible to your target and to passersby? (Pro Tip: Protesting in a dark alley isn't likely to be very effective. Also, getting busted for trespassing can put a real damper on your event.)

- **Know your agenda.** You can't predict everything, but you can set the tone for your event. Will there be speakers? If so, what will each of your speakers talk about, for how long, and how will you make sure people can hear them? Will you be handing out literature on animal abuse or just getting attention through signs? Are you marching, rallying, or planning a quiet-but-visual protest? Think through the details of how your event can turn heads. Do you want to use banners, street puppets, or other art to get attention? Should everyone wear the same color or have T-shirts or buttons with your message on it?

- **Know your message.** Spread the word ahead of time to get your fellow protestors on the same page about your tone and demands. If people show up to your peaceful demonstration with antagonistic signs or bring signs against animal testing to your puppy mill protest, it can be awkward at best and damaging to your cause at worst. Also, make sure you have designated spokespeople prepared to talk to your target if he or she comes out to respond to your demonstration, and people to talk to the media (though sometimes the media will mingle through the crowd, making it extra important that everyone knows why they're there).

- **Know your expected outcome.** Are you hoping to influence potential customers or ticket-buyers? Are you hoping to push Big Jim into meeting with you? Are you hoping to get media coverage? Thinking this through can change the tone of your signs and any other art or literature you bring with you, as well as how you promote the event.

- **Know who you expect to be there.** If you're the only one who shows up to your protest, that can be worse than not showing up at all. Big Jim will use it as a sign that the rest of the community is okay with the Puppy Emporium. Bring your family and friends. Call in favors. Create a Facebook event. Partner with other activists (and if they support your cause, it's important to show up for them, too). Hold a sign-making party ahead of time for people to get to know one another or have a Power Planning Potluck to bring everyone in on the master plan, get new ideas, answer questions for first-time protestors, and build relationships with other animal lovers in your community.

- **Know what you need.** If you need a permit for where you plan to protest, find out what you have to do to secure it ASAP. If you need megaphones or other sound amplification for speakers or chants, get it ahead of time. If you're planning on leading chants, someone has to write them. If you want people to have talking points or flyers or other literature, someone has to create and print them. And don't forget basic logistics: If you're going to be marching or standing outside for a few hours on a hot day, bring water, hats, and extra sunscreen. Throw a few granola bars in your bag in case anyone is hit with low blood sugar mid-protest. Take care of each other out there.

It's important to know the regulations and rights of protesting in your community. Sidewalks are generally fair game for protesting as long as you don't block pedestrian traffic or building entrances. You can usually pass out literature, but if you're setting up a table, plan to use amplified sound, or expect a large crowd, look into getting a permit. Same goes for protesting in the streets—you'll need a permit if you want to shut down a street for a march or rally, or set up a stage with microphones and a sound system. If you're protesting in a park, size matters—find out how many people are allowed to protest in the park you've picked out before a permit is required. You can also protest in government spaces as long as you're not interfering with business. You can hold a rally on courthouse steps, but not in the middle of a courtroom; you can have small signs or T-shirts and buttons expressing your opinion at a city council meeting, but you may get stopped at the door if you have a giant poster or banner that will block others in the room from seeing what's going on.

In any of these scenarios, if a permit is required, it's a good idea to get one to avoid having your protest shut down before it's even begun. Some people believe permits shouldn't be necessary, because the First Amendment guarantees freedom of assembly, but if local laws require a permit, demonstrating without one comes with risks. Whether you choose to permit or not to permit, know what you're getting yourself—and your supporters—into. Similarly, obey traffic signals and other laws, and stay on sidewalks.

As long as you're not breaking any laws and you're in a public space, you have the right to record what's going on, even if Big Jim comes outside to yell at you or calls the police. If you're unsure about your rights, if you're told you aren't allowed to be in the public spaces you've chosen, or if you want to know more about civil disobedience, the American Civil Liberties Union is a great resource for all things protest, before and after the fact.

Comment and Share

Change doesn't always require a big, public protest or viral campaign—old-fashioned outreach through talking with church groups, social clubs, and other community gatherings can be a very effective way to educate people on your issue and get them to join your cause. If you do start an online campaign, plan a protest, or organize a meeting, make sure people know about it. In addition to the usual Facebook posts, tweets, memes, emails, and other online outreach, consider the offline route, too. Post flyers, take out ads, get your event in the local paper, and talk to people face-to-face.

Get to know what's happening in the campaign world of the issues you care about. You can learn a lot from what others are already doing in your community and elsewhere. Take note of what campaigns you're drawn to and what made you share them to get ideas for your own campaigns. And if someone else is already taking on Big Jim's Puppy Emporium, see if you can join forces instead of duplicating efforts.

Boost your campaign with creativity. If you're having an in-person protest, a big visual element like street art or people in costume can attract more attention, especially when it comes to the media. Clever signs can get shared far and wide. Or reinvent the entire concept of your protest—instead of just holding signs, hold a parade of rescued dogs in front of the Puppy Emporium. Getting everyone to wear the same color clothing or bringing a specific accessory or prop can create a stronger sense of solidarity—think of the tens of thousands of pink pussy hats that united the Women's March around the world in 2017.

There are laws around protesting, but when it comes to running an effective campaign, there are few hard and fast rules. Think about what would grab your attention and what motivates you and put that to work.

! Action Alert

THREE THINGS YOU CAN DO TODAY

1 • Do your research. Pick a cause, identify who's making the decisions, and plan out how you can have the most influence.

2 • Join a protest. There are a lot of animals and people facing injustice in the world, so whether it's a pet store protest, a climate rally, a social justice march, or a demonstration against government or corporate abuse of power, get out there to make your voice heard.

3 • Create a campaign plan using the Five Things You Need to Know Before You Launch Your Campaign and get started with an online petition.

ANIMALS YOU'LL HELP SAVE
Any creature who has faced injustice and is ready for your action.

3   Share the Love

Wildebeests don't always have it easy. They're a favorite snack for lions, cheetahs, wild dogs, and hyenas, and they rarely get the love in stories and art enjoyed by other African animals. But they're not isolated in their struggle for survival. They often hang out with zebras, since each species grazes on different parts of savanna grasses. Oxpeckers perch on their backs to eat ticks and parasites from their skin, helping the wildebeests with pest control and sounding the alarm when danger is near. And every year, as many as 1.5 million wildebeests are joined by hundreds of thousands of other animals in the Great Migration—the largest land migration in the world—to their summer feeding grounds. Wildebeests not only coexist with others on the savanna, but these different species need each other. The world of activism is also an interconnected ecosystem, where animal issues and human issues are deeply intertwined. Animal advocates and human advocates need each other to create a better world.

When you advocate for animals, you're advocating for people, too. Animal welfare and social justice are inextricably linked; where you find animal oppression, you'll find human oppression. Serial killers often start by torturing animals. The link between domestic abuse of people and animals is well established (see chapter 26). Factory farms are not only bad for animals, but they're notorious for exploiting immigrant workers and endangering the public health of surrounding communities. The pollution that threatens the existence of endangered species also disproportionately jeopardizes the health of communities of color and low-income neighborhoods.

Sometimes when we raise our voices for animals, we're accused of choosing other species over our own. But caring about animals doesn't happen at the expense of caring about your fellow humans. It's simply not true that we can't care about both the treatment of farmed animals and world hunger, or endangered species protection and poverty, or stopping companion animal abuse and child abuse. Empathy isn't a limited resource, and by understanding how human and animal issues fit together, we can help others see the connections, too. This can open doors for those fighting animal abuse, poverty, hunger, violence, and other social injustices to support each other, making all our movements stronger.

Even if you've chosen to focus completely on advocating for animals and donating to animal causes, and even if your dog or cat is your favorite person in the world, it's crucial to keep these human connections in mind and embrace compassion for both the animals and the people affected by animal issues. If we're going to change the world, we need to care about each other, listen to each other, and support one another.

Helping Animals Helps Your Community

Animals may not pay taxes, but they have an enormous influence on your community. Homeless or poorly cared for dogs and cats can be a drain on animal control budgets and pose public health risks, so promoting animal adoption and responsible care and training can save more than individual animals' lives. Conserving energy and water, and reducing waste to protect natural resources and wildlife also improves the natural capital and the utility bills of your community. Laws that are harmful to animals, such as dog breed bans and lethal wildlife trapping, tend to be more costly (financially and morally) and less effective than their humane alternatives. Advocating for animal-friendly policies is beneficial across the triple bottom line.

Animal abuse is never just animal abuse. It's an early indicator of child abuse, domestic violence, and other criminal and sociopathic behaviors. Not only is it a warning sign, it's often directly used as a psychological weapon to threaten and intimidate victims. By taking animal abuse seriously, human lives can often be saved. When an animal is neglected, oftentimes it's a sign that the humans in the home need assistance, too. If the dog doesn't have enough to eat, the kids might not know where their next meal is coming from either. And if we can provide social services to the animals, it can save their lives, keep them in their loving homes, and help the rest of the family meet their needs. (See chapter 26 for more on helping animals in hard times.)

Throughout our society, mistreating animals is out and respecting them is in, to the benefit of animals and humans. The pet care industry—from designer toys to specialty vet care—is a big slice of the economy that keeps on growing; what's good for our companion animals is good for our economic health. Services like grooming, dog walking, and veterinary hospitals are increasingly taking home a larger slice of that pie, too, leading the way for an economic model that's based on health and happiness rather than buying more and more stuff.

People are also willing to pay more for products from humanely raised farmed animals and those that have less of an impact on wildlife. Plus, improving their health advances our health: Buying organic means reducing pesticide exposure for wild animals and for farming communities, while ending the overuse of antibiotics on factory farms would improve conditions for farmed animals and reduce the risk of antibiotic resistance in humans. Animal testing has severe limitations, so the more we invest in animal-free alternatives that better mimic human physiology, the sooner we'll have relevant results to save human lives without sacrificing animal ones.

Protecting Wildlife Protects the Planet

We all share the same planet, so when we make choices that protect the environment for animals, we're also protecting it for ourselves. Freshwater species need clean water and healthy riparian ecosystems to survive. So do we. Grasslands and forests are home to countless wild animals and play a key role in keeping the planet's atmosphere and climate inhabitable for us. If we strip the landscape of the biodiversity and plant life that wild animals need, we lose the landscape that we need to grow our food to erosion, desertification, and soil degradation. And, of course, we lose the wonder of the natural world.

Nature is full of animals who are worth saving in their own right.

Each species is beautiful and interesting in its own way and makes the world a richer place. By helping wild animals, we help ourselves, too. We rely on each other for balance, and we don't always know which piece will cause the Jenga tower to collapse if removed. Protecting the future of all wild animals—not just the cuddly and charismatic ones—also protects our future.

Caring About Animals Cares for Your Health

Companion animals are as much caregivers for us as we are for them. Even if you don't have a registered service dog or emotional support animal, your dog or cat plays an important role in your physical and mental well-being. Infants who live with dogs or cats are less likely to develop allergies to animals later in life.[1] People who live with dogs report benefits of increased physical activity and social interactions (in many places, dog parks are a hub of social activity for both dogs and their humans), and a decrease in depression and anxiety.[2] One study found that dogs and cats were better at alleviating stress than friends and spouses.[3] While there's some disagreement about whether dogs scientifically make us more fit and less likely to suffer from cardiovascular disease, people who have canine housemates are generally happy to expound on how much their dogs have improved their lives.

Animals don't even have to be part of your family for you to benefit from their particular brand of nonjudgmental company. Therapy animals help comfort hospital patients and alleviate loneliness in senior living facilities. They help college students destress during finals and provide a sympathetic ear to help kids practice their reading skills. Programs that pair incarcerated people with homeless dogs and cats help both humans and animals prepare for the next steps in their lives. Pet-friendly office policies have been shown to improve employee morale, recruitment, retention, health, and productivity.[4]

And it's not just companion animals. The health of farmed animals, particularly removing them from the farming system, is closely tied to our health. Eating more plant-based foods and less meat and dairy is associated with a whole menu of health benefits, including reduced risk of heart disease, diabetes, obesity, and certain types of cancer.[5] Animal-friendly diets are better for everyone—people, animals, and the planet.

Comment and Share

The connection between helping animals and helping people isn't about joining hands for a rousing "Kumbaya" sing-along, but rather recognizing that there's a long list of ways that people benefit from improving animal lives, and vice versa—and, more importantly, that all species (including our own) deserve compassion. It doesn't even matter if everyone is motivated by the same love. If a major brand stops selling fur coats because it's no longer profitable and they're solely motivated by money, that's still a victory for those of us who wanted them to end fur sales because we love animals. Love can be a powerful motivator, but it's not, in itself, a strategy for change. Harness your love of animals into effective campaigns and changes in your personal life—and as a bonus, you'll often find that it's mutually beneficial with other things you love (such as your own longevity) and issues that inspire non–animal lovers. Everyone wins.

Seek out common ground. You may not be able to convince people who don't care about faraway narwhals (or who may not even know that unicorns of the sea are real) to act on climate change to help save these unique animals. But they may care about climate change for other reasons, and while you're standing together at the next climate march or calling your representatives to demand clean energy, you can chat with them about your favorite arctic animal and learn about what inspired them to get involved. The important thing is that you set aside whether narwhal extinction or displaced coastal communities is the more urgent issue to focus on the action that's needed to save both.

Sharing the connections between what you love and what others love can build a bigger, more compassionate network for change. Figuring out what motivates others creates opportunities to work together toward the same end goal. You may choose to eat less meat because you love cows while others may choose the veggie burger to save the planet or lower their cholesterol—you can all band together to demand more meatless options at your favorite restaurant and celebrate together with dairy-free ice cream when you succeed. These connections are also an important reminder of how central the well-being of animals is to our own lives.

Be an ally for other causes that champion compassion and love. It's no longer unusual to see animal protection groups at gay pride parades or wildlife organizations fighting for social justice. Where there's injustice toward animals, there's injustice toward people, and you can care about both. Embrace the intersections of these issues and show up for other causes. Not only does fighting oppression create a more compassionate world for everyone, but when you stand with others, they're more likely to stand with you when you need them.

! Action Alert

THREE THINGS YOU CAN DO TODAY

1 • Embrace your love of animals—celebrate how much you care about making the world a better place for other living creatures.

2 • Remember that humans are animals, too, and make an effort to recognize where animal causes and human causes intersect.

3 • Share the love. Be there for your friends if they ask you to join their cause and they're more likely to be there for you. What goes around comes around.

ANIMALS YOU'LL HELP SAVE
Humans.

4   The Political Beast

Giraffes are some of the most amazingly awkward-looking mammals on the planet, with their six-foot necks, stilt-like legs, and comically long blue tongues. They have a reputation for being gentle giants, but, like most animals, when mating season comes around, it's on. Male giraffes show off their prowess with a Battle of the Necks—officially and amusingly referred to as "necking"—where they whip their necks around to whap each with the bony nubs on top of their heads. (Seriously, Google giraffe necking *if you've never seen it.) Despite their gangly glory, giraffes face many of the same threats as their more notorious neighbors on the savanna, and they've been quietly disappearing; there are fewer giraffes than elephants left in Africa.*[1] *If only necking could save them from extinction, but giraffes need politicians to stick out their necks to enact and enforce legal protections from habitat loss, hunting, and trade in trinkets made from giraffe skin and bones.*

The fate of giraffes and other wildlife, as well as the animals who live with us and those who are raised for food and other industries, is embedded in human society through laws and systems that determine whether they're processed, possessed, or protected. We have to change the system if we hope to create lasting change for animals. There's a lot we can do as individuals—in fact, our actions every day have an impact on animals one way or another, whether we're making conscious decisions or not. But you and I choosing to never buy a giraffe-bone carving isn't enough to save the species. Oftentimes, Endangered Species Act protection and international laws against trade and poaching are the difference between whether a species will make it to the next generation or not. Justice really is blind when it comes to meat and dairy production—she looks the other way from factory farm abuse, because much of the animal suffering is perfectly legal and considered standard practice. Laws, passed by representatives voted into office by people like us, determine how severely animal cruelty is punished and even how cruelty is defined.

Politics may be the realm of humans, but it shapes the lives of animals. From protecting neighborhood dogs and cats from abuse to determining whether we'll get our greenhouse gas emissions in check in time to save the arctic home of puffins and polar bears, every animal everywhere on the planet is affected by human political systems one way or another. Every animal welfare issue covered in this book persists because of weak, poorly implemented, or flat-out inhumane and outdated policies. We can urge individuals to make better choices and pressure companies to voluntarily change their ways, but at the end of the day, laws play a significant role in determining the freedom or ease with which people can choose animal-friendlier lives, whether industries comply with compassionate practices, and whether humane trends are fleeting or here to stay.

If you haven't been doing your civic duty as a citizen, it's time to get engaged in politics as an animal lover. The U.S. political system may have its flaws, but you get to vote, your representatives work for you, and, if things are going south, you get to protest. You don't have to run for office to save animals (though it is an option), but the animals need you to be their voice as a citizen and member of the community.

Bark the Vote

After presidential elections, it's usually not just humans who move into the White House. Dogs have historically been the preferred choice of presidents, but there have also been a number of cats, a few birds, hamsters, horses, ponies, donkeys, sheep, cows, goats, rabbits, raccoons, and opossums taking up residence at the White House, too. Some presidents, such as Theodore Roosevelt and Calvin Coolidge, had extensive menageries including exotic pets.[2] John Quincy Adams had an alligator who lived in a White House bathroom.[3] In his victory speech, President Obama promised his daughters a puppy when they moved to Pennsylvania Avenue. His words launched an online campaign urging the new First Family to adopt their White House companion from an animal shelter. President Obama indicated that he would like a shelter dog, but due to his daughter's allergies, the family ultimately decided on a six-month-old Portuguese water dog. (A second Portuguese water dog was added to the family in Obama's second presidential term.)

Very few presidents have run the country without companion animals by their side. Martin Van Buren was given a pair of tiger cubs by a sultan, but they were sent to a zoo; James Polk reportedly loved horses, but he didn't have any companion animals, equine or otherwise; and although Andrew Johnson had no pets, according the Presidential Pet Museum, he had a soft spot for White House mice. Donald Trump has shown no signs of being an animal lover, personally or politically; he has, however, frequently called people "dogs" as an insult in his tweets. (See chapter 7 for how language affects animals.)

As a country of animal lovers, we pay attention to how our politicians interact with nonhuman animals. Mitt Romney's 2012 presidential bid was haunted by the story of a road trip nearly three decades earlier when he'd made the family dog, Seamus, spend twelve hours in a carrier strapped to the roof of the car. Seamus became famous that election year and was viewed by animal lovers as an indication that Romney was uncaring and untrustworthy. Political signs began to include canine opinions, with dogs being against Romney or for Obama.[4] Animal cruelty wasn't the only issue that plagued Romney, but it didn't help. (Spoiler Alert: Romney lost the election.)

Animals don't get to rock the vote, but you do. Despite the media fame of Seamus Romney, animal issues are rarely given priority in political debates or on the campaign trail. But politicians have a track record of how they've acted when faced with animal-related legislation in the past. Some of them have responded to policy questions posed by constituents and humane organizations. Some are active with animal protection groups, while others are cozy with animal industries. Some of them are out kissing babies *and* puppies, while others are out hunting wildlife between campaign stops. Look for signs that they're a fellow animal lover, and if you don't know their stance on the issues you're most passionate about, call up their campaign office and ask.

Find out which candidates share your values and will stand up for animals, and vote for them. Vote in every election. Presidents and federal legislators are responsible for laws that protect wildlife and all animals across state borders. State policy-makers determine anticruelty statutes and bills that affect the way farmed animals are treated. Local officials can influence how animals are treated in your community, such as whether nonendangered wildlife can be harmed, if dogs can be left chained outside, or how your local animal shelter is run. School board members can help determine if dissection takes place in your district. As you'll see over and over again throughout this book, everything we do affects animals, so every election matters.

Embrace Your Inner Legal Beagle

State and federal laws can be confusing. Legislators come up with catchy names for bills that are often intentionally deceptive—and sometimes downright Orwellian—to gain support from people who aren't paying close attention. Take the "Right to Farm" laws that have been sprouting in states recently. Who would want to take away the rights of farmers to grow food? No one. Which is why farmers are already protected from frivolous lawsuits. This new crop of bills and amendments isn't about protecting innocent family farmers, as the name implies, but about shielding industrial factory farms from being held accountable for animal abuse, environmental pollution, and potential public health threats, earning them the more apt nickname of "Right to Harm" among animal advocates who oppose these policies.[5] Or the federal "DAIRY PRIDE" Act, introduced in January 2017, which stands for Defending Against Imitations and Replacements of Yogurt, Milk, and Cheese to Promote Regular Intake of Dairy Everyday. It was quite the acrostic poem and quite the political acrobatics intended to make plant-based dairy alternatives less competitive by making them harder to market. People aren't really choosing almond milk over cow's milk because they're confused by the label (they're choosing it for

health, animal, and environmental reasons), but that's what the bill's supporters wanted you to believe.[6] And once you get past the titles, bills and
ballot proposals can have vague or misleading wording intended to influence your vote one way or another.

Thankfully, a lot of people have dedicated their lives and their careers
to trudging through the policy swamp so you don't have to. Many national animal and environmental advocacy organizations have lawyers
and policy experts on staff who monitor animal-related legislation and
alert their supporters when there are laws that need support or opposition. You may have state-focused chapters or homegrown state-based
groups watchdogging legislation and politicians' track records more locally.
Look to these groups for help in interpreting policies and the complexities of the political process. Talk to local animal protection organizations
to find out what legislation they're working on and how your citizen
power can help get good laws passed and bad ones blocked. And support
these groups however you can, since they're instrumental in making
sure our legal system is there for nonhumans, too, which provides the
foundation for national advocates and local rescuers to do their lifesaving work. (Or become one of them—if you're considering a career or
career change in law or public policy, the animals can always use more
legal defenders.)

Several websites have sprung up to make it easier to search for bills related to the issues you care about, and see why people are for or against
them, read a plain-language explanation of what's in the legislation, and
click on media coverage (which often includes the perspective of national
advocacy organizations). Once you've done your reading, you can easily let
your representatives know where you stand through the sites or by contacting them directly.

When doing your own research on proposed legislation—whether at
the federal, state, or local level—follow the money. The internet can reveal
a lot of information to help you sleuth out the truth behind proposed legislation, from top political donors for a bill's sponsor to the real identity of
people behind friendly-sounding front groups. Be wary of supporting
animal-related policies that are backed by any groups that use animals for
profit.

Big Fish, Little Pond

It's important to speak out on federal and state laws, but oftentimes your voice is louder at the local level. You have more access to your elected officials—and with fewer constituents, your vote has more weight. There are a lot of ways your town can protect animals. AnimalLaw.com has a list of model laws, from banning abusive animal circuses from coming to town to saving animals locked in cars during extreme weather. And that's just scratching the surface. Innovative, animal-friendly communities have officially supported policies that increase the transparency and success rate of their animal shelters and that recognize Meatless Monday or include meat reduction as part of their climate action plans.

Whatever issue you're passionate about, do your research and see if you can find a town that's already passed the animal protection law you're looking for. They're proud to share their language for others to adopt. If no one else has passed the law you want to see in your community, put together a packet of information on why it's important, and start pounding the pavement at city hall and with local nonprofits to find an ally to help you blaze new trails for animals.

Get to know your city council members. They usually have meetings that are open to the public, where you can find out what they're working on and bring new issues to their attention. If you're advocating for or against a specific policy, ask to meet with your council members, the mayor, or other appropriate city hall staff to educate them on your perspective and let them see that there's a rational, caring person behind the political request. Important note: Be a rational, caring person. A lot of animal protection issues can be very emotional, but if you prepare ahead of time with relevant information and a fact sheet or letter to present them for reference, it can go a long way. You should be knowledgeable and respectful, but don't just be a fact robot—your personal story brings the "person" to the equation and helps representatives see how their policies affect real people's lives.

Consider running for office. You don't have to be the mayor, but you could be. Or you could start with city council. Or join a task force addressing a particular problem. A friend of mine who's passionate about protecting and expanding options for safe, off-leash dog parks in her town joined the city parks commission to help influence rules and budget proposals related to the community of canine park users. You can also get political by joining local nonprofit boards. The animal shelter is an obvious one, but on the board of a social service organization, you can help create connections to provide support for families struggling to care for their companions, and on the board of your library, you can help influence learning programs to promote kindness toward animals. Use your unique perspective as an animal lover to bring compassion to every corner of your community.

Comment and Share

Getting politically involved on behalf of animals is all about making your voice heard. Keep a cheat sheet of all your representatives' phone numbers—from city council to Congress—so you're prepared to call them when an issue arises. (To get you started, here's Congress's switchboard, where you can be connected with your senators or representatives: 202-224-3121; you can also find their information at senate.gov or house.gov.)

Phone calls make a difference. Emails are a good start and online petitions help show a groundswell of support or opposition to a bill, but when you pick up the phone and your representative or one of his or her staff hears from a Real Live Person, it has a greater influence. Always respect the staff you talk to in your representatives' offices—they may be as close as you get to speaking to your representative and they can be either your ally or your enemy in getting the legislator to pay attention to your issue. And don't just call when you're mad—if your legislators are animal heroes, give them a shout-out with a call, email, letter, or tag on social media letting them know you appreciate the positive things they do for animals and want them to keep at it.

Go to city council meetings and, during congressional recesses, attend town hall meetings to represent the Real Live People of your community. Many animal protection organizations host lobby days, where they'll get a group of people together to visit state or federal legislators to discuss animal-related issues, training included. Or create your own lobby day and set appointments to meet with your representatives. As with approaching local officials, make sure you do your research and prepare ahead of time, be professional and respectful no matter how much you might disagree with their politics, and be clear about what you're asking them to do. These rules apply to *all* communications with government officials—animal protection laws aren't passed nor do legislators tend to change their positions because of an email sent in all caps, written in textspeak, or riddled with insults.

Help others get politically active for animals. Get to know the voter registration rules in your state and join or host a voter registration drive. Check out the Humane Society Legislative Fund's humane scorecard to get to know the voting records of your members of Congress and share the results on social media. Let them know you're paying attention. Host a letter or postcard-writing party with your friends—like phone calls, the extra effort that goes into sending snail mail carries weight. As a bonus, you can post photos of your pile of outgoing mail on social media to inspire others and show that people care about whatever issue or bill you're writing about.

If you're working on a local issue, think about who is influential in your community, such as business owners and religious leaders. Veterinarians can be powerful spokespeople for animals. If you're working on dissection in schools or another education- or youth-related issue, reach out to teachers and animal-loving kids. They won't all be able to attend city council meetings, but you can gather testimonials, letters of support, and petitions from your movers and shakers to support your own testimony. The media can help you spread the word, too. If there's a policy that's up for vote, give the local paper and news stations a call to make sure they know this is something that matters to the community. Be prepared with talking points and background information to make their reporting job easier. You can also write an op-ed or letter to the editor of your local paper to present your side in your own words.

However you choose to do it, at whatever level of government, use the megaphone democracy has given you. And never miss an opportunity to vote.

! Action Alert

THREE THINGS YOU CAN DO TODAY

1 • Register to vote. If you're already registered, check to make sure your information is up to date.

2 • Write down all the contact info for your elected officials and use it to ask them to support laws that protect animals, or thank them if they're already fellow animal lovers.

3 • Check out your public city council meetings to get to know the process and identify your local animal allies.

ANIMALS YOU'LL HELP SAVE

Parliaments of owls, convocations of eagles, conspiracies of lemurs, consortiums of crabs, coalitions of cheetahs, and all the herds, packs, and other nonpolitically named groups of animals affected by human law.

Money Talks

Humpback whales are known for their haunting melodies under-water and smooth dance moves above the waves. But humpbacks are also occasionally known as saviors to other marine mammals. These forty-ton bodyguards have a reputation for ganging up on or-cas (aka killer whales) to stop them from killing other animals. In one dramatic scene caught on camera, a humpback whale was spot-ted carrying a defenseless seal on its belly to safety through a pod of killer whales who had planned on seal for dinner.[1] Don't feel too bad for the killer whales all dressed up in their flashy tuxedo coloring only to miss out on their meal. They're powerful apex predators, and they know it—killer whales are the only cetaceans known to attack sharks. But humpback whales keep them humble, and when it comes to big corporations—including those that keep orcas captive and harm whales in the wild—it's up to us to remind them that they don't rule the seas.

Governments aren't the only ones setting policy that affects animals. Companies have policies independent of what they're legally required to do. Clothing designers that refuse to sell fur coats have done so voluntarily, and largely because of public outcry making fur unfashionable. More and more restaurants are switching to cage-free eggs and including humane promises in their investor reports, rarely because there are laws telling them to do so, but because they know people care about how farmed animals are treated. And sometimes, when enough companies in an industry voluntarily make changes in response to customer demand, it can spur lawmakers into action to make those changes required and permanent.

Corporations raking in billions of dollars a year may seem untouchable. But beneath all that cash and power, all companies have the same weakness: They need money to survive. In order to get and keep paying customers, clients, or investors, they need to protect their image.

Websites and social media have made corporations more accessible and more vulnerable to customer feedback than back in the day when your only option was calling a toll-free number or sending an actual letter on paper. Those are still valid ways to let companies know what you think, but you have a lot more options in your customer opinion arsenal these days. Call on your inner humpback whale and stand up for innocent animals threatened by corporate policies and products. Because every purchase you make—or decide not to make—affects animals, whether it's choosing not to buy products made from or tested on animals, or choosing to support companies (big or small) with strong humane and environmental values. Just like you have a civic duty to get out and vote, you also have a responsibility to vote with your wallet. Your money and what you do with it matters.

The Customer Is Always Right

If you decide to stop buying a product because you find out it's tested on animals or because the company's CEO posts photos of himself on Instagram posing with an endangered rhino he just killed, the company probably won't notice the lost sale. But thanks to the internet, your defection can be a lot bigger than a blip in this week's receipts. You can tell companies in all kinds of ways why they lost your business. Send them an email, then post their response on social media. Tweet at them, post on their Facebook wall, comment on their Instagram photos, leave terrible Yelp reviews. You can also still go offline and visit the store to talk a manager, send snail mail, or call corporate headquarters.

When a company disappoints you, try reaching out to them. Sometimes, changes may already be under way. Or they're not aware of the problem or why people would care about it. Or they're willing to change, but aren't sure where to start or how customers would respond (bringing it full circle to why they need to hear from you). Sure, this may prove to be overly optimistic, but you want to give companies a chance to do the right thing before a big public showdown. The option of avoiding negative press and jumping straight to the accolades can be a pretty powerful motivator for a company that sees itself, or wants to be seen, as trying to do good in the world. And skipping straight to positive press can encourage them to keep making positive changes.

When you reach out to companies—whether it's the first attempt, a public post, or recruiting others to contact them—let them know what you once loved about them and how they betrayed your love. Losing a loyal customer hurts a lot more than a complaint from someone who clearly never planned to give them money in the first place. Many animal lovers have long appreciated that Starbucks is vegetarian-friendly and the majority of its drinks are easily veganized. So, when they learned that the Strawberries & Créme Frappuccino and other pink products were colored using crushed bugs (listed on the ingredient label as *cochineal extract*), thousands of customers signed online petitions and contacted the company to express their disappointment. In response to the outcry (and in a victory for the little guys used as food coloring), Starbucks announced plans to switch to a tomato-based extract. The company's then president blogged, "We've learned that we fell short of your expectations. . . . As our customers you expect and deserve better—and we promise to do better."[2] Starbucks has done better for animal lovers since then, not only removing the bug extract, but adding almond and coconut milk options and more plant-based foods in its stores.

You can still protest an inhumane company if you're not a customer, but it's a much steeper hill to climb since, frankly, they won't value your opinion very much. If you protest a steak house with vegan guns blazing, they're not likely to take your complaints to heart. But if the pet store where you buy dog food every month hears that you're going to take your business elsewhere unless they stop selling puppy mill dogs or exotic animals, you'll probably get their attention. And just like when you're writing your representatives, make sure to clearly and respectfully state your case. The only thing that's less likely to impress a CEO or part-time customer service department receptionist than a noncustomer is someone who is screaming all-caps accusations at them.

Once you've let a company know why you aren't supporting them and lay out the animal-friendly values you expect them to uphold to win you over or win you back, let them know that you don't plan to stay quiet about it. Tell them that you'll tell your friends, coworkers, extended family, neighbors, the cashier at the grocery store, the other soccer moms, and everyone at the dog park about why you've taken your business elsewhere. For all the money companies spend on advertising, they still rely on word of mouth and demographic groupthink for their brands' staying power.

Now, take all of the above and flip it around for the companies that deserve a pat on the back. Companies are always looking for ways to get more new customers and more money from their existing customers. This is why companies like Apple have big product releases only months apart—they're constantly innovating, hoping to capture more people and more sales. As animal lovers, we need to make sure that humane and sustainable policies and practices aren't innovated out of the picture. So let companies know you appreciate their efforts to offer more plant-based menu items, to reduce their product packaging so there's less waste polluting wildlife habitat, to ensure none of their ingredients are tested on animals, or to support animal adoption or conservation. Let them know that their role in creating a more animal-friendly economy is *why* you're a loyal customer.

And don't just reserve the gold stars for companies with a mission fully dedicated to helping animals. Let companies that have taken meaningful steps in the right direction know that you support their efforts and hope to see them keep walking along the animal-friendly path. (Now that McDonald's has committed to cage-free eggs, maybe there's hope for a McVeggie Burger headlining the menu someday?) Your virtual gold stars can help companies testing out new policies and products stick with them.

Brand Name Blemishes

Calls, emails, and social media posts may be small actions by themselves, but companies are desperate to impress on social media. They invest a lot in cultivating their online brand and trying to be hip on the internet. Everyone wants to score the next viral video, meme, or hashtag. If people start taking over corporate feeds with criticism, making them look decidedly uncool in front of other potential customers, they'll pay attention.

And because the nature of social media is to allow for open dialogue, if they delete negative posts or block critics, it often only makes them look worse.

Keep an eye out for hashtags the company is promoting—they often rely on vague "conversation starters" that inadvertently provide an opportunity for you to use their social media campaign for your cause. There are plenty of hilarious examples of ill-conceived corporate hashtags gone wrong. McDonald's started a promoted #McDStories hashtag, but it was quickly taken over by people telling the story of how unhealthy McDonald's food was for people and animals. McD's pulled the promotion, admitting it "did not go as planned."[3] Similarly, SeaWorld launched an #AskSeaWorld campaign in an attempt to seem transparent in the wake of their abusive practices being exposed by the documentary *Blackfish*. The open invitation for questions was answered by animal lovers around the world criticizing SeaWorld's track record of animal exploitation.[4]

Social media and online petitions also give you the opportunity to show the company you're not alone in wanting them to ditch animal cruelty for more humane practices. Let others know why you're upset with the company, what you're asking them to change, and how they can get involved, whether it's signing and sharing a petition, writing or calling the company, or tagging them on social media with a particular message on a particular day. Suddenly, their problem has become bigger—sometimes a lot bigger—than just one unhappy, lost customer. And that means their brand can start looking tarnished to other customers, investors, stores that stock their products, and everyone else who's an ingredient in their recipe for success.

All those people beyond the customers themselves who play a role in helping get the company more customers can be influential secondary targets when the company refuses to listen to your reasonable feedback. You can urge stores to stop carrying brands that are known for animal cruelty, such as asking boutiques and department stores not to carry designers who use fur. You can ask websites and media outlets to refuse to accept advertising from inhumane companies. And you can work with socially responsible investors or shareholders to push for change and introduce shareholder resolutions for animal-friendly policies.

Companies rise and fall on their brands. And some brands are more vulnerable than others. If a company has made its name as an animal-friendly venture and is exposed for causing animal suffering, it can cause real damage to its reputation and profits because it feels like a betrayal of what customers expect from them. On the other hand, a rifle manufacturer criticized for sponsoring contests to see who can kill the most coyotes and other carnivores (a real thing known as predator derbies) isn't likely to feel much of an effect from the criticism because everyone already knows they're in the business of killing animals. (However, stores that carry that rifle brand while also trying to appeal to animal-loving outdoor enthusiasts could be convinced to stop stocking that company's products.) When you're reaching out to or calling out companies, keep their brands in mind. They may respond to different talking points or different types of campaigns depending on whether they've tried to position themselves as humane, sustainable, socially responsible, reliable, adventurous, affordable, or luxurious.

By ourselves, we're often the lone customer taking on the giant corporation, and we may feel like little more than a nuisance or inconvenience. But together, we're a swarm of termites chomping away at the foundation of cruel businesses.

Spend Thoughtfully

Whether your wallet is haute couture or duct tape chic, it holds real power. What you choose to buy and what you choose not to buy can both contribute to creating an economy that animals don't have to pay for. Unfortunately, sometimes the animal-friendly option can be more expensive. You'll usually pay a few cents more per egg for cage-free eggs. Nut cheeses can be several dollars more than dairy cheeses. You may pay less for comfortable leather shoes than a decent pair of non-leather kicks. Companies that go the extra mile to ensure no animals were harmed along their supply chain often face higher costs (which are passed along to the customer) for that distance. This isn't because kindness to animals is inherently more expensive, it's just become a rarity in many industries where animal cruelty is heavily subsidized directly and indirectly so companies aren't paying for the animal suffering their business is built on. The way to change this is to make animal-friendly policies the norm. The more people refuse to purchase cruel products, the quicker humane practices will reach the economy of scale for prices to drop.

But don't get discouraged from cruelty-free products because you expect sticker shock. Animal-friendly isn't universally more expensive. It might just take a little planning and comparison shopping to find the animal-friendly choice that meets your needs and your budget. I don't like to cook, so it's worth it to me to budget expensive nut cheeses into my grocery bill, but other people make their own on the cheap. When you buy fruits and vegetables in season and get your protein through beans and legumes, you can come up with very cost-effective, delicious meals. Maybe you can't buy organic everything every month, but you can become more conscientious about buying organic when you can and buying fewer animal products overall. You might be looking around your bathroom and ringing up how much it'll cost to replace every bath and body product you use with ones that weren't tested on animals. You don't have to do it all at once—finish using what you have, then replace items one at a time as you're able to find alternatives that you like. Thanks to the internet, if your local stores don't carry cruelty-free cosmetics and cleaning products or non-leather accessories, you can find places that do at a price that fits.

All this extra effort isn't a bad thing—when you step back to research your options, compare costs, and watch for sales, it gives you a chance to consider whether you really need to make that purchase at all. Big-box stores like Target and Costco may be convenient, but they're famous for luring you in to buy necessities, then spitting you back into the parking lot with a cart full of stuff you didn't plan to buy and, in most cases, don't really need. I know what it's like to be chewed up by cleverly placed displays and sale signs. But our rampant consumer culture takes its toll on wildlife, and sometimes not buying anything is the most animal-friendly choice you can make. (More on that in chapter 9.) Work with your friends and family to take back your wallets. Start a Facebook group or other community network to share your animal-friendly finds, ask for help researching products, and buy in bulk when you find a good deal for animals and your budget.

Besides spending or not spending your hard-earned cash, you can also change the world for animals by giving away your money. Whatever your favorite animal or cause, there are nonprofit organizations out there working tirelessly to save lives. There's a lot that you can do as one person to help animals, but in order to end the animal suffering that's built into society, we need organizations that can take animal abusers to court, lobby government officials, ramp up the pressure on companies, and educate people beyond our networks on how they can help animals, too.

While many organizations need volunteers and donations of supplies for any animals in their care, every organization needs money to keep the lights on. Whether you're able to give monthly or once a year, every dollar matters, so if you're looking to make your money work for animals, make a donation. You can also help fund-raising teams meet their goals by volunteering at special events or stuffing envelopes for mailings. If you're not sure what groups to support, ask your animal-loving friends or check out sites that rate nonprofits, like GuideStar or Charity Navigator. And if you have any questions about how your money will be used, give the groups a call—animal protection groups tend to be staffed by animal lovers who are happy to talk with you about their work.

Comment and Share

Become a feedback machine. Be that squeaky wheel that tells companies and their customers what's hot and what's not. And pay special attention to places that aren't perfect but have earned points for effort. For example, don't save your rave reviews for vegan-only restaurants—celebrate the places that offer a few good options on a mixed menu so they stay veg-curious and welcoming of people who don't necessarily want meat at every meal.

Get your friends and family involved in your market campaigns, whether it's signing petitions, calling customer service, posting on social media, leaving feedback cards in person, or swearing loyalty or disloyalty to a company. Customers are much stronger when we work together, and companies know it.

If you have a retirement plan or other investments, find out where your money is going. There's an entire sector of sustainable and responsible investing, and some of those investors are even paying special attention to companies with strong animal ethics. There are a lot of different ways to build an animal-friendly portfolio, and your financial advisor should be able to help you design a sustainable and responsible investing plan. If your workplace doesn't give you options to choose humane, socially responsible investments for your retirement plan, talk to your human resources director about how you can help make that happen.

Tell people where you like to donate. I know talking about money can be taboo, but you don't need to flash dollar signs. Share what you love about the organization's work, fess up that you're a donor, and ask your friends and family to support them, too. Start a fund-raising campaign on Facebook or GoFundMe. Ask for donations to your favorite charity in lieu of gifts for your birthday, wedding, or the holidays. If you're attending a housewarming, share your favorite local organizations to help your friends connect with the community. Word of mouth has as much of an influence on our charitable giving as it does on our purchases.

! Action Alert
THREE THINGS YOU CAN DO TODAY

1 • Start tracking the businesses and brands you support, and make note of how they treat animals in their policies and their products up the supply chain. If you spot something shady, reach out to the company with your questions and concerns. If they're doing something good you'd like to see more of, send positive feedback.

2 • Leave online reviews. Be specific and clear about what a company is doing right or wrong for other customers who care about animals.

3 • Make a donation to the animal charity of your choice. If you're not able to donate today, start a list of groups you'd like to support by the end of the year.

ANIMALS YOU'LL HELP SAVE
Farmed animals, lab animals, captive animals, and all the others who pay for our spending habits.

6 Compassion in the Classroom

Bullfrogs can lay up to twenty thousand eggs at a time. With so many siblings, it would be all too easy to give up and embrace anonymity, especially when it takes two to three years to grow from a tadpole into a mature frog. (During which time they have to grow their limbs and lose the tail—talk about an awkward adolescence.) But scientists have found that tadpoles have distinct personalities, and they hang on to those traits as they grow up.[1] So those bold bullfrogs singing their famous tunes at the edge of the pond were likely the boldest swimmers during their legless youth. Unfortunately for bullfrogs brave and timid, they're the most widely used animals in classroom dissections. But their biology isn't a mystery, and interactive, virtual alternatives can provide at least as good an educational experience for kids as breaking out the dissection trays, without harming any amphibians in the learning process.

No matter how hard you work to teach compassion at home, all bets are off once your kids go to school. The debate over dissection is the most notorious animal controversy in schools, but it's not the only one. Some school reading lists and libraries are better stocked with animal-friendly stories than others. In some rural high school classrooms, kids are given baby chicks to raise, then are told to slaughter them five weeks later for a lesson in food production. Other classes get humane education programs provided by local animal shelters or wildlife organizations. Some take field trips to SeaWorld or zoos, while others write letters asking representatives to protect sea lions. And as schools become increasingly cash-strapped, it makes it easier for powerful animal industries to step in with a curriculum telling the story of happy farmed animals or for cafeterias to offer meat- and dairy-heavy menus without plant-based options because those food are easier to fit in their government-subsidized budgets.

By taking an active role in your children's humane education, you can make sure they don't stop learning about animals and how they're treated once those children walk out the front door. Even if you homeschool or don't have kids of your own, it's still important to advocate for animal-friendly school policies in your community, such as virtual dissection in the lab and meatless meal options in the cafeteria, or offer up your expertise or volunteer services to help provide humane education programs. After all, the future of animals and the planet depends on raising the next generation of compassionate kids.

Step Away from the Scalpel

Millions of animals are dissected in high school classrooms across the United States every year, plus an unknown number used in elementary and middle schools and college courses. Frogs are the most common science lab subjects, along with fetal pigs and cats, but various other fish, rodents, birds, amphibians, small mammals, and invertebrates like earthworms, squid, and sea urchins are also used. The animals are taken from the wild or purchased from animal industries (such as animal shelters or slaughter-houses), then sold to biological supply companies, which kill and preserve them to be shipped to classrooms.

There are a lot of reasons why students struggle with dissection day. Kids are natural animal lovers and don't love the idea of cutting open animal corpses. Some may also express ethical concerns about where the animals came from, knowing that many wild frog species are in peril or that fetal pigs are a product of factory farms. Some may just be grossed out by the idea of dissection, and while that may not have the noble ring of the other objections, it's still valid, as it can be hard to absorb a lesson when you're focused on keeping your lunch down.

Whatever the rationale, there's no reason why kids need to know how to wield a scalpel to earn their middle school or high school diplomas. Studies have shown that alternatives like computer programs and virtual dissection are just as effective—if not better—for teaching students about anatomy.[2] And where there are similar learning outcomes, the humane alternatives have a frog leg up on animal dissection since the lesson can be repeated with no additional cost to the school, to animals, or to students' gag reflexes.[3]

Even at higher levels, a lot of veterinary and medical programs are moving away from wasting animal lives on dissection and other lessons; as of June 2016, every medical school in the United States and Canada has stopped using live animals to teach surgery. They didn't all do it for ethical reasons—many determined that human simulators made more sense for future human doctors to learn on than pigs, cats, or dogs—but the decision saves thousands of animals a year.[4] And if simulators and other models are considered superior for training future doctors, they're certainly suitable for teenagers.

Eighteen states and Washington, D.C., have laws or policies that give students the right to opt out of dissection. These dissection choice laws make it easier to avoid having to dissect animals and to convince your school to switch entirely to virtual dissection, but you don't need to have a law in place to take it up with your teacher and the school board. With so many effective alternatives out there that can teach the exact same lesson, save money, and avoid unnecessary trauma for students, teachers should be hopping at the opportunity to end dissection. But oftentimes they need parents advocating for change to make it happen.

Find out your school's policy on dissection and urge them to switch to virtual labs. Get the teacher on your side, if you can. Get support from other parents and the student government. If your middle or high school students don't want to dissect, support their decision and help them advocate for humane alternatives. Adults have a tendency to chalk up making kids do things they're uncomfortable doing to character building, especially when it's in the name of education. But standing up against dissection is an opportunity for young activists to find their voice, stick by their values, and protect animals. Encourage your kid to write a letter to the school paper or community newspaper about why he or she opposes dissection. A student's testimony at a school board meeting can be more powerful than hearing from parents or community members who aren't in the school every day.

If your state doesn't already have a dissection choice policy in place to help students whose parents may not be as vocal and supportive as you are, contact your state representatives and department of education to ask for one.

Do Your Homework

A friend's son came home from second grade one day with a coloring book and bookmark from a social studies lesson promoting the pork industry—not just cheering on pork consumption, but also celebrating the use of farrowing crates and the practice of separating piglets from their mothers after just three to four weeks. Farrowing crates, along with gestation crates, are among the cruelest forms of confinement on factory farms, so small that sows can't even turn around. Pigs are at least as smart as dogs, and these cages literally drive them insane. But of course the Pork4Kids materials in her son's backpack—provided by the National Pork Board—depicted happy pigs, not the miserable animals in undercover video footage.

When my friend questioned why her son had been given pork propaganda, the teacher's initial response was to offer an alternative activity during the lesson next year when my friend's daughter would be in the class. My friend pushed back, pointing out that her kids already knew the truth about how farmed animals were treated; the bigger problem was that every second-grader was getting exposed to a false, sugarcoated perspective on how food gets to the table. She offered to help find another speaker who could talk about sustainable farming. The school agreed to stop using Pork4Kids lesson plans in all their classes.

My friend's success in getting compassion into the classroom had three basic steps that every parent can replicate. First, she paid attention to what was coming home in her kid's backpack, and when she saw something sketchy, she asked questions. Second, she spoke up, clearly explaining to the teacher why the lesson concerned her—not just because they were a vegetarian family of animal lovers, but because the educational value of the lesson itself was problematic. Last, but definitely not least, she offered to help find an alternative. This is the most challenging and most important step.

School funding is often tied to a set of specific metrics determined by the state or federal government, and many schools are so strapped for cash that it's hard to make space for creative lesson plans. That makes it easy for programs like Pork4Kids to sneak into the classroom by providing free materials to get kids engaged and give teachers a break from textbooks. So if you're asking a teacher to remove a lesson plan, whether it's a required unit on dissection or a bonus interactive activity on food production, you're more likely to be successful if you can provide a replacement. There's no shortage of simulations, virtual alternatives, and community members like local farmers who can help replace inhumane curricula.

As a parent or educator, look for teachable moments that can help animal-loving kids change the world. If your classroom already uses virtual dissection, spend a few minutes talking about frog conservation and how choosing not to dissect frogs helps amphibians and aquatic ecosystems. If the lesson is about wolf behavior or the class is reading one of the classic tales starring wolves, use the opportunity to talk about the threats to wolves in the wild. Add a bonus activity—if not in the classroom, then at home as a family—writing letters to lawmakers asking them to protect endangered wolves. Use lessons on civic engagement, social services, and charitable giving to highlight animal causes and how students can get involved. Students can start their own petition or adopt an existing one to support as a class project. Kids have powerful voices, and it's never too soon for them to learn how to use them.

Compassion in the Cafeteria

Tens of millions of lunches are served every day in school cafeterias, giving them a huge influence on nutrition and the food system. There's no time like childhood to learn good eating habits that are healthier for us, for animals, and for the planet. Unfortunately, a lot of cafeterias fall back on chicken nuggets and burgers as staples. Granted, it's not always easy to get kids to eat more fruits and vegetables or to try new things, but cafeterias dedicated to healthier, better-tasting lunches are cracking the code every day.

Plant-based versions of old favorites like tacos and sloppy joes make popular meatless meals. Salad bars that let kids create their own concoctions by mixing and matching the veggies they actually want to eat can entice them to eat more fresh produce than just offering pre-plated options. Getting kids engaged with recipe contests, taste tests, and voting on featured dishes can drum up excitement for expanding the culinary horizons of the lunch line to bring in more veg-centric meals. And it all leads back to millions of meals a day that are better for animals, the planet, and the students themselves.

Hundreds of schools have started making their cafeterias more compassionate (and healthier for students) by joining the Meatless Monday movement.[5] In some schools, this means a commitment to serving only meat-free meals every Monday. For others, it's about promoting meatless options at the start of every week and using it as an opportunity to teach kids about the health, animal welfare, and environmental benefits of plant-based meals. Ask your school to join the movement. If your school is already on the Meatless Monday train, ask them to take it even further by increasing meat-free options throughout the week, reducing the amount of meat while increasing plant-based proteins in dishes, offering nondairy milk alternatives, and displaying posters, recipes, and other educational materials to promote meatless meals. Encourage families to join the school in taking the Meatless Monday pledge at home.

If your child's classroom needs snacks, help him or her find donations to keep snack time healthy and meat-free. If your district has an after-school program that uses volunteer teachers, offer to teach a cooking class. Help your school start a garden so they can start growing their own fresh veggies on-site.

Schools can also help animals by taking steps to reduce the amount of food wasted in the cafeteria. In some schools, trayless dining can encourage students to take only the amount of food they plan to eat (though other schools make kids take certain foods, such as milk, whether they want it or not, to fulfill the requirements of meal assistance programs). Share tables allow them to leave any leftovers for classmates who may not have had enough. On the other side of the warming trays, tracking food waste can help staff adjust purchases and recipes to ensure no food is left behind. But one of the best ways schools can reduce food waste is by adjusting lunchtime. Moving recess before lunch can increase fruit and vegetable consumption by more than 50 percent.[6] And longer lunch periods that actually give kids time to finish their lunches can reduce the amount of food that's thrown away.

Comment and Share

Even when it's not the year of biology and the dreaded dissection, it's important to know what they're teaching your kids at school and use your right as their parent to question decisions that may not be in your animal-loving students' best interest. Don't miss parent-teacher conferences and other opportunities to find out what's happening. Join the PTA and go to school board meetings to get humane education in the classroom. When you find an animal-friendly alternative lesson plan or resource, share it with the other parents and teachers in your community.

When you're trying to help animals, the world is your classroom. Get your kids involved in the things you're doing to change the world, whether it's finding family-friendly volunteer opportunities, visiting farm sanctuaries and wildlife refuges, cooking meatless meals together, challenging them to save energy or water, building a backyard bird oasis, or encouraging them to make their own protest signs to stand with you at the next climate march or circus demonstration.

Most kids, when given the chance, provide a powerful, honest perspective on why we shouldn't mistreat animals. Seek ways to help kids learn about their impact on the world and foster their desire to make a difference at school and at home. Ask them about their favorite animals and use their interest to guide your conversations and activities. Don't be afraid to talk openly about issues that affect animals, what harms them, and how they can be kept safe. Help kids understand the problems animals face and ask them how they want to get involved to be part of the solution.

! Action Alert

THREE THINGS YOU CAN DO TODAY

1 • Contact your local school district about their policy on dissection and urge them to shift to animal-free alternatives.

2 • Review your kids' syllabi and talk to their teachers about integrating more animal-friendly concepts and materials into lesson plans. If you don't have kids in school, offer to help your school district identify opportunities and resources for humane education.

3 • Talk to your local school about joining the Meatless Monday movement and serving daily meat-free options for students.

ANIMALS YOU'LL HELP SAVE
Frogs, cats, piglets, and all the other animals who are more than the sum of their anatomical parts.

The Power of Words

Snakes can be more social than people think. Arizona black rattle-snakes, for example, choose to bunk in groups and have been observed hanging out with friends on a regular basis. They care for their own children—something reptiles usually aren't given much credit for—and they've been known to babysit other rattlers' kids.[1] Turns out some snakes have family dynamics that rival mammal social systems. In fact, their family dinners may be more pleasant than a lot of people's Thanksgiving meals. Even those snakes who aren't social just want to be left alone. As with most maligned animals, they're more afraid of us than we are of them. Yet being called a snake *isn't considered a compliment. Going all the way back to the Bible, snakes have been cast as the villains. The way we talk about snakes and tell stories about them influences the way people think about them, and as a result, snakes are persecuted and often denied conservation protections they desperately need to survive. Words can hurt as much as sticks and stones, after all.*

Back in the eighteenth century, when powdered wigs were finally going out of style and steam engines were still state of the art, it would have been considered scandalous to talk to your butcher about breasts and legs. Out of prudish necessity, terms like *dark meat, white meat,* and *drumsticks* were born.[2] Fast-forward a couple of hundred years, and these euphemisms have come in pretty handy for the meat industry. The words we use to describe food distances what's on our plates from the animals it comes from. People want to know that farmed animals were treated humanely,[3] but they also don't want to think about it. Researchers found that replacing the word *beef* with *cow* on the menu made people less willing to eat meat.[4] Apparently, it's not as appetizing to order cow with a side of roasted potatoes.

Beyond terms that mask the origin of animal products, language is peppered with phrases about other species, many of which aren't flattering. Calling distrustful people *snakes* puts those qualities back on the animals—the snakes are just minding their own business, but they're characterized as untrustworthy and dangerous, and therefore it's easier to justify eradicating them. Describing aggressive people as *pit bulls* fuels the misconception that pit bull dogs should be feared and therefore banned from communities. Why would we want to kill any birds with a stone, let alone two of them? Why do we casually talk about beating a horse, alive or dead?

Language matters. Every time we repeat phrases and idioms that cast animals in a bad light, we reinforce stereotypes and objectification that can perpetuate animal cruelty. As animal lovers, we can start paying attention to the words we use and what they're really saying. Changing the way we talk can help change the world for animals.

Slip of the Tongue

When I think of pit bulls, I picture my sweet, goofy, snuggly dogs. But that's not usually what people mean when they call someone a pit bull. At the same time, many—if not most—people who use *pit bull* as a slur aren't dog haters. They may even know and love a few pit bulls. I have friends who have casually called someone a pit bull in conversation, and it's only because I'm such a vocal pit bull advocate that they usually catch themselves, backtrack, and come up with an alternative moniker. The point is that most of the time it's unintentional. Sometimes it isn't even meant as an insult, but it still reinforces negative stereotypes that put pit bulls in danger. Similar to the efforts to remove words from our vocabulary that are offensive to marginalized groups of humans, we need to work at holding our tongues when it comes to words that malign or objectify animals.

It's easier said than done. We all have phrases that we've used for so long that we don't even think about the words that make them up. Every so often, I catch myself falling back on an old animal metaphor or idiom that I've been hearing my whole life, and it takes a conscious effort for my brain to retrieve an alternative. This isn't about being politically correct. It's about speaking up for animals. Their fate lies in the way we use our language to talk about how they should be treated, to understand their needs, and to write policies that will either protect or exploit them.

You don't have to scrub your entire vocabulary of everything animal-related. That would be impossible, considering how many of our words are rooted in appearances, colors, and behaviors of the animal kingdom. And not all animal phrases are bad—some are neutral or describe positive characteristics. There's nothing wrong with taking a cat nap, having a nest egg, watching someone like a hawk, or not wanting to hurt a fly. We don't need to be boring conversationalists; we just need to be more aware of the way our relationship with animals influences and is influenced by what we say, and use our power of speech for good.

Happily Ever After

If individual words and idioms about animals have an impact, imagine what can happen when words are piled together in stories. Humans have always used storytelling as a way to understand the world. The roles animals play in fairy tales, legends, children's books, movies, and other narratives can shape the way we perceive them. You probably don't literally expect to visit your grandmother and find a wolf wearing her nightgown, but the pervasive Big Bad Wolf stereotype has stepped off the page when it comes to how we treat real wolves. These types of stories psychologically predispose us to fear wolves, resulting in persecution instead of protection.[5]

Animals are particularly significant in children's stories—both in their presence and in their impact on the reader. All those nonhumans acting like humans in storybooks help kids process difficult topics and cope with emotions.[6] Books like *Animal Farm* and *Planet of the Apes* serve a similar function for adults, but our shelves aren't as packed with animals as the children's section. While the moral of most of these stories isn't directly about the animal species themselves, if certain animals (like the Big Bad Wolf) are always typecast as the evil bad guys, that leaves an impression that can change our relationships with those animals from an early age.[7]

Pay attention to how animals are portrayed in the stories you share, especially with kids. There are plenty of books out there for all ages that explicitly impart a message of kindness toward animals. The classic book *The Story of Ferdinand* is about a peaceful bull who would rather smell the flowers than go into the bullfighting ring. *Oh, Theodore!* and *The Forgotten Rabbit* teach kids about caring for guinea pigs and rabbits, respectively. As kids get older, there are books about animal rescue, like *Buddy Unchained* and *Shiloh*. Or, my personal childhood favorite, *Mrs. Frisby and the Rats of NIMH*, where rats are the heroes who escaped animal testing and help save a family of mice from a farmer's plow—so much material to help kids relate to animal issues. Whatever you read with your child, ask them about the story to discover how they interpret it and the world around them. Sharing stories with your children is an opportunity for both of you to learn. Find out what they're learning at school, too—check out the books they're reading in class and organize a book drive to get more animal-friendly stories in local classrooms.

There's no shame in reading these children's classics as a grown-up, either. But there are also timeless stories like Richard Adams's *Watership Down* or *The Plague Dogs* for older audiences. Carl Hiaasen and Eliot Schrefer have written books with strong wildlife conservation themes for young adults. If nonfiction is your thing, there are tons of books to learn more about animal issues or particular species, heartwarming stories of rescued dogs or cats, or personal looks at less familiar animals, like Sy Montgomery's *The Soul of an Octopus*.

I haven't even scratched the surface of stories that help us better understand animals and how they're treated—and, by extension, better understand ourselves. Whatever your age, support stories that help animals, and when you find one you love, share it on Goodreads, Instagram, Litsy, or wherever you post your reviews, bookstagrams, and shelfies. If there's an animal-friendly movie you love, take your friends to see it and leave a positive review on Rotten Tomatoes and other review sites.

Pop Culture Clash

There are stories we're told by books and movies, and then there are the subplots of our lives that surround us in advertisements, on fashion runways, in magazines, making cameos in TV and film, and embedded in news reports. These everyday exposures to messages about animals are addressed throughout this book. But there's one pop culture phenomenon that deserves special attention: celebrities.

Celebrities have always had an influence on trends. They're the ultimate cool kids—if an A-list celebrity is seen eating at a certain restaurant or wearing a certain designer label, that place or outfit takes on a new sheen of coolness. If that restaurant happens to be vegetarian or that designer is fur-free, that's pretty cool for animals, too. *Travel + Leisure* calls vegetarian restaurants an "innovative, celebrity-espoused scene,"[8] and when Kanye West and Kim Kardashian dined at Woodlands Vegan Bistro, it made headlines in *The Washington Post*.[9] We don't even have to wait for gossip magazines anymore to know what's trending. Between blogs tracking celebs' every move and the celebrities' own social media, we know what's in as soon as it happens.

That's not necessarily a good thing. Celebrities are people, too, and not always known for making the best decisions. Whether it's Michael Jackson or Justin Bieber hanging out with the captive primates they kept as pets, Kardashians sporting fur coats, or Michael Vick busted for dogfighting, fans are taking note. While the bust of Vick's kennel brought dogfighting into the national spotlight and helped give the victims a second chance they didn't always get in lower-profile cases, the fact that he so quickly returned to the privilege and prestige of his pro football career didn't exactly send a message that animal abuse has serious consequences.

Celebrity is a brand—a scandal can cost them work, while being beloved can increase their earning potential. If celebrities are doing something that harms animals, call them out on it. After the *Blackfish* documentary aired, online petitions sprang up asking entertainers not to condone marine mammal captivity by performing at SeaWorld or its affiliated parks. Pat Benatar, the Beach Boys, REO Speedwagon, Trisha Yearwood, Willie Nelson, Barenaked Ladies, and other musicians withdrew from a 2014 concert series tied to the park in Orlando, leaving the summer festival pretty high and dry.[10]

Celebrities don't have universal appeal when it comes to influencing our decisions,[11] but they do get a lot of airtime. Thankfully, a lot of celebrities love animals (they're just like us!) and lend their names to good causes, joining campaigns as spokespeople and models, writing letters, speaking at rallies, or just showing off their animal-friendly lifestyles and adorable adopted companions. When *Harry Potter* actress Evanna Lynch Instagrams her visit to a farm sanctuary, her 1.3 million followers take notice. Ellen DeGeneres has used her platform as a top talk show host to advocate for dog and cat adoption and other animal issues. *Vampire Diaries* star Ian Somerhalder started a foundation to help animals and the environment, with a focus on getting his younger fans engaged in changing the world.

Celebrities can be powerful allies for animals. Sharing the good decisions and calling out the bad choices made by celebrities can reach people in your network in a way that other stories may not. We all know people who can't resist the guilty pleasure of celebrity tabloids and clickbait. Maybe your friends haven't been swayed by your rave reviews of meatless meals, but knowing their favorite actor goes out for late-night vegetarian cuisine could pique their interest in giving it a try.

Comment and Share

It's important to walk the talk of caring about animals through your actions, but talking the talk can help others understand how their lives affect animals and what they can do to help change the world. Sure, buying all your friends a copy of *The Animal Lover's Guide to Changing the World* is one way to spread the word about how to be a force of good for animals, but there are a lot of other ways to get the message out and inspire friends, family, and followers to join you in taking action. From responding to news stories on social media and with letters to the editor, to creating animal fan art, you can be a voice for the voiceless and a positive influence on the people around you who love animals, but aren't sure what to do next. With the rise of social media, regular individuals can have as much or more influence than celebrities on what people think.[12]

Raise your voice beyond social media, too. Volunteer to give a presentation or lead a discussion group at a local school, community center, or library. Organize vegan potlucks to show your friends that compassionate diets are easier and more delicious than they may think. Have a letter-writing party or an outing to bring donations to the local animal shelter. Share book recommendations and give animal-friendly books as gifts.

Whichever animal issue has captured your heart and imagination, talk it up and welcome others to join the conversation.

! Action Alert

THREE THINGS YOU CAN DO TODAY

1 • Take note of how you and those around you use animal-related lingo, and make a conscious effort to expand your vocabulary beyond negative animal talk.

2 • Support animal-friendly literature by starting an animal lover's book club or donating books that positively portray animals to libraries and schools.

3 • Be a superfan for animals—cheer celebrity compassion, jeer celebrity cruelty.

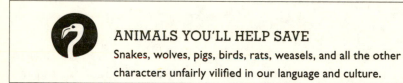

ANIMALS YOU'LL HELP SAVE
Snakes, wolves, pigs, birds, rats, weasels, and all the other characters unfairly vilified in our language and culture.

Find Your Pack

Prairie dogs live in an intricate system of burrows where they form tight-knit groups known as coteries. The guys may have several families, but the sister wives stick together to raise their young. Prairie dogs are known for being chatty; their name comes from their doglike yips and squeaky barks. But they're not just having idle conversation—research has shown that prairie dogs have a more complex language than what's known about chimpanzees, dolphins, or orcas. They have different sounds for different predators, and not only will they discuss whether to be on the lookout for a coyote versus a hawk versus a human, but they'll also describe the specifics, like whether it's the human in a blue shirt or the one wearing green headed their way.[1] While researchers don't know everything that prairie dogs are saying as they're gossiping about our fashion choices and other happenings in prairie dog town, we do know that social animals like prairie dogs—and humans—need each other for safety and sanity.

Social change happens on three levels. I've already talked a bit about the role of your individual choices and the need for policies that advance change on a larger scale, and those themes will keep coming back in each chapter. To recap: Aligning your actions with your values is key to taking responsibility for the impact of your decisions and doing your part to create a cultural shift toward animal-friendly trends. Using your voice and your vote (at the ballot box and with your wallet) creates society-level changes that make the animal-friendly option more readily available, affordable, and even inevitable for everyone else. But in between changing your lifestyle and changing policy is creating change as a group.

You can't change the world in a vacuum. Your individual actions have the strongest impact when they're multiplied by the actions of others. Those actions become even stronger when they're bonded together to create a movement of people coordinating pressure on companies, politicians, and other decision-makers. If you decide not to go to the rodeo, you've made an ethical choice not to support animal abuse, but your absence isn't likely to shut down the event. If you and a group of people decide to boycott the rodeo and show up with signs against the abuse of calves and other animals, the event organizers, sponsors, and the venue start to take notice. And if your crew works together to inundate your city council with requests to ban the rodeo from town or let sponsors know that they're losing customers over their support of calf roping and steer wrestling, you'll have a much greater chance of preventing future abuse on your home turf than if your protest had been a solo act.

Networking saves lives and your sanity. Animals face an army of threats around the world, often backed by governments and huge corporations, so Team Animal needs strength in numbers. Thanks to the internet, it's easy to find people who care about the same issues you do, as much as you do, to create a support system to help you change the world.

The Introvert's Guide to Pack Behavior

It's not unusual for animal lovers to feel like they relate better to animals than to other people. You may feel like the last thing you'd ever want to do is host—or even attend—a meeting of complete strangers, even if you all have a common cause. Luckily, we have the internet, allowing all of us introverts to unite separately from our own homes. The internet goes a long way toward coordinating campaigns and sharing experiences with other animal lovers. It was years before I met the majority of people whom I volunteered alongside to combat misconceptions about pit bulls and fight against breed-specific legislation. I still haven't met many of my fellow pit bull advocates, but I know I can count on them when the dogs need us to be their voice.

Look for online groups that are active, welcoming, and engaging. Some groups are all signature-gathering business, sharing petition after petition. These can be good resources to stay up to date on the latest campaigns, but you're not as likely to create meaningful or lasting connections for the long haul. The groups where people are chattier and get to know each other on a personal level are more likely to yield strong alliances—and maybe even friendships—with people who will help out when you need letters, phone calls, social media actions, ideas for ways to increase pressure, or someone to listen when you're feeling frustrated or disheartened.

Be open to getting out of your comfort zone for the sake of the animals. I'm not saying you need to agree to protest naked or go door-to-door for a ballot campaign if those things make you break out into a cold sweat. But consider some of the more outgoing tactics that may not be on your list of favorite things to do, and find ways to make them tolerable.

Many introverts hate the phone, but making calls to legislators is far more effective than sending an email. Write out a short script for yourself so you don't have to wing it (in most cases, simply stating the bill or issue, your status as a constituent, and how you want them to vote is enough). Maybe you could never stomach phone banking, but you'd be willing to send texts on behalf of animals. If you're unsure about attending a protest, bring along a friend and make fun signs ahead of time to get into the spirit. Same goes for attending a meetup or other local gathering—even if your trusted friend isn't as passionate about the issue as you are, they'll probably be willing to come along as moral support (especially if you throw in an animal-friendly dinner on the way). They might even get into it and decide to join the campaign with you.

The Extrovert's Guide to Pack Behavior

You might be an animal lover who thrives as much on being around other people as you do being around animals. Humans are, by nature, social creatures. (Even most introverts aren't actually reclusive.) As an extrovert, you're particularly well suited to bringing people together, especially when it comes to building IRL communities and driving offline actions. Whatever your mode of communication—listservs, Facebook groups, meetups, protests, craft nights, happy hours—you can help your pack of fellow animal lovers stay in touch.

Look for opportunities to keep your allies connected. Social events can be a great way to strengthen your bond with other animal lovers and get advice or new skills to help you on your journey toward an animal-friendlier lifestyle. Welcome others to the table when hatching plans for animal campaigns. Working as a team can bring fresh ideas and energy that can be the difference between success and burnout.

In my experience, extroverts are often great at making sure everyone feels included and has something to contribute to the cause. However, it's important to recognize that people will want or need to participate in different ways. So if you're organizing a happy hour to plan your big protest, have a way for people who can't or don't want to attend the meeting to get the notes and participate at the protest itself when you need them the most.

Follow Your Passion

Ask a roomful of animal activists to name their favorite animals, and you'll get as many different answers as if you'd asked a room of toddlers. Maybe more. There's nothing wrong with having favorites. We need to be strategic about our efforts—the same actions or policies to save chickens from battery cages won't save rhinos from extinction. Not only can specialization make us more effective, but following your passion can make you a more authentic, compelling advocate. If you're just not all that interested in polar bears, but you've been an avid coral reef diver since high school, you'll have a lot more to say about why we need to fight climate change to save the reefs than focusing on the arctic. Your excitement will shine through as you geek out about all the different animals you've seen underwater, making your plea for the cause that much more colorful and contagious.

So if you're not sure where to begin changing the world, start with what you love the most. Those animals will thank you, and you can always come back for the others as your appreciation for them grows, too.

It's not just your favorite animal or what you love about them that's uniquely you. Your voice is also unique. Everyone brings a different perspective and different skills to a campaign. Maybe you can offer a religious viewpoint or a scientific perspective, or express why the issue matters to you specifically as a parent or a student or a doctor or a professional basket weaver. If you come from a background that's different from what's expected from animal lovers or you once stood on the other side of an issue, being an unusual suspect gives you a powerful voice. At agency hearings about wolf management, ranchers who refuse to kill wolves are often able to get the attention of conservative decision-makers in ways that lifelong animal lovers and animal protection organizations cannot. If you grew up hunting, once had a summer job at a slaughterhouse, or used to be afraid of dogs (or even still are), don't be ashamed to talk about your journey. Share the story of how you became an animal advocate or how you came to love your favorite animal.

Everyone has a story and yours can help inspire burgeoning animal lovers and activists. Showing how an animal issue affects us on a personal level can engender empathy from others in a way that fact sheets alone cannot, and can show the diversity of people who are coming together to unite for a cause.

Think about the other things in your life that you're passionate about and how you can use your knowledge and skills to help animals. If you love fashion, organize a fashion show of cruelty-free designs. If you love photography, your images can help draw attention to campaigns or help adoptable animals find homes. If you love sewing, convince your sewing circle to spend a day making blankets for the animal shelter. If you love to cook, provide informal cooking lessons to help others expand their meatless culinary horizons. Whether it's writing or painting or graphic design or gardening, use your art and your hobbies in your animal advocacy.

Comment and Share

You don't have to do it all on your own. Whether it's online or offline, seek out other animal lovers who care about the same things as you and join forces. Sharing lifestyle tips, skills, campaigns, and commiseration all help animals in ways that you can't do alone. Make new friends to expand the circle of people who can help you create change—your love of animals is a pretty big common interest. Recruit old friends, too. Let people know what you're up to and why you need their help—you might be surprised by the people already in your circle who are willing to stand beside you to save animals.

Not everyone in your existing friends list will be a part of your animal lovers' pack. It's likely that you interact with and care about a variety of people with different interests and lifestyles, and you can help make sure they don't feel alienated by your efforts to change your own life and the world. Instead of slamming your friend's decision to order the surf-and-turf special, offer to take him or her out next time to your favorite restaurant to share a veg-friendly meal. Instead of shaming your coworker for his or her new leather boots, talk about why you've changed your style and where you like to shop. If your brother just bought a dog from a pet store, love that dog like a niece or nephew and encourage your brother to join the fight against puppy mills or volunteer with you at the local shelter. They're not bad people for making these choices; they're just people caught in the system you're trying to change. Remember that your existing pack is on your side, and you want them to understand why you care about the things you do rather than feeling constantly criticized by your cause.

Don't ignore the more established packs—namely, the nonprofit organizations working 24-7, 365 days a year to help animals. Join their email lists and follow them on social media to learn from them and so you know when they need your voice in a campaign. Share the good work they're doing. If you're able to, donate money or your time as a volunteer. These groups may seem big and powerful, but they need members and supporters to keep caring for homeless animals, advocating for stronger anticruelty laws, pressuring corporations for animal-friendly policies, and fighting to save animal lives.

! Action Alert

THREE THINGS YOU CAN DO TODAY

1 • Join an online animal lovers' community. Whether it's a Facebook group, a listserv, or a Twitter list, find your people and know you're not in this alone.

2 • Identify what skills you have to contribute to the cause and polish them up for the next campaign that needs your help.

3 • Follow your favorite animal-saving nonprofits on social media and sign up for their email lists so you're ready for action when they need signatures, calls, volunteers, or donations.

ANIMALS YOU'LL HELP SAVE

Prairie dogs, domestic dogs, wolves, lions, elephants, chimpanzees, and all the other animals—including animal lovers—who depend on their packs for survival.

Get Wild

When nature suffers, we suffer. And when nature flourishes, we all flourish.

—JANE GOODALL

Green Is the New Black   9

Birds have been recycling long before the cool kids started. They use fur, lint, and hair when building their nests, and many are into interior design, adding colorful shells and berries, as well as bits of string, plastic, and other found treasures to make their bachelor pads more attractive to the ladies. But our towers of trash have become way more than birds—or any species—can handle. It's time to go beyond curbside (or nest-side) recycling and rethink how we consume things in the first place and how our choices may affect millions of wild animals we'll never meet.

If you're the kind of person who enjoys things like eating, breathing, and having water to drink, you already have plenty of good reasons to care about protecting the planet. But if you're an animal lover, you have exponentially more reasons to care. From aardvarks to zebras, the wildlife that fascinate us (and teach us our alphabet) are in trouble. We're destroying their environment in endless and diabolically creative ways: tearing down rain forests to make cheap hamburgers, paving over wild homes for Walmarts, sucking up desert water sources to keep golf courses green, filling our oceans with plastic, and changing the climate with our planes, trains, and automobiles. The list goes on, but suffice it to say we've made a mess of the earth, and we kind of need this place.

Despite your sci-fi dreams, this is the only planet we have. But our interest in the earth runs deeper than self-interest. I'm pretty sure that even the biggest polluters in the world aren't tucking their kids in with their favorite stuffed oil rig. Wild animals are amazing in their own right and make our world a more amazing place to live. We might congratulate ourselves for inventing a few gadgets that make life more convenient, but nature invented flight, camouflage, hibernation, and bioluminescence first. Nature has given us elephants and fireflies, three-toed sloths and humpback whales, chameleons and flamingos. Yet for some reason, wildlife is often left out of the conversation when we talk about how to help animals, or the spotlight is on the abuse suffered by animals in captivity—which is no small thing—but the wild animals who suffer from our abuse of the planet deserve more than that. These are the creatures who gave us fairy tales and legends, jungles and coral reefs, inspiration for product design and pattern ideas for fabric. We need to pay a lot more attention to making the world a better place for all of us.

There are a lot of different shades of green. Some actions have a greater impact than others, and sometimes our ability to create change in our own lives is dwarfed by the damage caused by industries and policies that make it nearly impossible for us to avoid some of the biggest polluting pitfalls. The next few chapters will help guide you through where you can have the greatest impact and how to influence the system that's pushing bears and butterflies off the planet. But let's start with the basics.

Less Is More

We all have an environmental footprint—the measurement of how big a mark we leave on the planet as we go about our daily lives. Your footprint is determined by what you eat, where you live, your energy use, your transportation habits, and how much trash you create compared to how quickly the earth can clean up after you by absorbing your carbon emissions and regenerating forests, fisheries, and the other natural resources you use. Those of us in the United States are stomping around in giant clown shoes compared to the rest of the world. The average American has an environmental footprint about 60 percent larger than most Europeans and nearly 700 percent bigger than the average person in most African countries.[1] If everyone lived like we do, we'd need nearly four and a half planets to support our lifestyle. Yet we still only have one. It's time for us to wake up from the American

Dream of multiple cars, sprawling homes, and supersized everything if we want to stop the nightmare of the endangered species crisis.

We're obsessed with stuff. The breaking news of a new gadget release often eclipses reporting on humanitarian crises. After 9/11, we were told that shopping was one of the best ways to show our patriotism. We regularly hear terms like *retail therapy* that convince us happiness can, indeed, be bought. And that's not even getting into the mania of Black Friday. What's even worse is that we live in a disposable culture. Electronics are made to become quickly obsolete by design changes, cheap materials that can't stand the test of time, irreplaceable spare parts, or by being so expensive to repair that it's cheaper for you to just buy a new gadget. Even our clothing has become about "fast fashion"—clothes that are cheaply made to cycle quickly through stores and our closets, landing in the landfill to make room for next season's trend. And that's just one industry in a sea of industries that spend a lot of time telling us we're "consumers" instead of people.

Everything we buy—and throw out—required resources to create it in the first place. Resources like water and land that were taken from wild animals. Just because something isn't made from fur or a chopped-down tree doesn't mean it's wildlife-friendly—the production of plastics and the minerals that go into electronics are often responsible for polluting or outright destroying wild habitat. And once you no longer need something, donating and recycling are better than simply trashing it, but those actions don't erase the environmental cost that went into making the thing in the first place or the resources that will go into repurposing it. The best way to deal with waste is to not create it in the first place. If we stop buying so much stuff, companies will have to cut back on production—they don't want to waste money or get stuck with piles of useless products either.

Before you become paralyzed with guilt over buying this book (it's one more thing in my house!) or donate all your worldly goods and make a promise you probably won't be able to keep to live a spartan existence from now on, you don't have to swear off all material objects or a little luxury and convenience to live a greener lifestyle. The key is to start paying closer to attention to what you buy, what you actually use, and what you throw away.

When you're making a purchase, ask yourself three questions:

1. Do I really need this?

2. Can I buy it used or borrow it, or can I invest in a higher-quality version that will last longer?

3. No, seriously, is this really something I need?

By simply asking yourself these questions and becoming more mindful about unnecessary excess in your life, you can make big strides in shrinking your environmental footprint. Plus, you'll save money you can use to invest in better versions of the things you really need, or to take a vacation or donate to animal charities.

And if something breaks, try to fix it. YouTube is a treasure trove of DIY videos for minor repairs and learning new crafts, and there are repair shops that can help wherever you're not so handy (which, for me, covers just about everything). Small electronics, however, are becoming harder and harder to fix, designed so they can't be easily taken apart, while companies are refusing to share service manuals or supply parts to third-party repair shops. This means when your smartphone is on the fritz, you may have no choice but to take it to the manufacturer, who may decide to charge more than a new phone is worth. You may get the latest, shiniest new technology out of the deal, but your old phone joins the growing heap of e-waste—about sixteen billion pounds a year of hazardous, high-tech trash in the United States alone.[2] So if you can't fix your electronics, recycle them to keep their toxic materials out of waterways. Then write the company to demand longer-lasting products and support for fair repair laws that require manufacturers to make it easier for you find someone to fix your gadgets.

Make a commitment to tread lighter on the planet by hauling around less stuff, because every time your eco–shoe size drops, wild animals get a little more breathing room.

The Cost of Being Trendy

All those Prius-driving celebrities and designer reusable tote bags for sale are signs that green really is the new black. Caring about the planet has gone mainstream, and *environmentalist* is no longer a four-letter word (except when uttered in the boardrooms of those who want to profit off the planet and other animals). The more eco-conscious people become, the more we can change our polluting ways. Politicians realize they can earn much-needed bonus points by protecting the planet and endangered species. Researchers can get funding to figure out where we're doing the most damage and how to stop it. Innovators can harness technology and creativity to slash the environmental cost of all kinds of things. And for those of us keeping the eco-score at home, it's much easier to find greener products. Maybe a little too easy.

Earth Day has become so mainstream that it has sales events named after it. If you're buying stuff you don't really need just because it's billed as eco-friendly, it's the same as any other excessive or wasteful purchase. Clever marketing has made it easy for us to believe we're doing good simply by buying a product that's less bad for the environment. But if your Prius is your third car in a family of two, it's not going to save the world.

Everything has a production cost, even reusable grocery bags made from recycled plastic bottles. Those tote bags are an excellent way to cut down on single-use plastic bags, which get tangled in trees, swept into the ocean, and swallowed by animals. But they require more resources to make than disposable plastic bags, and they've become so popular that companies have rushed to get their share of the market. As a result, many of us have more tote bags than we can ever put to use, making them start to feel, well, disposable. I still occasionally get tempted by a clever design (how is it that a tote bag gets me so perfectly?) or one that benefits a good cause. But then I remember all the totes crammed into every nook of my car and piled in my closet (many of them from well-intentioned conferences wanting to give out useful swag), and how even when I was grocery shopping to feed seven people for a weeklong retreat, it required fewer than ten bags . . . and the new tote doesn't pass the three-question test. If it's for a good cause, I donate the money instead of buying the bag.

By definition, trendiness is fleeting. Protect wildlife in ways that will never go out of style.

Greening Your Pets

Once upon a time, domestic animals lived near human homes, finding their own food or eating scraps, running through the woods, scaring off predators, and hunting small animals. Today, dogs and cats have become companion animals who sleep in our beds and reap the benefits of a nearly $70 billion a year,[3] recession-proof industry of premium kibble, gourmet treats, and a variety of toys that puts Santa's hardest-working elves to shame. Our pets have become unwitting allies in our bad overconsumption habits.

In recent years, greener pet products have also become trendy. Some of these are investments that can truly help wildlife while keeping your less-wild companions happy. For example, the clay used in common kitty litters is extracted through strip mining, which leaves wild habitats devastated and desolate. But now there are better alternatives (that are also healthier for your cat), made from wheat, corn, pine, or recycled newspaper. Choose organic foods and treats, so your pet's diet isn't contributing to pesticide use, and toys made from natural or recycled materials that won't contribute to plastic pollution. When spoiling your nonhuman family members, follow the same guidelines as you would for your own purchases: How badly does Fluffy really need it, and is there a better alternative?

Once your dog has digested his organic, free-range dog food (or whatever you feed him), make sure you pick up after him. Domestic dogs and wild animals carry different pathogens, which means leaving your dogs' feces lying around could expose other mammals in the area to disease. Parvovirus—a deadly illness that started in domestic dogs—was suspected of killing 65 percent of Yellowstone's wolf pups one year.[4] Dog poop also pollutes water sources, including the ones we rely on, with bacteria and excess nutrients. Picking up after your pup protects local wildlife, though we're often stuck using plastic bags to dispose of it. The Environmental Protection Agency recommends flushing it, if you happen to be near a toilet; this way, like your waste, it'll get treated to minimize water pollution. There are also backyard compost systems designed to help break down your dog's feces. However, don't simply add your dog or cat's poop to your regular compost pile since it may carry unwelcome diseases to your garden.

There's no getting around the poop problem or the fact that our companion animals demand resources. Based primarily on the carbon cost of kibble, two large dogs in the United States can have a bigger environmental footprint than the average person living in Haiti (but significantly less than the average American toddler, for those of you whose dogs are your kids).[5,6] One of the greenest things you can do is prevent unwanted litters by spaying or neutering your animals and adopting from your local shelter.

Our four-legged family members can't make eco-conscious decisions on their own . . . but they're also not the ones choosing overconsumption. Your dog doesn't really want (or need) an entire wardrobe. They have a pretty simple and green wish list to start with—basic care to keep them healthy and all the free attention and love you can give them.

Comment and Share

Everything you do has an environmental impact, from how long you shower in the morning to what you eat throughout the day to the temperature on your thermostat when you go to bed at night. Pay attention to things you do or buy that might be unnecessary or excessive and try to replace them with more environmentally friendly habits. Research says it takes an average of sixty-six days to create a new habit[7]—so whether you're taking on a more earth-friendly diet, refusing to buy plastic, or changing the way you get around town, in just a little over two months you can be on your way to a greener lifestyle.

Challenge your friends to reduce their ecological footprints, too. Check out the appendix for online tools and apps that can help you track and compare your environmental impact. When the people around you share your good habits, it helps keep you on track, creates a sharing community that can cut down on consumption, and multiplies your sources for new ideas on how to make your life more wildlife-friendly.

Your smartphone can help increase your eco-intelligence with apps that rate the environmental impact of products, so you know the full cost of what you're buying. There are also plenty of apps that make it easier for you to join the sharing economy—using less (and usually spending less) through carpooling, clothing swaps, equipment rentals, and trading services. Use your social networks to let people know if you have tools and appliances they can borrow to help them avoid one-time-use purchases.

Do your part to create new trends by sharing your favorite resources and greener habits and helping raise awareness about the dangers of our disposable culture on wildlife. Most people don't make the connection between buying a sweater just because it's on sale and their favorite endangered species feeling the squeeze from the combined habitat loss, water pollution, and greenhouse gas emissions that went into all those sweaters that will only be worn once and then thrown away. Encourage your friends to skip the sales and have a clothing swap or crafting night instead. If your friends have kids, set up a toy swap with wildlife-themed stations. When fixing up your nest, check out secondhand stores, garage sales, and local classified ads like Craigslist—other people's trash could be your treasure.

Buck the trend of consumerism and commit to making purchasing decisions with wildlife in mind. Raising your eco-consciousness is the first step in helping wild animals, with the added benefit of saving money and protecting the planet we need to survive, too.

! Action Alert
THREE THINGS YOU CAN DO TODAY

1 • Before you make your next purchase, ask yourself the three questions: Do I really need this? Can I borrow it, or buy it used or better quality? And, really, do I need it?

2 • Leash the temptation to make your companion animal an accomplice to your overconsumption. Use the same green principles when purchasing for your animals as you do for yourself.

3 • It's easier being green with friends—set up a swap-and-share network with others who want to support your new non-shopping habit.

ANIMALS YOU'LL HELP SAVE
Lions and tigers and bears, and all wild creatures great and small.

Tigers can run as fast as sixty-five miles per hour and jump sixteen feet in the air. Faster than a speeding Buick, leaping tall branches in a single bound, these powerful hunters are practically Supercats. But despite their strength and striking-yet-stealthy appearance (those stripes aren't just camouflage, they're also as unique as fingerprints), the hunters have become the hunted. There are now more captive tigers in the United States than there are wild tigers left in the world. The majority of these tigers are being kept in backyards, basements, and roadside zoos; some are being shown off as team mascots and others displayed as a cheap gimmick, like Tony the tiger, who spent his days inhaling exhaust fumes as he paced his cage at a Louisiana truck stop.[1] We're their kryptonite, and if we don't stop deforestation, trophy hunting, and the use of traditional remedies made from tiger bones and other parts, the only tigers left will be the ones behind bars.

People argue that seeing a real, live Amur tiger or Chinese crocodile lizard is the only way to inspire people to want to save Amur tigers or Chinese crocodile lizards from extinction. Maybe you have your own story about the first time you saw a giraffe or rhinoceros in the zoo and how the experience of seeing a creature so unlike anything else in your regular life stuck with you ever since. But how much did that experience define your love of animals versus tap into a natural love that would have blossomed in other ways? How much did you really learn about how giraffes and rhinos behave in the wild and how you could help save them? And what about the experience of the animals living on the other side of the cage, plexiglass, or moat? Are the potential conservation benefits enough to outweigh the moral cost of captivity? These and other questions are part of an increasingly hot debate among animal advocates, scientists, and the public about whether zoos really play a role in educating future conservationists or are just telling a tragic tale about captive animals.

Modern zoos have been around for a couple of centuries, and people have been "collecting" wild animals for thousands of years. Lately, though, our desire to get up close and personal with wildlife has spiraled even further out of control. It's bad enough that our expanding human population is taking over wild habitat, but our ability to travel anywhere, anytime has people trampling in previously untouched wilderness. We're leaving big, muddy boot prints all over the place and picking up exotic animals like they're souvenir snow globes. And those killer selfies are literally killing wildlife.

Maybe stuffed animals and storybooks aren't enough to foster the love needed in enough people to save endangered species from extinction. But there have to be better ways than putting live animals on display to expose people who aren't born animal lovers to the magnificence of wildlife. There's no captive animal experience that will show you the drama and love that you'll see in a Disneynature documentary. Or that will immerse you in the wildness of their worlds the way an IMAX screen or virtual reality experience can. Through sharing stories and art, we can understand how connected we are to wildlife and how wild animals have shaped our traditions and cultures. We have so much creativity and technology at our fingertips—let's put it to use to learn to love wild animals without causing them harm.

Zoos: The Good, the Bad, and the Horrifying

There are ways you can distinguish between zoos with a commitment to conservation and those more committed to cashing in on your love of animals. The worst excuses for zoos are easy to spot. Look for the depressed animals behind bars or in concrete enclosures with cracked paint, as if a polar bear will be fooled into thinking he's home by a splash of arctic blue on the walls. These zoos are often in places that are unexpected for a reason, like shopping malls or tacked on to a go-kart/mini-golf complex.

You know the horrifying when you see it. Don't go there. (But if you do stumble upon one, and you can snap photos without giving them your money, take a few pictures to send to local authorities and animal protection groups that can fight to shut them down and send their captives to sanctuaries.)

It gets trickier in the territory of larger, nonprofit, accredited zoos. You'll notice a pattern in this book that certifications should be taken with a big grain of salty skepticism, and it's no different when it comes to zoos. The main organization in the zoo world is the Association of Zoos and Aquariums, which makes institutions fill out a lengthy application about their animal care and other activities. It's a start—none of the zoos in the horrifying category would pass muster—but then again, SeaWorld was granted AZA accreditation with its orcas living in too-small tanks and being forced to perform tricks. (For more on animals used in entertainment, see chapter 18.)

The best place to save wild animals is, without question, in the wild. But the wild is rapidly disappearing. While I wish there was no need for any conservation efforts beyond respecting wild habitat and reducing our greenhouse gas emissions, I also wish for world peace and an oven that magically produces delicious-but-healthy vegan doughnuts while I sleep. We've made life a lot harder for endangered species in the wild, and now they need us to help fix it. Zoos have played an important role at times in helping species recover, particularly if you look at the broader definition of *zoo* as a place that keeps a collection of wild animals for study and rehabilitation and not just as a place that puts them on display for field trips and family outings. Through captive breeding and reintroduction programs, California condors went from only twenty-two birds left in the wild to a population of two hundred and growing.[2] The last five surviving Mexican gray wolves in the American Southwest were taken into captivity for a breeding program, and now there are more than one hundred in the wild.[3]

These species may have been pulled back from the brink of extinction, but they're still hovering pretty close to the edge. And once captive-bred animals are released back into the wild, they don't simply go trotting, flying, or slithering off to happily ever after. There's often a significant death or recapture rate, and we need to make sure they have wild homes to return to as well as protection from the threats that caused their decline in the first place. Still, being temporarily taken into captivity gave them a better chance at truly recovering than if they'd been left to just die out.

But not all captive breeding programs have the goal of repopulating wild habitats. Some are more concerned with keeping zoos populated. In some cases, animals are bred purely as an enrichment activity—and because baby animals draw crowds—even if it means the zoo will wind up with more animals than it can sustain. When that happens, healthy animals are culled. Zoos may argue that these programs help them better understand reproduction in endangered species and raise awareness about those animals, but if they're not actually protecting wild animals in the wild, then it's a means without an end.

Here are five characteristics of zoos trying to do right by wildlife:

1. **They take conservation seriously.** Saving wildlife habitats and helping the animals living on the outside should be core to any zoo's mission, from investing in fieldwork to providing meaningful educational programs that confront the real-world challenges faced by endangered species.

2. **They recognize their limitations.** In 2004, the Detroit Zoo became the first major zoo in the country to voluntarily retire its elephants, Winky and Wanda, to a sanctuary because the director decided it was unethical to keep elephants in zoos.[4] The deep intelligent, social, and emotional lives of elephants have been well documented. Plus, these are huge animals who need room to roam—in the wild they'd wander a minimum of several miles daily and sometimes several dozen miles a day, which is impossible in a zoo setting. The largest zoos in the world are only a few square miles *total* (and most are much smaller); no amount of enrichment will make an elephant believe his or her corner of the zoo is just like home.

3. **They love the scalies, slimeys, and creepy crawlies** as much as the big, cuddly critters. The most popular guy isn't always the one

who needs saving the most. Zoos should work to save all kinds of species and to help people understand why sometimes snakes, snails, and spiders are even more important to other animals and the environment than species like pandas, who may have lots of charm but limited range and influence on ecosystem health.

4. **They educate people** on how to help wildlife once they go home. If conservation work doesn't end for the zoo at its gates, it shouldn't end there for the visitors either. Zoos should take advantage of the love people felt during their visit by providing information on what they can do in their day-to-day lives to help save the animals they just spent the afternoon with.

5. **They practice what they preach.** Caring about animals means providing the best possible care with natural habitats and enrichment. You can tell when an animal in captivity isn't doing well psychologically when they show stereotypic behaviors like relentless pacing and swaying. If a zoo claims to care about lions as a species, but the lions in its care are miserable, then they've failed. They've also failed if they don't care for the planet that wildlife need to survive by ignoring sustainability in their operations, such as offering only disposable plastic, not recycling, not having meat-free options on their menus, and doing nothing to improve energy and water efficiency or reduce their carbon footprint.

If you're still uneasy about seeing wild animals in cages—even if they're in pretty cages with real trees and water features—you're not alone. Donate the price of admission to an organization working directly to conserve wildlife in the wild instead.

The Mixed Bag of Ecotourism

Ecotourism promises a unique experience with wild animals in their natural habitat, usually someplace off the beaten path, where you can commune with nature and increase your environmental awareness while supporting conservation efforts to keep some amazing, biodiverse ecosystems thriving. Basically, it's the opposite of a weekend in Vegas.

For wildlife lovers, ecotourism can be a dream vacation. And for some countries that previously relied on killing animals for money, ecotourism and other animal-friendly ventures are cashing in on conservation. Consider whale hunting: Despite the international moratorium on commercial whaling, a handful of nations continue to hold annual whale hunts, which they struggle to subsidize in the face of public distaste and lack of demand for whale products. Whale watching, on the other hand, has become a multibillion-dollar industry and a convincing argument to end whaling for good. Countries with famous wildlife like great apes, big cats, and elephants have found that protecting these animals can be a bigger tourist draw than hunting them.

Some argue that the draw has become too big. The more people want a piece of the action, the more greedy companies will make greenwashed promises to provide an ecotourism experience that's actually bad for the ecology. There are three main concerns to watch out for to make sure you're not stepping into a tourist trap: disturbing wildlife, trashing the environment, and exploiting local people.

One of the greatest threats of the growing popularity of ecotourism is interference with wild animals. Be skeptical of any tour that guarantees you'll see animals eating, mating, playing . . . or that you'll see any animals at all. Wild animals don't care about the tour bus schedule, and they shouldn't have to. They should be left to their own agendas. When tours start feeding animals to guarantee that customers get the photo ops they paid for, the wild animals become dependent on humans and specific feeding station locations, which makes them vulnerable.

You also shouldn't interact directly with the wild animals on your tour. The more they get used to humans, the more it disrupts their natural behaviors, social systems, and survival skills, and the more likely there is to be a human-wildlife conflict (which rarely ends well for the wild animals). And as tempting as it is to believe the advertising that says you can have your ecotourism cake and eat it, too, be wary of any trips that involve a bonding experience with wildlife. Hint: If you're swimming with dolphins in a seaside pen, that's animal entertainment, not ecotourism.

Any trip—whether it's a one-day excursion or a two-week safari—that promises to be environmentally friendly should, in fact, be friendly to the environment. Pay attention to whether a company is constantly taking large groups of people through wild habitat and whether they pay attention to their environmental footprint, both on the tours and in their operations. Also, consider your own carbon footprint when deciding whether to travel to the ends of the earth for a rare wildlife sighting. Getting to know some of the local wildlife a little closer to home might be a better option for your carbon and your cash budget.

Last but not least, be conscious of the impact that all this wildlife tourism can have on the local human communities. When big international tourism companies come to town, it can lead to the locals being forced to give up traditional work for exploitative, low-paying jobs. Make sure your eco-travel choices support biodiversity and cultural diversity and that it benefits the local communities.

Shop smart for your animal dream vacation. Scratch beneath the surface of the ads, and don't be shy about asking the companies for the specifics on how they're not just showing off wild animals, but helping wildlife and people in the region. Read the reviews on TripAdvisor, Yelp, and all your favorite reviewer sites, and search for local reports on the company's reputation.

Trading Lives

If you're a self-described animal lover, you're probably not reading this book while sipping a glass of tiger bone wine and lounging on your snow leopard fur rug. It may even seem absurd to you that people will pay for ground-up rhino horn, dried pangolin scales, or ivory-inlaid jewelry. But wildlife trade is the third-most lucrative black market business behind drugs and weapons. The efforts to fight the wildlife trade are becoming pretty impressive in their own right. Apps are helping law enforcement officials better identify animal products and more quickly connect with wildlife enforcement networks. Between drones to stop poaching and DNA matching to determine the origin of smuggled animal parts, it's basically *CSI: Wildlife* out there.

But it's the less dramatic, often entirely legal wildlife trade that you're more likely to encounter. Birds, turtles, frogs, and salamanders are stolen from their homes to become pets in ours, which is both cruel and has led to unsustainable declines in wild populations. Even the aquarium trade has its dark side, as tropical fish are harvested using devastating practices. For example, cyanide is dumped into coral reefs to stun fish, making it easier to catch them, and killing as much as 50 percent of nearby fish, along with corals, in the process.[5] From there, tens of thousands of fish may die on the journey from the ocean to the tank and will simply be written off as the cost of creating that soothing aquarium atmosphere in homes, offices, and restaurants.

Wild animals shouldn't be pets. Ironically, smaller wild animals like frogs, turtles, and lizards are often given to children as "starter pets" for families who aren't sure if they're ready for a dog or cat, even though amphibians and reptiles can be hard to properly care for, resulting in unnecessary suffering and untimely deaths. All too often, people realize they can't (or no longer want to) care for their reptiles and amphibians and release them into the wild. Since these exotic animals didn't come from your local pond or park, if they survive out there, they can cause an invasive species problem that competes with native wildlife. Instead of getting your animal-loving kids a wild pet, expose them to wildlife by spending time in parks and at local nature centers, where they can learn about animals in their natural environment and from people who understand their unique needs.

Pet trade problems aren't limited to aquarium-sized creatures. It may be harder, legally and logistically, to smuggle a tiger cub in your suitcase (though it's been known to happen), but there's a booming trade of captive-bred exotic pets. As difficult—and potentially dangerous—as it is to attempt to care for wild animals, fewer than half of all states ban exotic pets, and a handful have no restrictions at all, essentially making it as easy to get a tiger as a terrier.

Comment and Share

If you happen to already have an exotic pet—big or small—whom you can no longer care for, contact a rescue group that specializes in that species so they can help find proper placement. In Florida, the Fish and Wildlife

Conservation Commission has an amnesty program to encourage people to relinquish their exotic pets to qualified caregivers instead of turning them loose; in ten years, they've rescued more than 2,500 animals. If your local zoo, sanctuary, or wildlife agency also offers amnesty days, help spread the word in case there's anyone in your network with a wild animal who could use better care. The best choice is not to support the pet trade in the first place. That also goes for skipping any businesses that think a captive tiger or bear is a draw for customers—if you ever find yourself in Louisiana, fill your tank anywhere other than a truck stop with a caged tiger. Support local and state laws that ban exotic animal ownership to help get animals like Tony out of their cages and into sanctuaries.

If your local team has a live wild animal mascot, ask them to retire him to a sanctuary. Start a petition of sports fans, get a tweet storm going on game day, and bring signs to the stadium to spread the message that compassion is the winning play. A goofy guy in an animal suit is better for team spirit than a miserable mascot on the sidelines anyway.

And before you go anywhere, even to the next chapter, we need to talk about wildlife selfies. Wild animals have increasingly become victims of our selfie culture. If you're in a park and a squirrel photobombs you, that's fine. You've won the selfie lottery. But if you pull a porpoise out of the water for a photo op or try to buddy up to a bison for the perfect pic, you're putting the animal—and oftentimes yourself—in harm's way. The rule here is simple: Don't do it. Respect the personal space bubbles of wild animals. You don't want to test the patience of a two-thousand-pound bison, no matter how docile she may seem while grazing. You don't want to see just how close you can get to fit that bear in the frame before she decides it's too close. And there have been far too many stories of young dolphins being selfied to death as they're dragged out of the water and passed around for everyone to get their shot. There is no amount of likes and shares that makes that photo worth it.

! Action Alert

THREE THINGS YOU CAN DO TODAY

1 • Support organizations that save wild animals in the wild.

2 • Stay away from stores and other businesses, including sports teams, that keep exotic pets. Urge them to send their wild animals to a sanctuary.

3 • Skip the selfies. Keep a respectful distance from wildlife.

ANIMALS YOU'LL HELP SAVE

Elephants, tigers, gorillas, snakes, turtles, dolphins, and a menagerie of awe-inspiring animals who belong in the wild, instead of cages and aquariums.

Neighborhood Bird-Watch

Hummingbirds are the smallest birds in the animal kingdom, but proportionally they have the biggest brains, weighing in at more than 4 percent of their body weight. By comparison, our human gray matter is only about 2 percent of our weight. These tiny, zippy birds can see and hear better than we can. They're smart enough to remember the flowers they visit and when those flowers will be ready for dining again. So if your backyard hummingbirds seem to know when you refill the feeder, it's not your imagination. Turns out it's not so bad being a birdbrain, and not just if you're a hummer. Unlike the wild animals you might encounter on an ecotour or hike in the wilderness, birds and other urban wildlife have been forced to adapt to some pretty massive changes we've made to their landscape, including skyscrapers and power lines, tens of thousands of airplanes invading their skies every day, and concrete paving over their paradise. While we work to save the world's remaining wild places, making our yards a little more welcoming for the animals trying to get by where humans have already taken over is really the least we can do.

We humans have a tendency to see the world in terms of boundaries—the countries, states, cities, and neighborhoods where we live, our houses or apartments, and the yards and other outdoor spaces that we claim as an extension of our homes. But property lines don't mean much to the birds and the bees. We've already trespassed in their habitats, so it's only fair that we should be sensitive to how our habitat and habits affect their lives.

As we fight to protect pandas and penguins who most of us will never see in the wild, sometimes we fail to remember that we're surrounded by incredible wild animals wherever we live. Especially once we grow up, we forget that we were once enchanted by monarch butterflies and lightning bugs. That we once noticed lizards scurrying between the stucco cracks and we didn't take birdsong or cricket symphonies for granted. We used to watch squirrels play, and we would freeze in place to avoid scaring off rabbits. Each of these animals has their own unique existences and quirky characteristics, and they all play a role in our local ecosystems. Even in the concrete jungle, there's a food chain of birds, small mammals, insects, and plants, and there are ways that you can lead the neighborhood watch to keep them safe.

These Are the "People" in Your Neighborhood

One day, while people were eating lunch at a Quizno's sandwich shop in Chicago, a coyote strolled through the door and decided to chill out in the cooler beside the juices and sodas.[1] Since wily coyotes don't usually order off the menu in broad daylight, many people don't realize that they're in nearly every major city in the United States. And they're not the only hidden wildlife among us. Mice and rats have learned to lie low, birds stick to rooftops and treetops, and raccoons sneak around like they're actually masked bandits. There are entire animal worlds around us, and when we discover those animals, they're often viewed as pests. Our relationship with our closest neighbors is complicated at best and hostile at worst. Even many animal lovers have a tendency to ignore the way local wildlife are treated as we invest our attention and advocacy in distant, exotic species.

No matter their size or species, get to know your wild neighbors. You might be surprised by the biodiversity in your own backyard—endangered birds have been known to take up residence amid skyscrapers, and rats are among the most intelligent, underappreciated animals on the planet. Local critters can help keep parks and gardens healthy. But more importantly, they keep life interesting. Urban animals are incredibly clever—they've figured out where to get the best food scraps, to find cover among buildings from natural predators, and to hide in plain sight from humans. They remind us that even when we surround ourselves by electronics, steel, and plastic, we're part of a larger, wilder world. And when a mountain lion wanders into Los Angeles from the foothills or a black bear walks out of the woods and into a New Jersey suburb, we're reminded of just how much we've encroached on habitat that once belonged to someone else.

Learning to appreciate your wild animal neighbors doesn't mean you have to welcome them into your home. Generally speaking, it's not the best solution for you to invite a colony of mice into your walls or let chipmunks take over your attic. But knowing what kind of animals your trash cans might attract, what your local birds prefer in the feeder, how to keep uninvited guests from becoming permanent squatters, and what kind of park spaces can provide good homes can foster peaceful coexistence in your neighborhood.

Be a Better Neighbor

The whole family has a role in protecting backyard wildlife. Teach your kids to be compassionate to all living creatures, including insects. Kids can also get involved in creating pollinator-friendly gardens, cleaning bird feeders, and building bat houses. These activities are a great way for them to learn about local urban wildlife and get invested in caring for their nonhuman neighbors.

Your family cat may be adorable, but there's a good chance he's a serial killer. A recent study estimated that cats are responsible for killing as many as 4 billion birds and 22.3 billion mammals every year.[2] Keeping your cat indoors not only protects wildlife, but also protects your cat from disease and the threat of getting hit by a car or attacked by a larger animal. (Not to mention protecting your neighbors' gardens and sandboxes from being turned into litter boxes.) If you want to give your cat some time outdoors, use a leash and harness or create an enclosed patio to keep her safe and avoid putting potential wild victims in harm's way. Dogs, as a species, aren't generally as bloodthirsty as cats, but if you have a dog who likes to chase wildlife, keep her on leash when wild animals are around. If you're walking in a local park where wildlife have made their home, keep dogs and kids close and on designated paths, fields, and playground areas to keep from crushing anyone's living quarters.

When it comes to animals trashing your trash cans, remove the temptation by keeping your garbage cans in the garage or shed until pickup day. If you have to keep the trash outdoors, secure lids with bungee cords and weights or get a wildlife-proof can. You can also try motion-detector lights or sprinklers to scare off the garbage thieves. Make your yard less appealing to raccoons and other scavengers by never leaving dog or cat food outside, cleaning your barbecue after every use, and sweeping up under bird feeders. These tips help avoid attracting bears, too, though if you live in bear country and don't want them hanging out in your yard, you may need to rethink having a bird feeder at all.

Most animals are just looking for an easy food source—once they've decided your home is the local convenience store, it's hard to convince them otherwise. With raccoons and other smaller animals that coexist in our cities and suburbs, this can be a nuisance, but when it comes to bears, once they become acclimated to human neighborhoods, they're often considered too big of a risk for wildlife officials to let them live. For your own safety and theirs, don't feed the bears, even unintentionally.

If a family of squirrels, raccoons, or moles has taken up residence in your home or garden, leave them alone if you can. If it's spring or summer and they're nesting, the best thing to do is to let them raise their babies in peace. Unlike humans, young animals don't take eighteen years to move on—usually within a few weeks, the little ones are self-sufficient enough for the family to no longer need your comfy chimney or shed for their den, and they'll head back out into the big world. If you don't want future squatters, figure out how they got in and seal off the entrance. If you can't wait for them to graduate from their den or if they're just hanging around to snack on your garden, you can kindly ask them to leave by annoying them with bright lights, blasting your worst pop or heavy metal playlist, or leaving stinky rags soaked with something strong but nontoxic (such as cider vinegar) lying around. They'll usually get the hint and move the family to a more peaceful pad.

The most important rule of being a good neighbor is: Don't poison your neighbors. If mice or rats take up residence in your home, the most humane thing you can do is to make it less hospitable for them. If there's a rodent Yelp out there, your goal should be to have a one-star home. Remove food sources, keep your house extra clean, and seal up any cracks they may be using as a secret entrance (mice can fit through spaces about the size of a dime, so seal up every little potential entryway you can find). The internet is full of suggestions and products with varying reviews to deter rodents, including peppermint oil–soaked cotton balls, ultrasonic or strobe light devices, and asking a friend to supply you with used kitty litter if you don't have a cat of your own. Whatever you try, avoid rodenticides, particularly the supertoxic second-generation anticoagulants. Not only do these anticoagulants kill slowly and painfully, but the chemicals move up the food chain, so if that mouse is caught by a cat, snake, or raptor, those animals may also be poisoned. If you live in a rural or suburban area, setting up barn owl boxes and bat houses can help provide night patrols for natural rodent and insect control.

Build a Backyard Oasis

The monarch butterfly's iconic orange-and-black-spotted wings used to be spotted in backyards across America. They were regular visitors to picnics and pool parties. But in recent years, their population has plummeted.[3] One of the biggest culprits in their disappearance is the loss of milkweed plants to herbicides sprayed on genetically modified crops. Supporting policies to limit and label GMO products before they can be snuck onto your plate can help save monarchs.

You can also help them in your yard by planting milkweed and avoiding pesticides (including chemical weed killers) to give monarch caterpillars a chance. Add other native, pollinator-friendly plants to create a garden that will help butterflies and bees who have lost their habitat to development and industrial agriculture. Make sure you buy organic plants, though, as many nurseries sell plants—including, disturbingly, those marketed for pollinator gardens—that have been pretreated with deadly neonicotinoid pesticides linked to colony collapse disorder in bees.[4] Beware of products with acetamiprid, clothianidin, imidacloprid, and thiamethoxam listed as active ingredients. If a plant's tag says it's protected from aphids, that's bad news for bees and butterflies who visit your garden. Planting a vegetable garden can be a great way to supplement your animal-friendly meals with less pressure on the planet, but stick with organic fertilizers and weed control, and use fencing, chicken wire, and other nonlethal deterrents to keep away hungry deer, rabbits, and moles.

If you're not growing food for you or pollinators, consider xeriscaping—landscaping with native plants that need little or no irrigation—especially if you live in a dry, arid climate. If you have a lawn, avoid toxic herbicides and cut back on watering. Learning to live with less green in the yard can put more green back in your wallet and save water for local wildlife.

Bird feeders can be a fun and easy way to hang out with your feathered neighbors. Instead of holding an open house with generic, all-purpose birdseed, specializing based on the birds you hope to attract gives them higher-quality food and wastes less, since all-purpose bird food tends to have a lot of fillers the birds ignore. Plus, you're less likely to have awkward, parasite-spreading interactions between different bird species who don't normally fly in the same social circles. Clean your bird feeders regularly, including any spilled birdseed around the feeder, to prevent mold and bacteria that could make birds sick. We're all about the hummingbird feeders at my house, regularly reporting to each other which birds we've seen and when. It feels like we've gotten to know them in a way that's different from the beloved but distant hawks soaring over the yard.

Putting bird feeders close to windows may seem counterintuitive, but it can actually encourage birds to slow down for landing, making them less likely to mistake your window for open sky. You can also shatter the tempting illusion with decals, ribbons, or other decorations that break up your windows' reflections. Get creative with some origami birds or get convenient by purchasing thin films or screens sold for this purpose. Keeping your curtains drawn can also cut down on reflection, with the added bonus of keeping your house cooler in the summer (although drawn curtains may not be the most desirable solution if you're hoping to watch the birds visiting the feeder near your window).

Pay attention to how wildlife needs change with the season. They may need more food during mating season or when they have small mouths to feed in the springtime. Summer heat may have animals seeking shade or wanting to go for a dip in birdbaths; different animals benefit from baths on pedestals than those left on the ground level. In the fall, leave your leaves alone, or rake them under bushes and trees to create a mulchy shelter for small animals. Provide water in winter, when natural sources may be harder to find.

Comment and Share

When it comes to wildlife-friendly lawn care, the grass doesn't always have to be greener on the other side of the fence. Challenge your neighbors to join you in watering less during heat waves. Set a good example with organic yard care and native plants that don't require a lot of water. Start an animal-friendly garden club. If you get enough of your neighbors on board, you can create corridors to help animals like monarch butterflies and birds in their long migrations. Use Nextdoor and other neighborhood social networks to share tips, including humane critter control methods, animal-friendly lawn services, and warnings about larger wildlife sightings to avoid conflicts that might put coyotes, cougars, or bears in danger as they're passing through.

Talk to your local nursery about promoting organic yard care and gardening practices. Ask them to commit to stop selling plants pretreated with neonicotinoids, or any other products containing these bee-killing pesticides, and to take the deadliest rodenticides (brodifacoum, bromadiolone, difethialone, and difenacoum) off the shelves to protect wildlife, pets, and children.

Contact your city council and ask them to support nonlethal wildlife management, such as community education and hazing to keep predators at a distance instead of resorting to deadly trapping, and to replace deer culls with contraceptive vaccines or other methods of humane sterilization. Ask your local parks service to protect smaller animals and your community's health by ditching pesticide treatments. It's easy to overlook the beauty in what you see every day. Share your local wildlife photos on social media to help people see the animals in your community as neighbors, not nuisances.

! Action Alert
THREE THINGS YOU CAN DO TODAY

1 • Learn about your local wildlife to help better meet your wild neighbors' needs.

2 • Ditch the pesticides and switch to natural lawn and garden care.

3 • Tell your local nursery to stop selling plants and other garden products with neonicotinoids. Plant your own butterfly garden using organic, native plants to attract pollinators.

ANIMALS YOU'LL HELP SAVE
Birds, butterflies, bugs, and more small, savvy mammals than you'll ever know.

Unplug Climate Change **12**

Pikas are small, potato-shaped critters who face down enemies with fierce squeaks. These rabbit relatives may be one of the cutest animals you've never heard of and can be harder to catch sight of than catching Pikachu. The name isn't a coincidence, either: Pikachu is loosely inspired by pikas, though pikas aren't known to have the ability to harness lightning. While Pikachu lives safely in your Pokémon GO app, climate change is eating away at the cool alpine habitat that pikas need, making them one of countless species threatened by our addiction to fossil fuels.

Pikas are just the tip of the melting iceberg. Carbon pollution causes ocean acidification, which is causing clownfish (like the title character from *Finding Nemo*) to get lost more easily. Ocean acidification harms the fish's sense of smell and hearing, and young clown fish like Nemo not only are having a harder time finding their way home when exposed to carbon dioxide pollution, but it actually makes them more likely to find their way into the jaws of predators.[1] Then there's the polar bear, poster cub of climate change, which may only survive in beautiful photos if we don't do something about greenhouse gas emissions.

From mountaintops to coral reefs, if we don't change our climate-disrupting ways, more than a third of animal and plant species will face extinction by midcentury[2]—and up to 70 percent by the end of the century.[3] As animal lovers, we need to take the climate crisis seriously. Though it's also worth taking seriously if you're into self-preservation, since climate change is disrupting human communities, causing sea-level rise, aiding the spread of disease, triggering catastrophic weather events, and complicating agriculture.

Taking the Heat Off Wildlife

The power struggle between human energy needs and wildlife survival starts long before our greenhouse gas emissions reach the atmosphere. Getting oil, coal, and natural gas out of the ground only happens through disaster movie levels of destruction. Pipelines plow through thousands of miles of habitat while a single spill can dump hundreds of millions of gallons of oil into the environment, choking wildlife, coating them in deadly oil, and contaminating oceans and coastlines. Entire mountaintops are literally sheared off to get to coal. Fracking for natural gas pumps toxic chemical stews into water supplies and, along with wastewater injection, has been shown to increase the risk of earthquakes.[4] Extracting, refining, and transporting fossil fuels is a dirty process that takes up huge swaths of land and massive amounts of water, and produces toxic pollution. And that's all before we even get to the part where we burn it to drive to work, turn on the lights, and charge our smartphones. Then comes more pollution, including the greenhouse gas variety that's led to the whole climate catastrophe.

Before you run out to stock up on candles and cancel your Netflix, we don't have to return to the Stone Age to save animals (and ourselves) from the climate crisis. There are dozens of ways that we can use less energy, waste less energy, and support energy from renewable sources that have minimal impact on wildlife.

Although it's critical that we ditch fossil fuels as quickly as possible, not all types of renewable energy are created equal when it comes to protecting wildlife. For example, some legislators and power companies want to count burning trash as renewable energy. Just because we produce a lot of garbage, that doesn't mean it's a renewable resource. (Not to mention that burning tires and other trash creates toxic smoke full of pollutants and the greenhouse gases we're trying to avoid.) A lot of cities boast about hydropower from rivers, but those massive dams change the natural flow of waterways, altering ecosystems that wild animals are counting on. So, unless you're a beaver, leave the rivers to find their own way at their own pace. Fuel from trees and other plants—known as biomass—has gotten a lot of credit for being a clean and green alternative to fossil fuels, but that credit is borrowing from the climate. It turns out that burning biomass often emits more carbon dioxide than coal and gas because you have to burn a whole lot more of it to get the same amount of energy. And consider where that biomass came from—forests or crops grown on ex-habitat that used to belong to wildlife.

But there's an abundance of energy we've barely tapped into that's truly renewable and wildlife-friendly. Solar and wind energy harness natural phenomena without altering them and produce truly clean power free of carbon emissions and toxic pollutants. Wind turbines have been responsible for killing birds and bats, and large solar farms have displaced desert wildlife and burned-up birds, but the number of animals killed by wind and solar is far less than the number killed by climate change, fossil fuel production, pesticides, cell towers, windows, and even cats.

Still, we should strive to minimize the danger to wildlife. In addition to placing wind farms away from migratory flyways to avoid high traffic, the wind energy industry has been working to design turbine blades that are less hazardous to wildlife and changing everything from the paint color to the speed to minimize collisions. We should produce energy close to where we're going to use it to reduce the need for transmission lines that fragment habitat. And when it comes to the best source of energy for wildlife, worship the sun.

Solar panels on existing human habitat—like using rooftops and parking structures—solve the problem of taking over additional wildlife habitat to meet our energy needs. Plus, photovoltaic solar panels require virtually no water to generate energy and produce minimal emissions, including in the manufacturing process. Good for the planet, good for the planet's critters, and good for people, too; rooftop solar and small local solar installations don't pollute and give communities more power over their own power generation.

The Future Is Now

From oil-covered birds to starving polar bears, the effects of our fossil fuel habit become more apparent every year. Climate change is happening now—but so is the renewable energy revolution. In the past five years or so, rooftop solar prices have plunged 50 percent, and they're expected to continue dropping.[5] Technological improvements have made solar panels lighter and more efficient. More and more tools are coming online, like

Google's Project Sunroof and MIT's Mapdwell Project, to help you determine the solar potential of your home and what it'll cost for you to install rooftop solar panels. Programs are expanding to make solar energy more accessible for everyone, from businesses to renters.

Solar panels used to have a reputation for being the high-tech eco-power of the future, but the future is here. The technology already exists. It's no longer reserved for Silicon Valley CEOs and A-list celebrities. And wildlife can't wait for us to expand it and back off fossil fuel development. Right now, solar accounts for just a small portion of our energy generation, but look around—we're surrounded by rooftops. There's a huge amount of untapped energy on top of our homes, businesses, industrial parks, warehouses, malls, and parking lots and garages.

The further you look into the future, the brighter it gets. Scientists are working on superthin, transparent solar cells that can turn windows into solar panels and integrating photovoltaic technology into roadways. They're also working to improve battery technology so that whether you live in Seattle or Sarasota, you'll be able to save up the sunshine for a rainy day. With these new technologies in various stages of prototypes and pilot tests, mainstream applications are still a few years away, but it's important to let your utility company and elected officials know that you support a solar future so we can start rolling out the political welcome mat for rooftop solar that's available today, as well as the emerging clean energy advancements of tomorrow.

Slay the Energy Vampires

Even with prices dropping and more rebate and financing programs available, not everyone can afford to put solar panels on their home, and if you rent or live in an apartment, the rooftop isn't necessarily yours to panel. But that doesn't mean there aren't ways to shrink your carbon footprint. Everyone can help flip the switch on climate change by wasting less energy. After all, the most wildlife-friendly type of energy is the energy we don't use in the first place.

Don't look now, but your house is full of vampires. Your computers, televisions, cable boxes, music equipment, microwaves, toasters, and other electronics with clocks suck electricity from the outlets even when they're powered off. As long as their fangs are in the wall, they're pulling energy, and a lot of it—nearly a quarter of the electricity consumed in American homes is lost to appliances that are plugged in and not in use.[6] Slay these vampires and you'll reduce your home energy use, save money, and help save climate-sensitive wildlife. And there's no risk of splinters from whittling stakes—all you need for this slaying is to start unplugging your electronics when they're not in use, or use a power strip that allows you to stop multiple appliances from feeding with the push of a button. My personal Dracula is my laptop—as a writer, I have a bad habit of leaving it on so I can leap into action whenever the muse shows up. I have to regularly remind myself to power down and unplug; the muse probably won't run off in the ten seconds it takes to boot up, and, in an emergency, pen and paper can still do the job.

There are a few other simple things you can do to keep your home energy use from sucking. If you thought your ugly Christmas sweaters only had a purpose one night a year, think again. You can wear them around the house all winter to bundle up and turn the thermostat down. Heating and air-conditioning are the biggest energy users in buildings. Grab a few extra blankets and keep your house at sixty-eight degrees when you're home during the day, and aim for sixty-five degrees at night or when no one is home. You could save 1 percent on your heating bill for every degree you drop the temperature for eight hours a day.[7] In the summer, show a little skin and keep your air conditioner at seventy-eight degrees when you're home and eighty degrees when you're not. Programmable thermostats can automatically change the temperature depending on the time of day and the season—some of the newer ones even sync with your phone to determine when you're out and let you change the temperature remotely so you're not overheating or cooling an empty house.

Unplugging electronics, adjusting your thermostat, washing your clothes in cold water and line-drying in the summer, and turning off lights all help reduce your climate impact at no cost. You can spend a little cash to upgrade to energy-efficient light bulbs and weatherize your home with caulk, weather stripping, and insulation to keep your heat and air-conditioning from ghosting through cracks around windows, boards, and pipes. If you're in the market for new appliances, invest in a more efficient model with the Energy Star label. Apps can also help you monitor your energy use, so you can see where you can save more. Or you can get a good, old-fashioned energy audit to better understand your home energy use from an in-person expert.

Tame Your Road Rage

Electricity and heating are the biggest pieces of the energy pie, but they're not the only ones. Animal agriculture also bloats your carbon footprint (see chapter 15 for more on the environmental impact of your diet). And, of course, there's transportation. Traffic jams aren't just bad for your stress level, they're also bad for the climate. Ultimately, the best way to stop stressing out the planet will be for us to move to a fully electrified transportation system—powered by solar energy—with more public transportation and fewer cars on the road. That's not going to happen overnight, so in the meantime, drive less. Get on board with public transportation whenever possible; Google Maps and apps from the local transit authority make it easy to get to know the system even if you're traveling in an unfamiliar city. Walk or bike where you can, which also helps eliminate the likelihood of any wildlife collisions.

When you do drive, use mapping apps to find the most direct route and combine errands to reduce the number of trips (which also saves time and money). Unless you're in the market for a new car, don't run out to buy a hybrid, since you don't want to unnecessarily waste all the resources that go into producing and disposing of cars. But if you are in the market, pay attention to fuel efficiency whether you're buying new or used, hybrid or regular. You can boost the efficiency of the car you already have by 10–40 percent or more by keeping it tuned up, keeping the tires properly inflated, and driving in the responsible, speed limit–abiding, easy-on-the-accelerator-and-brake way that would make your driver's ed instructor proud.[8] Driver feedback apps can help keep you honest. And remember, carpools aren't just for kids.

Comment and Share

Climate change is real, it's caused by us, and it's happening now. There is no debate among scientists about this. And considering that the same actions that can stop climate change also reduce pollution, protect wild-life, and save money, there's no reason not to kick the fossil fuel habit (unless you happen to be profiting from it, in which case you have some serious demons to face if you want to make the world a better place for animals). In fact, we don't really have a choice—it's becoming increasingly dangerous and costly to extract oil, gas, and coal, and climate change is already taking its toll on our future as well as the animals we love. There's a lot that we can do on our own to help the shift to clean, renewable energy, but as individuals, we can't do it all on our own. The energy system is a complicated tangle of wires and politics, and everyone from your local utility to the federal government has a hand in determining whether we can curb our carbon in time to save endangered species.

Decision-makers need to hear that clean energy is important to you. Write your local utility company and ask them to invest in renewable energy. Ask your city council to adopt a climate action plan with concrete steps to reduce emissions in your community, such as committing to operating on 100 percent wildlife-friendly renewable energy, increasing rooftop solar targets, and expanding public transportation. Urge your state representatives to support policies that make local solar more affordable and accessible, such as net metering and community solar projects. Demand that the federal government stop allowing fossil fuel leases on public lands and waters and that they lead the way on international climate goals. Support policies that fight energy waste, such as energy-efficient appliance standards, labeling and education projects, better building codes, and programs that help people audit their energy use and weatherize their homes.

Ride-share to work (a great way to get to know your coworkers and catch up on friendly office gossip), run errands as a team, and head out for a night on the town together instead of meeting there. Or stay in: Put on that ugly Christmas sweater and host a movie night about climate change—take your pick from documentaries like *An Inconvenient Truth* or *Chasing Ice*, or a "cli-fi" disaster movie like *The Day After Tomorrow* or *Snowpiercer* to inspire climate action. Share energy-saving tips and action alerts with your friends. Look up photos of pikas so you can think of them whenever you take steps to reduce your carbon footprint. (Really, they're adorable. Let's save them.)

! Action Alert

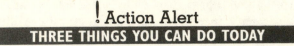

THREE THINGS YOU CAN DO TODAY

1 • Change up your commute—carpool, take public transportation, bike, or walk when possible.

2 • Get in the habit of unplugging electronics when not in use and dialing down your heat or air-conditioning at night.

3 • Call your representatives and let them know that fighting climate change matters.

ANIMALS YOU'LL HELP SAVE

Polar bears, pikas, clownfish, and all the other climate-sensitive mammals, fish, birds, amphibians, lizards, plants, and insects.

Plastic Detox

Sea turtles face the greatest threat of their life right after they hatch, when they have to leave their cozy nest on the beach to make a mad dash for the water, where they'll spend the rest of their days. Imagine running for your life across sand on flippers, as a newborn, through a gauntlet of predators waiting to pick you off before you reach your home for the first time. No one ever said nature was fair. Also unfair is when sea turtles survive that epic beach race and have the chance to grow up, then one day they think they've found a tasty jellyfish snack and wind up getting a deadly mouthful of plastic bag instead.

Haunted by images of birds and turtles shackled by loops of plastic, I became a dedicated cutter of six-pack rings from a young age. I felt better knowing that if an animal came across that particular six-pack ring, I'd provided an escape hatch. But then I learned about the Great Pacific Garbage Patch, sometimes referred to as the Pacific trash vortex (which appropriately sounds like it's the portal to an alternate dimension full of trash demons), where bits of plastic from toys and bags and bottles and clothes and countless other things collect in the ocean's currents. I realized those six-pack rings were a drop in the tsunami of the plastic problem wildlife was facing.

We live in a plastic world. Right now, wherever you are, you're surrounded by plastic—it's in electronics, medical equipment, cars, building materials, furniture, yoga mats, fleece jackets, drinking straws, toothbrushes, action figures, games, packaging, and millions of other products. Plastic has become one of the most ubiquitous materials in our lives, thanks to its durability and convenience. Except it's not so convenient if you're a wild animal.

Plastic doesn't belong in nature. It's easily mistaken for food, but it's not digestible. In its many forms, it can tangle birds, turtles, seals, dolphins, whales, and other marine life. Plastic is also full of toxic chemicals, including persistent organic pollutants (POPs). As the *POP* name implies, not only does the plastic itself not go away, but its toxicity hangs around in the environment, threatening the health of animals and accumulating up the food chain (which isn't good news for those of us at the top of the food chain: the toxic chemicals eaten by little fish are eaten by bigger fish, then eaten by even bigger humans, bringing our pollution full circle).

And there's that one not-so-small fact that plastic manufacturers would prefer our climate-concerned society continues to ignore: Modern plastics are made from petroleum, contributing to our fossil fuel dependence. Imagine every plastic bottle of water filled one-quarter of the way with oil—that's how much fossil fuel it took to produce the plastic and process and ship the bottled water to the store.[1] So, in addition to saving ocean life, a plastic detox will also help fight climate change.

Warning: Choking Hazard

Modern synthetic, carbon-based plastics came on the scene in 1907 with the invention of Bakelite. The next few decades brought the invention of polystyrene (such as Styrofoam restaurant carryout containers), polyester (the favorite fabric of workout clothes and cheap uniform designers), PVC (used in everything from pipes to shower curtains), nylon (found in ropes, rugs, and rugged clothing), and polyethylene (the most common plastic in the world, primarily manufactured to package other manufactured things). With each decade since then, we became more and more dependent on plastics.

Here's the really scary part: Since plastic takes somewhere between several decades and several centuries to decompose, most of the plastic that's been created since 1907 still exists in the world. In fact, the majority of plastic ever created was produced in the past ten years, so it'll still be around for your great-grandchildren.

Actually, it gets scarier: By 2050—less than 150 years after plastic was invented—there will be more plastic than fish in the sea[2] and every shorebird in the world will be eating the stuff.[3]

Our oceans are choking on plastic. Six-pack rings are just one of the dangers. Plastic shopping bags float in the water, looking like jellyfish and entangling unsuspecting sea life. Bright bits of plastic trash on the beach look a lot like insects, small fish, crustaceans, crab eggs, and other shore-bird delicacies. Sometimes these plastics, like the jellyfish-imposter shopping bags, can pose an immediate choking hazard. But even more frequently the small bits of plastic—the pieces that have broken down but will never biodegrade—slowly fill the stomachs of birds, fish, and other marine animals so they think they're getting food while they're actually starving to death. One recent study by Swedish researchers compared young fish chowing down on plastic to teenagers hooked on fast food, finding that even when they have access to nutritious alternatives to eat, the kids just can't resist the lure of plastic.[4]

At this point, you might be thinking, *I'd never throw plastic in the ocean. Littering was so 1970s.* I believe you, but sadly the litterbug has not gone extinct. As recently as 2008, more than 25 percent of people interviewed admitted to littering in the past month, and 35 percent of people were observed being litterbugs in action, though they flat-out denied it when asked a few minutes later.[5] Whether they didn't want to fess up or didn't consciously realize what they'd done, it's clear that we've still got work to do to make sure garbage gets into bins instead of the mouths and beaks of wildlife.

For those of us who dutifully put trash where it belongs, our detritus still has a way of blowing around, tipping over, and being raided by raccoons and other wildlife. Although recycling programs have grown, they're very limited when it comes to plastic products that aren't bottle-shaped. Only 9 percent of plastic is recycled in the United States, compared to 26 percent in Europe, while as much as twenty million tons globally finds its way to the ocean every year.[6] The only way to be certain you're not contributing to plastic pollution is to stop contributing to plastic production.

Keep Away from Children

There's been a lot of attention in recent years on lead, phthalates, and PVC in toys exposing kids to toxic chemicals. As a result, toy giants like LEGO and Hasbro have been working to get toxics out of their products and reduce their plastic packaging. Unfortunately, they're still producing millions of games, dolls, and other cheap, virtually disposable plastic playthings that will outlive you and your children and your children's children. LEGO has invested a lot of money into researching alternative materials for its famous building blocks, but the deadline for the sustainable switch isn't until 2030. In the meantime, companies will keep churning out plastic products as long as people keep buying the stuff (that goes for toys made for kids and adults).

New plastics that claim to be biodegradable are a good idea in theory—unlike petroleum-based plastics, these alternatives are capable of breaking down, but it only works under certain conditions and high temperatures. Just like petroleum-based plastics, these alternatives often wind up in the ocean, where they're insulated from the conditions they need to decompose, so they hang around waiting to be consumed by wildlife. Similarly, compostable, plant-derived materials are available in place of plastic plates and flatware, but there aren't many waste disposal facilities that will accept them. Most of those compostable sporks still wind up in the landfill. Your best bet is to avoid any kind of disposables when possible. For parties and other events, break out the reusable dishes and silverware. The extra dish duty is worth it to protect birds and fish.

Products made from recycled plastic are another idea that's a little too good to be true. While recycling is a better option than littering, plastic recycling takes an enormous amount of energy, and generally the plastic is degraded in the process. So plastic water bottles usually don't become new plastic water bottles. Instead, they're recycled into toys, pens, shoes, bags, and clothing. It seems like a cool idea, but then we're back at square one with plastic products that can't be recycled. And when it comes to clothing with plastic-based fibers, recycled or virgin, every wash releases microscopic pieces into the water system to be eaten by wildlife. (See chapter 20 for more information on microfibers.) As long as oil and gas prices stay low, it's cheaper for companies to make new plastic than to invest in recycled-plastic products anyway.

Depending on where you live, the types of plastic that can be recycled—even if it has the little triangle on the bottom—may be limited. Attempting to break down plastic through burning trash releases toxic chemicals and greenhouse gases into the atmosphere. There's really no good way to get rid of it. So, despite all these efforts at ingenuity, the best plastic is no plastic.

This Bag Is Not a Toy

If we keep demanding that companies get rid of extraneous plastic packaging, we can start reducing the wasteful plastic pollution that's taking over our oceans. When Hasbro stopped pointlessly wrapping game instructions in plastic packaging, it saved eight hundred thousand pounds of material.[7] Seemingly small changes can have a huge impact when a company applies them across their product line.

While most electronics come swaddled in plastic, Apple replaced the majority of the plastic wrappings and tabs from its products in favor of minimalist recycled-paper packaging. They also recently phased out the once-iconic plastic bags from its stores. Businesses and cities across the country are starting to offer plastic bags by request only or even charging a small fee per bag to make customers think twice about whether they really need one. These nominal fees or upon-request policies have been effective in reducing single-use bag consumption.[8] Sometimes all you need is to hit pause on your old habits long enough to form new ones.

Comment and Share

Think of how many times you've had to fight through plastic packaging within packaging to get to a product. It's possible to do better—and for the sake of sea turtles, birds, and fish, we need to demand better. Next time you purchase something with unnecessary layers of plastic, post a photo of the unnecessary waste on social media and tag the company. Send a message to their customer service department with your concerns and the photo, too. Leave a negative review on the website of the store where you purchased it. Start an online petition. In as many ways as you can, let them know they need to stop the plastic madness. Less plastic will save wildlife and save money.

Start paying attention to how plastic comes into your life, and avoid it whenever possible. I can't avoid the plastic built into my car or computer, but I can make the radical choice to put my kale and apples directly in the shopping basket or in a cloth tote instead of separating each in its own plastic produce shroud. I take my reusable water bottle with me everywhere and get inordinately excited about water fountains with bottle-filling stations in airports and parks. And I religiously refuse to use straws in restaurants, even at the risk of waitstaff taking it as a personal rejection. How did drinking directly from the glass go out of style? Americans use five hundred million plastic drinking straws every single day. If we all declared a straw-free Sunday, we'd save twenty-six trillion straws, enough plastic to fill about 6,500 school buses a year.[9] In addition to just saying no to straws, ask your local restaurants to only provide straws and plastic lids upon request. We shouldn't be foisting plastic waste on people or wildlife simply out of habit.

If you have a choice when making a purchase, go with the option with less or no plastic in the product or the packaging. Plastic six-pack rings should be a thing of the past; ask companies to stop using the plastic rings, and stores to stop stocking them. Instead, buy a two-liter or a case of cans in recyclable cardboard (it's not as if those carbonated beverages are going to expire anytime soon). Avoid snacks individually wrapped in plastic; buy in bulk, then repackage in reusable snack packs for convenience. Invest in your own reusable water bottle that you love and stop buying bottled water—you, too, can become a water fountain connoisseur. Take a travel mug to the coffee shop. Bring your own reusable containers to restaurants for leftovers. Refill printer cartridges and other office supplies. Keep tote bags in your car instead of accepting plastic shopping bags. For larger, more durable plastic products like toys and household goods, consider whether it's something you can borrow from a friend or snag as a hand-me-down or secondhand purchase. Ask around online before you buy or before you toss bigger plastic goods in the trash.

You may be one person trying to change the world, but policies that ban single-use plastic shopping bags and bottled water have successfully changed the behavior of entire communities. San Jose, California, passed its Bring Your Own Bag ordinance in 2012, which bans single-use plastic bags at the checkout and makes stores sell paper bags for a minimum of ten cents. Just a few years later, 48 percent of shoppers are using reusable bags and 43.8 percent are opting for no bag at all, compared to 3.1 percent and 12.9 percent, respectively, before the ban. Plus, there's 76 percent less plastic bag pollution in local creeks and rivers.[10] In 2009, Washington University in Saint Louis became the first university to ban the sale of bottled water and since then, the campus boasts a BYOWB (Bring Your Own Water Bottle) culture and overall bottled beverage sales have dropped by 39 percent, taking half a million bottles out of the waste stream each year.[11] Ask your campus or city council to tackle its plastic problem with these types of policies.

Plastic is so pervasive that's it's hard to completely avoid it until we see some serious changes in how we produce and sell things. But by getting creative, we can get unnecessary plastic out of our lives. And by getting vocal, we can keep excess plastic out of the ocean.

! Action Alert
THREE THINGS YOU CAN DO TODAY

1 • Get used to using reusables—learn to love your water bottle, to bring your own bags and carryout containers, and to embrace doing a few extra dishes to avoid disposables.

2 • When making purchases, choose the option with less packaging whenever possible.

3 • Ask your city council and favorite stores to ban single-use plastic bags.

ANIMALS YOU'LL HELP SAVE
Sea turtles, shorebirds, fish, and other marine and freshwater animals.

14   Down the Drain

Amargosa toads are quieter than most other toads and frogs. These silent hoppers only give a croak when they're grabbed by predators and chirp their "Let me go!" call. Can't blame them for giving up their vow of silence in a life-or-death situation. Except their whole existence has become life or death these days. These rare toads reside on an exclusive ten-mile stretch along the Amargosa River in southern Nevada's Oasis Valley. The wetlands and river habitat they need to survive have been threatened by development, particularly the type that slurps up groundwater. In drought-plagued Nevada, the more that people and industries open up the pipes, the less water there is left for Amargosa toads and all the other animals who rely on the region's diminishing rivers and wetlands.

It's easy to take water for granted when it fills fountains, swimming pools, and toilets, and gushes from the tap with a flick of the wrist. But the historic droughts across much of the United States have raised some important questions: Do we really need golf courses in the desert? What's the shortest shower one can take without shortchanging hygiene? And if it's yellow, should you let it mellow?

American households guzzle more than twenty-seven billion gallons of water every single day through our faucets, showers, toilets, washing machines, dishwashers, sprinklers, and hoses.[1] That's more per person than anywhere else in the world, and an average of sixteen to twenty times more per person than what's needed to meet basic hydration, hygiene, and sanitation needs according to the World Health Organization.[2] This doesn't even count the water footprint that goes into our food and energy, and into manufacturing all the things we buy and use.

It's not like water just falls from the sky. Okay, maybe it does, but rain isn't an endless supply of magical unicorn tears. There's a limited amount of water on the planet, and unless you have a rain barrel (which isn't legal in some states),[3] the water falling from the sky doesn't go directly to your pipes. The water in your tea, your tub, and your toilet comes from rivers, lakes, and groundwater aquifers or wells. And the river systems, lakes, and wetlands that provide that water are full of wild animals just trying to get by. Our out-of-control water consumption is changing and draining ecosystems, leaving countless species in the dust.

Water Wars

Water is life. We can't survive without it, but four billion people worldwide face severe water scarcity at least one month each year, with as many as 2.9 billion living with insufficient freshwater sources for at least four to six months.[4] Water is wasted, mismanaged, and polluted. And when people get thirsty and don't have enough water to grow food or sustain their economy, they get desperate, increasing the risk of violent conflict. Sociologists say that water crises helped erode stability in regions like the Middle East and that future wars will be fought over "blue gold."

A future without water isn't just apocalyptic for humans—animals need water, too. Many aquatic species and other animals who rely on wetlands and watersheds for nesting, feeding, and migration are now threatened or endangered because of our reckless water consumption. The United States has been experiencing extreme drought conditions over the past decade; it's gotten so bad that with climate change forecasts, NASA researchers warn that we're likely headed for a decades-long "megadrought."[5] Meanwhile, corporations are hogging all the water they can get. People like to vacation in warm places, so companies build golf courses that require enormous amounts of water in the middle of the desert. Meat and dairy production gulps water in drought-stricken regions while produce farmers struggle to keep their crops alive. And bottled water companies are draining communities of their rightful water sources.

Our water demand has pitted us against charismatic creatures like sandhill cranes and kit foxes, and lesser-known but colorfully named species like the unarmored threespine stickleback (a fish) and Texas fatmucket (a mussel). It's really not a fair fight. We have more than 7.5 billion people and all the drills and pipes and dams up against cuteness and cool names. It's time to declare a truce and start saving some water for wildlife. We need to speak up for Amargosa toads and other thirsty animals who can't speak for themselves.

Every Flush Counts

The average American family uses the equivalent of 2,400 glasses of water every day.[6] Only a small amount of that is actually going into glasses for drinking. Your faucets gush one to two gallons of water per minute, so every time you leave the tap on while brushing your teeth or shaving, or if you get distracted while hand-washing dishes, the gallons add up. Showerheads spew even more water—the difference between a fifteen-minute and a five-minute shower can be as much as fifty gallons down the drain (the damage isn't quite as bad if you install low-flow showerheads).[7] There's something about rushing water that washes away my mental blocks and helps me think through problems—I even used to keep bathtub crayons in the shower to jot down my brilliant, if waterlogged, ideas. But then I realized how much water my wandering shower-brain was taking from wildlife. These days I challenge myself to speed showers and take my problems for long walks instead. If, like me, you're fortunate enough to live near rivers, streams, and waterfalls, you can still get into the mental flow by visiting rushing water (and the wild animals who share it) instead of making it come to you.

Automatic dishwashers use about half the amount of water as doing dishes by hand, saving time, money, and wildlife.[8] More good news: You can also do less laundry. Don't be ashamed of your sort-of-clean clothes pile or how often you employ the sniff test. According to Levi's, dirty is the new clean—the jeans giant recommends washing your denim after every ten wears to save water (spot-cleaning as needed, unless you've been up to something exceptionally grungy). Withholding your jeans from the washing machine between monthly spin cycles can save nearly two hundred gallons of water a year per pair of pants.[9] You're welcome.

And, of course, there's the toilet. If you have an older model, each flush whisks away enough water to sustain someone's drinking, cooking, and basic washing needs for a day. You might remember a popular meme a few years ago with a skeptical-looking kid, apparently from a village in a developing country, giving the side-eye to a well-dressed woman with some variation of "You do *what* in bowls of clean water?" No wonder we're headed for water wars. If you're in the market for a newer toilet—or already have one—porcelain thrones with the WaterSense label drop your flush footprint from six gallons to close to one gallon per flush. A WaterSense toilet can save your family nearly thirteen thousand gallons of water every year.[10] There are also dual-flush models—increasingly spotted in public bathrooms, but also available for homes—that let you choose your own flushing adventure depending on what kind of business needs to go down. Flushing etiquette calls for leaving the toilet clean and well rinsed for the next person in public, but in the privacy of your own home, why not let it mellow if it's only yellow? Every time you skip a flush, think of all the endangered salmon, frogs, and bald eagles you're saving water for. It's practically the patriotic thing to do.

One final note on toilets: A running toilet isn't just annoying, it's running away with a huge amount of water. A minor leak wastes about thirty gallons of water a day, but if you've got a big leak, you could be losing up to four thousand gallons of water every day it's neglected.[11] The average household has all kinds of drips and leaks that go unnoticed—or noticed and ignored—but those drops in a bucket can add up to more than ten thousand gallons of water a year.[12] Together, Americans waste a trillion gallons a year just through household leaks. Plumbers are the unsung heroes of water conservation. For the sake of fish, river otters, and thirsty migratory birds, give your local plumber a call.

If you want to save water for wildlife, it's also time to have a chat with your landscaper. If you have a yard, there's a good chance your lawn is siphoning a major chunk of your water bill. Our obsession with greener grass has led to inefficient and unnecessary watering that wastes as much as half the water that's used outdoors. Your lawn doesn't need water as much as your local streams do—if you cut down watering to just once or twice a week, you can save up to one thousand gallons of water a month. Brown grass isn't the end of the world. If you have a sprinkler system, automatic sprinklers can be installed with moisture sensors to avoid watering in the rain. And if you really want to be a water hero, trade your lawn for native, water-saving landscaping, known as xeriscaping, and save up to eighteen thousand gallons of water a year.[13] Let the Joneses try to keep up with that.

Unbottle Water

The fact that fresh, clean water is so readily available to most of us on demand, at little to no cost, has resulted in many of us taking it for granted. Yet we buy about $14 billion worth of bottled water each year, and that number keeps growing.[14] The previous chapter discussed the problem with the plastic bottles. Now let's talk about what's inside those bottles.

Bottled water companies are selling us a story. They want us to believe their water is fresher than what comes out of your tap and that it comes from idyllic places where life is better, cleaner, and healthier. Many of those places were better, cleaner, and healthier, once upon a time, before the bottled water factories came to town. However, tap water is actually better regulated than bottled water; even in communities where corruption has tainted the water supply, municipalities are required to regularly test for contaminants and report results to the Environmental Protection Agency.

An even bigger scandal is that nearly two-thirds of all bottled water is just repackaged tap water.[15] Huge multinational corporations come into communities and convince local officials to let them build bottling plants and tap into public water, which raises ethical concerns about privatizing the water supply as well as concerns about the impact of high-volume withdrawals on the health of ecosystems and sustainability of water sources. Then the companies mark it up nearly two thousand times above the cost of tap water, on average, and try to sell it back to residents in ocean-polluting plastic bottles.[16] If corporations could figure out how to bottle air, they would repackage and sell that back to us, too. Across the country, communities are fighting back to stop these behemoth water bottling plants from coming into their towns, taking their water, creating pollution, and damaging their local watersheds.[17,18]

As for the bottled water that comes from fresh mountain springs and other sources that aren't filtered through a municipal water supply, the ramifications for wildlife are obvious. A giant processing plant that sets up shop beside clean wildlife habitat to suck up profits isn't doing the resident fish, amphibians, and other animals who rely on that water source any favors.

Whatever you love, you can find a reusable water bottle that reflects your personality. Buy a bottle you're happy to carry around and get in the habit of bringing it everywhere with you. From the Detroit Metropolitan Airport to Zion National Park, water bottle–filling stations are sprouting in public places to make it even easier to refill on the go and avoid purchasing plastic bottles. Always choose tap water when dining out, and if you're a regular at a restaurant that offers bottled water for sale, ask them to do the planet a favor and ditch the bottle.

Comment and Share

Whether it's a rural community trying to stop a bottling plant from coming to town, an indigenous tribe trying to stop a pipeline from polluting their groundwater, or a city trying to get their neglected water supply cleaned up, support the fights for clean, community tap water by signing petitions, writing letters, sharing news on social media, and donating to the groups on the front line. Access to safe, drinkable water should be a basic human right. If we lose our water sources to corporations and pollution, there's no hope for the wild animals who need clean water, too.

Become a tap water evangelist. Urge your favorite parks and other public gathering spots to install water bottle–refilling stations. Lead by example—the more your crew sees how easy it is for you to carry your own reusable bottle, the more likely they are to get in the habit, too. Encourage friends and family to invest in the perfect water bottle and invest in wildlife by using it.

Eating less meat and dairy is an important step to shrinking your diet's water footprint. Go ahead and post that veggie burger online and brag about how it required 93 percent less water to produce than a beef burger.[19] But other than your animal-friendly food choices, no one wants to see pictures of how you're reducing water use in your kitchen or bathroom in their social media feeds. Photos of dishwashers and toilets aren't exactly Instagram gold. But there are a lot of great, shareable infographics online about saving water. You can also share photos of your favorite wild animals along with how you're helping them by cutting your water waste. Everyone can appreciate the importance of water; sometimes we just need a reminder that we're not the only ones who need a drink.

! Action Alert

THREE THINGS YOU CAN DO TODAY

1 • Turn off the tap. By shaving just five minutes off your shower time, you can save as much as 750 gallons a month.

2 • Call your plumber. It could save wild lives.

3 • Ask your local parks, community centers, stadiums, and other public places that sell bottled water to ditch the bottle and make water fountains and stations for refilling reusable bottles more available.

ANIMALS YOU'LL HELP SAVE
Everyone gets a little thirsty sometimes, but fish, amphibians, and birds are often the first to suffer when rivers, lakes, and wetlands dry up.

Take Extinction Off Your Plate

Bison may be North America's largest mammal, but it's their tiny tails that often reveal the best clues as to what kind of mood they're in. Tails down and twitching usually mean the bison is chill, but if the tail is up, he or she may be gearing up to charge. If bison could respond to what's been happening to their species over the past couple of centuries, it would be tails up all around. Tens of millions of bison once roamed across North America, but now there are fewer than 30,000 wild bison left on the continent and only one herd living in Yellowstone National Park that can still trace its ancestry back to prehistoric times. These magnificent mammals have lost their homes to agricultural development and their lives to the perception that they're problematic for cattle. To add insult to injury, thousands of Yellowstone bison have been killed over the past few decades because ranchers fear that if the animals wander out of the park, they'll transmit a disease called brucellosis to nearby grazing cattle—even though there's never been a known case of cattle contracting brucellosis from bison and bison got the disease from cattle in the first place. Bison may be America's official national mammal, but the American appetite for cheap meat has them under the knife.

When you sit down to a steak dinner, it's pretty obvious that there's a cow who didn't fare well for that fillet to reach your plate. But it's not just the farmed animal who had a bad day—meat and dairy production are the greatest threats to biodiversity worldwide. From climate change to habitat loss to the millions of wild animals killed every year to protect industry profits, wildlife pay the price for our addiction to burgers, bacon, wings, and cheese.

Industrial animal agriculture is growing even faster than the human population.[1] Everywhere we go, we take our farmed animals with us, and it's only going to get worse. Between grazing and feed crops, the world's cows, pigs, sheep, goats, and chickens have already taken over 30 percent of the planet's total land and 70 percent of all farmland.[2] In the United States, animal agriculture takes up half the land area of the lower forty-eight states.[3] More than thirty-five thousand miles of U.S. rivers have been polluted by factory farms,[4] and about half of our freshwater use goes toward meat and dairy production.[5] No matter what form of environmental destruction you look at, the meat and dairy industries top the worst offenders' list.

And the nightmare gets even worse for wildlife.

The U.S. Department of Agriculture has a little-known program called Wildlife Services. The main service provided is to kill animals by the millions, usually to protect meat and dairy industry profits. The annual death toll includes hundreds of gray wolves, mountain lions, black bears, river otters, and bobcats, as well as tens of thousands of coyotes—and those are just the ones we know about; others likely die when Wildlife Services destroys dens, and still more deaths may be unreported since there's little accountability or public transparency required of the program. And it's not just predators—nearly fifteen thousand prairie dogs were killed and more than sixty-eight thousand of their burrows destroyed in 2016 alone because they're seen as an expensive inconvenience to grazing cattle.[6] Pesticides are sprayed to kill native grasshoppers for eating grass that cows might want to eat. Nontargeted animals, including cats and dogs, get caught in traps or are poisoned by bait left for other animals.

In other words, millions of wild animals are killed every year just to make the world a safer place to raise hamburgers.

Not only is industrial animal agriculture cruel to wildlife and farmed animals (discussed in more detail in chapter 21), it's an incredibly inefficient way to feed people. The meat industry wants you to believe this is the only way to address hunger, but there has to be a better option than growing crops to feed animals in order to feed people, right? Of course there is. We can use far fewer resources—leaving more for bison and other wildlife—by growing more crops for direct human consumption. As an added bonus, research overwhelmingly shows that eating more foods from plants and fewer foods from animals is not only healthier for the animals, but for us, too.

The Meat of the Matter

As dietary changes go, putting beans and veggies in your burrito one day a week instead of chicken or beef isn't a big sacrifice, and it's a reasonable suggestion coming from the government agency that's supposed to promote healthy diets and support farmers. Especially since we don't currently grow enough fruits and vegetables in the United States to meet the daily recommended amount.[7] But when the U.S. Department of Agriculture name-dropped Meatless Mondays in a department newsletter, the meat industry cried foul. The National Cattlemen's Beef Association dramatically called the mere mention of a day without meat "a slap in the face." The USDA quickly distanced itself from Meatless Mondays, retracting the suggestion that forgoing meat once a week might be a good way to reduce your environmental footprint.[8]

Unfortunately, a newsletter retraction is far from the only favor the U.S. industrial animal agriculture industry gets from the government. While nations around the world are starting to integrate sustainability concerns and recommendations to eat less meat and dairy into their official dietary guidelines, the United States is not one of them. In 2015, during the latest revision to the U.S. dietary guidelines, pressure from the meat industry beat out advice from the government's own panel of experts stating that Americans should be eating more sustainable diets that are higher in plant-based foods.[9] In 2016, millions of taxpayer dollars were spent to buy surplus cheese that's been piling up in warehouses due to slow sales in the dairy aisle.[10] Subsidies on feed crops and grazing leases give producers steep discounts that lead to a Big Mac costing less than a salad at the drive-through.

This is where you come in. Despite all these favors, meat and dairy production ultimately rely on the market in the long run. As more people choose plant-based foods and smaller portions of meat, menus and grocery store shelves will reflect those preferences. We're already seeing a shift toward a greater availability of vegetarian options and nondairy alternatives like almond milk and soy cheese. It helps when you let the stores and restaurants you frequent know that you'd like to see more veggies and meat-free meals. Not only can this change their purchasing practices, but greater availability and visibility helps people who don't usually consider meatless meals become a little more veg-curious.

Isn't Grass-Fed Greener?

Grass-fed meat has gained a reputation as being the greatest thing for hamburgers since sliced buns. It's commonly touted as the alternative for anyone who wants more sustainable, more humane, healthier, and better-tasting meat. But when you look at the whole picture, the sustainability status of grass-fed meat is, well, complicated.

Factory farms are terrible for everyone—the animals, the workers, the surrounding communities, and the environment. Grass-fed is reminiscent of the bucolic days of red barns and green pastures with a few scattered cows, pigs, and chickens doing their thing. As long as the animals aren't grazing on sensitive grassland habitat, riparian areas, or forests, or contributing to wilderness being clear-cut to create new pastures, there are advantages to not having huge concentrated manure pits, wasting fewer resources on feed crops, and giving farmed animals a chance to see daylight and real pastures.

Except none of this accounts for the sheer scale of animal agriculture. The only reason we're able to raise billions of animals a year for food in the United States is *because* they're crammed into factory farms. If they were all living the Old MacDonald life, there wouldn't be space for them. Grass-fed is currently a very small part of the meat market; if it started cornering a bigger share without a drastic reduction in the amount of meat people eat, it would quickly become even more disastrous for wildlife. Cattle grazing is already one of the greatest threats to imperiled species—on public lands alone, more than 175 threatened or endangered wild plants and animals are further threatened by cattle tromping around their homes.[11]

To protect wildlife from our carnivorous cravings, we're going to need to adjust our attitude about food. It's time to go retro with our plates, back to the time when meat wasn't the default centerpiece of every meal. Animal agriculture can be part of a sustainable food system, but in a much more limited role than our current appetite for meat and dairy. There are too many people eating too much meat for any form of production to be truly sustainable without reducing our consumption. The best way to take extinction off our plates isn't to replace one kind of meat with another, but to dish out fewer animal products to start with. If you do eat meat, make it a side dish or save it for special occasions to help save a place at the table for bison, butterflies, wolves, prairie dogs, and all the wildlife affected by meat and dairy production.

There Won't Always Be More Fish in the Sea

To us land-dwelling humans, the oceans are vast and alien, particularly if we stop to think about some of the odd creatures of the deep, like fanged viperfish and giant tube worms. But that hasn't stopped us from being so merciless in our quest for seafood that we've turned the old idiom into a lie: There are not, in fact, plenty of fish in the sea. Ninety percent of the fish stocks that the seafood industry relies on have hit or exceeded the limit of harvesting that's considered sustainable.[12] Some of those have been hunted to the brink of extinction, like Pacific bluefin tuna. These powerful warm-blooded predators who sometimes hunt in groups (they're basically the wolves of the sea) have declined to less than 4 percent of their unfished levels due to an unfortunate popularity on sushi menus.[13]

It's not just the sea creatures people like to eat who are in trouble. In an effort to maximize profits, commercial fisheries use nets that can be a mile long or up to sixty miles of nearly invisible fishing lines with a thousand hooks. This giant fishing gear has a tendency to snag anything in its path, including endangered sea turtles, whales, dolphins, sea lions, and sea birds. All those mammals, turtles, birds, and fish who aren't headed for the seafood special are simply thrown away. Some estimates put the total of this deadly bycatch as high as two billion pounds of marine life every year just in the United States and sixty-three billion pounds globally.[14]

Fish raised on farms instead of taken directly from the ocean have their own school of problems. Fish farms are basically wet factory farms, causing many of the same threats to wildlife, including degraded habitat and water pollution, with the added threat of invasive species when farmed fish escape their seaside cages. Genetically engineered salmon add a host of new concerns, particularly around mutant escapees mingling with endangered wild salmon to cause genetic problems and other changes to the natural order of the ocean.[15] Also, farmed fish need to eat, which means they're either eating feed crops or smaller fish taken from the ocean, so their fate is either tied to industrial land agriculture or overfishing and bycatch.

Seafood is pushed as a healthy alternative to meat, but the marine life we've developed a taste for face the same sustainability conundrum as land animals: There are simply too many people eating too much seafood for the ocean to sustain our appetites. Like other animal products, reduce your consumption of marine animals, and if you do eat seafood, minimize your impact on ocean ecosystems by sticking to fish lower on the food chain, like tilapia, sole, scallops, and sardines, and avoid species that have been heavily overfished, like Chilean sea bass, Atlantic salmon, Atlantic halibut, and bluefin tuna. It's not easy to tell whether your sashimi or fillet came from a fishery with a bad bycatch record when you're ordering, but urge your favorite restaurant to ask the hard questions of their seafood suppliers and support smaller-scale fishing with gear that's safer for turtles and marine mammals.

Don't Waste Wildlife

There's something attractive about a heaping basket of fruit and bottomless buffets. Supersized meals are not only a good value, but they tap into something primal—as a species, humans used to have a lot less certainty, like other animals, about where our next meal was coming from. Yet even in the land of plenty, one in seven Americans still face food insecurity on a day-to-day basis. Meanwhile, 40 percent of perfectly good, edible food produced in the United States is wasted.[16] Trashed. Dumped. Left to rot on the fields and in landfills. It's shameful when so many people are going hungry. It's an affront to anyone concerned about wasteful spending, with about $218 billion worth of food tossed every year.[17] And it's an insult to all the wild animals who lost their lives or their homes to agricultural production for nothing.

Here's what we're throwing away each year: If global food waste were a country, it would be the third-biggest contributor to climate change behind China and the United States.[18] The amount of farmland wasted producing food that's never eaten takes up enough space to make the nation of Waste-landia the second-biggest country after Russia.[19] If we reverted the farmland growing uneaten food just in the United States back to wildlife habitat, we could create wilderness thirty-five times the size of Yellowstone National Park.[20]

Fortunately, food waste prevention is a rising star. Government officials and industry groups are taking steps to make it easier to donate leftover food to those in need and to standardize date labels to reduce the confusion that frequently causes people to throw out food that's still safe and delicious because they think it's expired. Grocery stores are starting to ease up their superficial beauty standards in the produce aisle by giving "ugly" fruits and vegetables a second chance in prepared foods or discount bins. Ending the beauty contest and selling more imperfect produce could save more than a quarter of a million tons of food per year that would have been rejected simply for being a little out of shape.[21]

But there's more to be done. Grocery stores and restaurants need to be more transparent about how much food is being wasted so we can work together to take bigger bites out of the problem. And we, the eaters, need to take an active interest in fighting food waste. More than 80 percent of wasted food is thrown out in the home or by restaurants, cafeterias, and supermarkets.[22] On the home front, a little planning goes a long way. Grocery lists, meal plans, and inventorying the fridge to use what you already have will cut down on overpurchasing, saving food, money, and wildlife. The USDA's FoodKeeper app tells you the best way to store everything from apricots to zucchini to keep them from getting prematurely funky. With foods like dairy products, juices, and sauces, ignore the date on the carton in favor of the sniff test. While grocery stores and decision-makers are working to end the confusion caused by date labels, keep in mind that, with the exception of baby formula, those "best by," "sell by," and other expiration dates are based on the producer's idea of peak freshness, not food safety.

Apps are getting in on the food waste fight with tools that help you track the food in your fridge and pantry, including when they were bought and when they're best used by. Keep an eye out for up-and-coming food redistribution apps, such as Too Good To Go, which launched in Denmark and the U.K. in 2015 to work with restaurants, bakeries, and other shops to sell leftover food that otherwise would've been thrown out at the end of the day to app users willing to pick up cheap takeout at closing time. If you don't like grocery shopping with a list, you can install a FridgeCam that takes a snapshot of your fridge's contents whenever you close the door, enabling you to check the latest image on your smartphone app when you're wandering the grocery aisles or deciding if you need to pick up dinner on the way home from work. (You can also go the lower-tech route and snap your own photo of the fridge and pantry before heading to the store.) Knowing what's on your shelves helps you avoid buying things you don't need and makes it easier to choose ingredients to fill out meals with whatever you already have.

Produce is the top source of wasted food. In addition to planning your meals and improving your storage techniques, buy smaller amounts of perishables more frequently, embrace ugly fruits and vegetables, and get creative to use as much of the plant as possible. Challenge yourself to use everything you buy—you might be amazed at what a wok or blender can do. And be realistic about what goes in your cart. I know many well-intentioned salad greens have met an unfortunate demise in my refrigerator. So, despite my inner diet police telling me I should want to eat salad at home, I've accepted that I rarely do and stick to buying versatile greens like spinach and kale that I can use in lots of different and, to me, more appealing dishes. If you ever find that you bought way more groceries than you could possibly eat or reasonably store, invite your friends over for a potluck to help rescue your food before it winds up in the dump.

Eat Local, Think Endangered

The local food movement has been going global, and with good reason. Eating locally produced food supports smaller farmers, builds community, and helps us reconnect with where our food comes from. If you eat animal products from local farmers, you can often find out details about how the animals were raised. When you eat local organic produce, you know you're not contributing to pesticide pollution that could harm fish, amphibians, birds, and other animals in your neighborhood. Since your food didn't have to travel very far, it's not contributing as much to climate change, with the added bonus of being fresher, tasting better, and allowing you to explore regional, seasonal flavors.

Before you run off to start living la vida locavore, remember that the term *local* only refers to one thing: geography. Grocery stores can advertise produce as "local" that came from anywhere within a five- to five-hundred-mile radius. Local farmers can still sell food that's laden with pesticides or genetically engineered crops that threaten biodiversity. If you happen to live near factory farms or a harbor that's home to whale-killing fisheries, technically, you could be eating a ham sandwich or shrimp cocktail that's both local and terrible for wildlife. One study from Carnegie Mellon University found that eating an entirely local diet still doesn't save as many greenhouse gas emissions as eating meat-free just one day a week.[23]

Take control of your dietary footprint by taking advantage of local produce and reducing your meat consumption no matter where it comes from. And don't fall for the marketing—without additional information, "local" is a meaningless label. Look for food that's local, organic, *and* seasonal, and if you're eating animal products, find out if the animals were raised in pastures and without routine antibiotics or other unnecessary pharmaceuticals.

Local food production can be the antidote to industrial farming. Instead of fueling more vast homogenous, wildlife-deprived fields of pesticide-drenched, genetically engineered crops being fed to animals crammed into dark warehouses, we can choose a food system built on smaller diversified organic farms that contribute to the economy, culture, and health of our communities and that promote conservation and coexistence with all wildlife. But only if we look for the wildlife hidden behind the labels.

Comment and Share

Changing our diets isn't easy. If it were simple, there wouldn't be a multibillion-dollar weight loss industry. But if we all start with small changes, it adds up. Reducing the meat in your diet by one-third—that could be a meat-free meal every day or smaller portions or eating vegetarian a couple of days a week—can save as much as 340,667 gallons of water, more than 4,000 square feet of land, and the greenhouse gas equivalent of driving

2,700 fewer miles a year.[24] Imagine if all your friends did that, too. Now imagine how much more water, habitat, and clean air that leaves for wildlife.

The easier it is to eat earth-friendly, the more likely you (and your friends) are to do it. Although more people are aware of and enraged by the mistreatment of farmed animals and the environmental footprint of animal agriculture than they used to be, the biggest factors in the trend of meat and dairy reduction tend to be health concerns and the availability and affordability of plant-based options like soy, coconut, and almond milk. As far as the animals are concerned, it doesn't matter so much why people eat fewer animal products, just that they do. That means meat-free and organic alternatives need to be more visible and readily available to normalize them and drive down cost. Although plant-based foods have a far smaller footprint than animal products, you can still choose the even-more-environmentally-friendly option when possible, such as organic instead of GMO soy and the dairy alternatives that require less water and energy to produce.

Leave positive reviews for restaurants that have good vegetarian and vegan options and ask those that only offer you a plate of iceberg lettuce and fries to do better. If you eat in a cafeteria, request plant-based options and ask them to participate in Meatless Mondays or Green Mondays or a similar program where, at least once a week, they feature meat-free meals for people to try. Trayless dining and buffets that aren't overflowing help cut food waste. Ask grocery stores to commit to zero food waste, to support clear, consistent date labels, to buy ugly fruits and vegetables, and to donate excess edibles so more food winds up in bellies than garbage bins. And ask stores and restaurants to track and report their food waste to keep them accountable.

Sustainability needs to be part of the conversation about food at every level before we eat ourselves and other animals out of house and planet. There are dozens of policies that influence what foods are available and at what cost, but the impact on the planet is rarely taken into account. Ask your representatives to include environmental considerations in federal food policies like dietary guidelines, labels, and subsidies. If your city or company is creating a climate action plan, urge them to include the footprint of food by encouraging programs to reduce meat consumption, make veggie options more available, and support local farmers. Ask your local environmental clubs and animal groups to adopt vegetarian meal policies for their events. Too many organizations dedicated to helping wildlife or encouraging compassion for animals undercut their own work with meat-filled menus at fund-raisers.

Last but not least, talk to others about the connection between food choices and wildlife protection. Most people aren't thinking about bison or butterflies when they sit down to eat, despite the direct connection between food production and threats to endangered species. There are a lot of different reasons why people make the food choices they do, and for those who haven't been convinced to eat less meat for their own health or to cut food waste to shrink their grocery bills, saving their favorite wild animal just might be the missing link. (For tips on sharing your animal-friendly eating habits to inspire others, see chapter 21.)

! Action Alert
THREE THINGS YOU CAN DO TODAY

1 • Reduce your meat and dairy intake by one-third by trying more meat-free dishes and making veggies the star of your meals while sending meat to the sidelines.

2 • Make a plan to put a lid on food waste at home with grocery lists, menus, and clean-the-fridge potlucks.

3 • Ask your favorite restaurant to up their sustainability game with meat-free options and more local and organic ingredients. Bonus points if it's not already a vegetarian hangout so you can reach more people outside the choir.

ANIMALS YOU'LL HELP SAVE
Wildlife losing their habitat to pastures and feed crops, wildlife poisoned by pesticides, wildlife who need clean water, and everyone affected by climate change.

16   Let's Talk About Sex

Bonobos are one of our closest relatives in the animal kingdom, shar-
ing almost 99 percent of our genes. These adorable endangered apes
are known for being smart, social, and randy as all get-out. Sex isn't
just for reproduction in Bonobo Town—they find all kinds of excuses
to get it on several times a day with different partners. They even
indulge in extreme make-up sex, solving their problems with pan-
sexual orgies. Except there's one problem bonobo booty calls can't
solve: Human reproduction taking over the planet.

When I say everything you do is an opportunity to create a better world
for animals, I mean *everything*. As an animal advocate, you never stop saving animals—even in the bedroom.

There are more than 7.5 billion people on the planet, and we're hurtling
toward nearly 10 billion by midcentury.[1] And in geologic time, this practically happened overnight. For about two hundred thousand years, human
population stayed well below the 1 billion mark; it was only in the past two
hundred years—thanks to industrialization, agriculture, and modern
medicine—that our population skyrocketed by the billions. There's
never been another large vertebrate animal whose population has grown
as much, as quickly, or with such devastating consequences for other
species.

In just the past fifty years, human population has doubled while wildlife populations have plummeted by more than half.[2] We're literally crowding other species off the planet. Not only with our sheer numbers, but all
that industrialization and agriculture that made it easier for humans to
survive are driving the sixth mass extinction, with species going extinct at
one thousand to ten thousand times the natural background rate.[3] The last

time this happened (a.k.a. Extinction Event #5) was around the time of the dinosaurs. And we all know how that worked out for them.

Without our massive, unsustainable human population, it would be a lot easier to address all the issues affecting wildlife in this book, as well as much of the suffering of domestic and farmed animals—after all, the continued expansion of factory farming is typically "justified" as feeding a growing population. This is a *big deal*, and one that's often swept under the rug. People tend to avoid talking about their sex lives, and there's an even bigger taboo around questioning how many children people should have . . . unless you're a woman in her twenties or thirties, and then everyone from your parents to the media has an opinion on why you haven't had any or when you should be queueing up your next. Double standard aside, the topic gets even more uncomfortable because as soon as you bring up the population issue, it evokes images of genocide and eugenics and other terrible policy experiments in human history.

There's good news and bad news on the population front. The bad news is that no matter how much we sweep, there's no rug on earth big enough to keep this problem contained. We keep growing, but the planet isn't getting any larger. The good news is that the most effective way to solve the problem isn't by triggering a dystopian plotline. Most women want to have smaller families, and when women are able to stay in school, have job opportunities, and have equal rights, they tend to start having children later in life and have fewer overall. And when everyone has access to contraception, family planning, reproductive health care, and education about how to use these things and why they're important, fertility rates drop.

In other words, more human rights lead to smaller families, which leads to more resources for those families and for wildlife. It doesn't get much more win-win than that.

Breaking the Taboo

At this point, some readers may be thinking this isn't what you signed up for—this was supposed be a book about helping animals, and even though you knew it involved personal actions, things are getting a bit too personal. (Others may find themselves unable to look away—after all, sex sells.) We're not supposed to talk about sexual intercourse in polite society. We're not supposed to talk about family-planning decisions outside of the family, except perhaps with the family doctor . . . and who would want to touch it with a ten-foot pole anyway, considering all the delicate religious and cultural complexities tied up in the topic?

Wildlife need us to break the taboo. So do women—225 million women in developing countries want to use modern contraception to delay, limit, or space their births and are unable to do so.[4] Nearly half of those women aren't using contraception because of concerns about health risks or specific types of contraception, or because they or someone close to them opposes birth control, often based on cultural or religious beliefs. The concerns can be addressed through increasing knowledge about the health benefits of family planning and the pros and cons of different types of birth control to help women choose the one that best meets their needs. Overcoming opposition gets a little more complicated, but isn't insurmountable.

Journalist Alan Weisman traveled the world for his book *Countdown* to ask the hard questions that would get to the root of the population problem, including exploring the role of cultural and religious norms. He wanted to figure out what it would take to convince people around the globe that it's in their best interest to have fewer children. Weisman says that although it was often difficult, "I still found everywhere I went some really eloquent cultural expressions or historical events that are part of the culture that indicate that we don't have to change people's beliefs or tell them that they're wrong."[5] From biblical stories of Joseph advocating for smaller families during the famine to the dramatic decline in Iran's fertility rate in the 1990s through voluntary family-planning programs supported by the country's religious leaders, most of the world's major belief systems recognize the role of having fewer children in difficult times. And we're living in those times now. The one major exception, Weisman notes, may be the Catholic Church, but the Vatican's views on birth control don't align with many Catholics—there's even an organization, Catholics for Choice, dedicated to challenging those views and advocating for reproductive rights.

Because, really, this is all about rights. It's way easier said than done, but population should be a nonpartisan, nondenominational issue—the entire point is to ensure that everyone has the ability to make their own family-planning decisions, so people of all cultures and animals of all species can thrive on our shared little planet.

If we started by preventing unplanned pregnancy, we'd be well on our way to tackling population growth. People often think this is a problem unique to developing countries, but nearly half of all pregnancies in the United States are unplanned.[6] Even though U.S. fertility rates are still lower than those in developing countries, our babies have a much bigger impact on the planet: An American infant is responsible for more carbon emissions in her first year than a Tanzanian will generate in her entire lifetime.[7] That's why we need to address both population and overconsumption as two sides of the same coin. If we reduced fertility rates but kept expanding our consumer culture and destructive industries, we'd still use up the planet's resources faster than the earth could replenish them. And if we got our nature-consuming ways under control but continued increasing our population by a million people every five days, we'd still wind up crowding wildlife—and ourselves—off the planet.

While unplanned and teen pregnancy rates have been dropping in the United States,[8] there's an alarming trend pushed by ultraconservative politicians toward policies to make it harder for us to make reproductive choices and to keep us ignorant about why that matters. So, in addition to taking care of your own business in the bedroom, help make sure everyone has the information and tools they need to decide for themselves if and when they want to have children, and how many. Talk to your friends, family, religious congregations, and other community groups about population and contraception misconceptions to help break the taboo. Support reproductive rights, family-planning services, and comprehensive sex education, and let your elected officials know this is important to you.

Safe Sex Saves Wildlife

So, go ahead, have all the sex you want. Get it on in honor of your favorite endangered species. Embrace your inner bonobo. As long as you protect yourself, you're doing your part to protect wildlife. Thanks to modern contraception, heterosexual intercourse doesn't have to equal reproduction.

Is contraception itself dangerous for wildlife? The pill has gotten a bad reputation for flushing estrogen into waterways and causing male fish and amphibians to switch genders. Condoms come with unavoidable trash, plus rubber plantations, like other industrial agriculture, are responsible for habitat loss. Every so often, the environmental impact of birth control makes a good headline, but don't give in to the clickbait. While endocrine disrupters in the water are problematic for wildlife, your sex life doesn't get all the credit. Hormones and other endocrine disrupters wind up in the water from a variety of sources, including factory farms. And, unlike anything you might flush from home, animal waste is virtually untreated to remove chemicals before it's dumped on wildlife. If rubbers are your thing, choose a condom brand that sources from responsibly managed forests. If you're looking for the most wildlife-friendly ways to prevent pregnancy— which also happen to be the most effective—check out long-acting reversible contraceptives (such as IUDs, which come with or without hormones) or getting a vasectomy.

But remember that no matter how sexually active you might be, you're still creating less waste and pollution than an entire unplanned human would create. In greenhouse gas emissions alone, according to an Oregon State University study, each additional child you have increases your carbon legacy by twenty times what you could save with a lifetime of energy-saving measures like driving a hybrid and using energy-efficient appliances and light bulbs.[9]

But Shouldn't Animal Lovers Make More Copies of Ourselves?

The world definitely needs more animal lovers and activists, but we're not going to get them through unprotected sex. Your love of animals, like your political views and your drive to make the world a better place, are not coded in your DNA. After all, you're probably not exactly like your parents—if you happen to be a carbon copy, I'm sure you know plenty of others who aren't—so there's no reason to expect that your children will automatically grow up with a passion to change the world. No matter how much you try to instill your values in your kids, they'll get information from other sources like school and the internet, just like you did.

Building an army of activists shouldn't influence if or how many children you have. Besides, even if you succeed, their ability to take action is at least a decade or two away. You're better off making activists out of the people who are already here by helping educate your friends, family, and community on how their daily lives affect animals and what they can do about it.

If you do want a big family, consider the adoption option. There are hundreds of thousands of kids in foster care in the United States alone, and they need people like you who care about what kind of world they're going to inherit. Nurture beats nature on this one. I'm not saying adoption is an easy way out of the family-planning problem—like many of the solutions to population growth, the concept is simple on the surface but complex in practice since adoption processes are often difficult, lengthy, expensive, and unpredictable. But like the other solutions that empower people and give everyone a chance at the life they dream of, it's worth it to keep fighting for policies and social services that support a just, equitable, and caring world for everyone.

Your Child-Free Card Isn't a Get-Out-of-Jail-Free Card

If you've already decided not to have children, wildlife thank you. That's not a judgment call on those who do have kids, but anyone who chooses to be child-free these days for whatever reason tends to face questions about their sanity, happiness, and value to society. Not everyone wants kids, and that's okay. You can still be a good person without reproducing. But despite the environmental benefits of having no children or a small family (think of the diaper savings alone!), it doesn't give you a free pass to consume everything your nonexistent children might have consumed. If you're bingeing on daily steaks, throwing away heaps of plastic bags, and traveling by private jet, you're not giving wildlife much reason to celebrate your child-free status. If you ask a starving polar bear swimming in search of disappearing sea ice where he might be able to catch some food, he doesn't care if the greenhouse gas emissions that put him in this position came from a bunch of large families or solo climate bombs.

We have to stop the false debate over whether our environmental problems are the fault of *either* population growth *or* overconsumption. Don't worry, there's plenty of blame to go around, and we're capable of addressing more than one problem. It's both our numbers and what we're doing with those numbers that are chasing wildlife to the brink. So, no matter how many kids you have, including zero, you still have a responsibility to help shrink our collective impact on other species.

Comment and Share

Fifty years ago, it was more widely accepted that our rapidly growing human population was problematic. The publication of *The Population Bomb* by Paul and Anne Ehrlich helped explode the debate around the issue, and population concerns made headlines at the first Earth Day. That was nearly four billion people ago. In recent decades, things have gotten very quiet. Too quiet. With the exception of a few articles marking the moment we crossed the seven billion threshold, the conflict between our growing population and the limits of our planet rarely makes the news and is even less likely to crop up in your average cocktail hour small talk. But it should.

Most people have a sense that there are a lot of humans on the planet, but they don't know what to do about it. Plus, it's awkward to talk about where babies come from. But it's time to have the population conversation. Figuring out how to do just that is one of the most amusing parts of my job as a population advocate for a wildlife organization. I talk to men about getting "whacked for wildlife" on World Vasectomy Day. I work with bold volunteers finding creative ways to get the conversation started, from giving away condoms at their church's Earth Day festival to dressing up like their favorite animal to talk to complete strangers about family planning. I get to come up with slogans for endangered species–themed condoms like "For the sake of the horned lizard . . . slow down, love wizard."

Yes, it gets awkward. Unbelievably awkward at times, as people share unsolicited details about their sex lives and reproductive organs with me. But unless we push past the awkwardness and start talking about our unsustainable human population and what reproductive rights have to do with saving whooping cranes and walruses, we're never going to be able to solve the problem. No matter what strange turns the conversation takes as people try to understand the issue, we need to be the grown-ups here and talk about sex out in the open. And we don't need to wait for a high-tech solution. While research continues to make contraception even safer, more effective, and easier to use, we already have a lot of good options to get this party started.

So write letters to the editor and repost stories making the connection between population and endangered species. Share actions and support organizations that defend reproductive rights, increase education and equality for women and girls, and conserve remaining wildlife habitat. Post photos of how population growth affects your own life and the wildlife in your neighborhood with the hashtag #CrowdedPlanet to make the conversation personal. And, of course, make it even more personal by talking to your partner about family planning, contraception, and saving wildlife in the bedroom.

! Action Alert
THREE THINGS YOU CAN DO TODAY

1 • Have "the Talk" with your partner. Kids are too big of a deal, for a lot of reasons, to leave it to chance.

2 • Defend reproductive rights. Whether it's joining the next women's day of action, volunteering at your local Planned Parenthood clinic, or calling your representatives, you can help women and wildlife by joining the fight.

3 • Break the taboo around population growth. Get your friends talking about family size, sex, and saving the planet.

ANIMALS YOU'LL HELP SAVE
All wild animals, but especially endangered species who can still be saved from extinction with a little breathing room.

17   The Call of the Wild

Wolves embody the idea of wildness, the impression magnified by stories of howling at the moon and my-what-big-teeth-you-have. But given the way we bond with our dogs, it shouldn't come as a surprise that wolves are also the embodiment of love. Wolf packs are closely bonded families. The so-called alphas are the parents, not the Ultimate Fighting Champions, and they're usually lifelong sweethearts. Lone wolves aren't rebels or rejects—they're out seeking a family of their own. (Some wolves stay with the pack they were born into for life, but someone eventually has to leave home to deepen the gene pool.) Wolves help each other out, care for their injured, and raise their pups together. As many as two million gray wolves once roamed across North America, but we've been losing wolves and other wildlife as we forget how incredible and important they are. To save them, we need remind ourselves what love is all about.

If you're feeling too connected to your devices and disconnected from nature, you're not alone. A recent Nielsen report found that American adults spend nearly eleven hours a day staring at screens.[1] And according to an EPA-sponsored survey, Americans spend 87 percent of our time indoors and another 6 percent driving or riding around in vehicles.[2] That only leaves 7 percent of your life outside. Not only do our lives keep edging closer to the robot-dominated reality all those sci-fi writers have been warning us about, but more than 80 percent of American families live in urban areas,[3] and it's not always easy to get to a place where you can safely experience how great the Great Outdoors can be.

We've fallen far from the trees, and we have to find our way back. Not just as individuals searching for wildlife in remote places, but as humans who are part of our local ecosystems. Everyone should feel welcome and empowered to enjoy nature and see why it's worth saving for our future and for wild animals.

With all the ways to save animals from the comfort of your home—not to mention the distraction of ridiculously adorable sloth videos and red panda gifs—it can be easy to forget to step away from the screen every once in a while. But one of the most important parts of being a wildlife advocate is remembering that we're part of nature, too. Go outside, get a little wild, and remember what you're fighting for. Seriously, no matter how high def your monitor is, it's more beautiful out there.

Choose Your Own Adventure

You don't have to go far to reconnect with nature. If you built a backyard oasis back in chapter 11, spend some time enjoying it. Use wildlife identification apps or books to help you start a journal of all the different species who share your neighborhood. Explore your local park system—check out your park department's website to discover places you probably didn't even know existed in your county. One of my favorite weekend activities is to swipe through the maps and reviews of trail discovery apps to pick new places to explore. Find out what state parks and federal lands are nearby. There are more than 417 places to check out in the national park system, from the big, famous parks like the Grand Canyon and Arches to lesser-known lakeshores, scenic rivers, recreation areas, and historic sites. There's a reason more than three hundred million people a year visit our national parks from around the world. They're worth the road trip.

Need a challenge to get outside? Try geocaching for a modern update on old-fashioned treasure hunting. There are two million geocaches worldwide to add a little adventure to your hike. Download the Geocaching app, choose the one you want to find, and start searching. Once you find the geocache, sign the logbook, and replace it for the next treasure hunter. If you're artistically inclined, join the family-friendly trend of spreading cheer through painted rocks. People around the country are hiding colorful, creatively decorated rocks around public parks for others to find, photograph, collect, or rehide, and sharing their artwork and discoveries in local Facebook groups. If you're hooked on gaming, Pokémon GO can give you a good reason to explore the outdoors in search of rare Pokémon—just keep an eye out for real wildlife, too. If you want a more social experience, seek out local meetups for hikers, bird-watchers, mushroom hunters, or whatever other outdoor adventure you prefer.

There are endless ways to connect with nature, from hanging out in city parks to backpacking through remote wilderness. Appreciating the outdoors means different things to different people, and for the most part, that's great, as long as your activity of choice doesn't harm wildlife.

Leave No Trace

There are seven core principles, created by the Leave No Trace Center for Outdoor Ethics, that have been widely adopted by outdoor enthusiasts to help ensure your walk on the wild side doesn't walk all over nature.

THE LEAVE NO TRACE SEVEN PRINCIPLES

1 • Plan Ahead and Prepare

2 • Travel and Camp on Durable Surfaces

3 • Dispose of Waste Properly

4 • Leave What You Find

5 • Minimize Campfire Impacts

6 • Respect Wildlife

7 • Be Considerate of Other Visitors

(© 1999 by the Leave No Trace Center for Outdoor Ethics: www.LNT.org)

Whether it's the official Leave No Trace principles or local regulations posted by wilderness areas, wildlife refuges, and local parks, follow the rules. Park rangers aren't on a power trip with their restrictions; they're just trying to protect wild plants and animals. Sometimes that means changing your dog walk route if there's a No Dogs Allowed sign posted, or sacrificing a backcountry experience where open fires aren't allowed for a campground with established fire pits if roasted marshmallows are a personal requirement before curling up in your tent.

The Leave No Trace principles don't just apply if you're taking a family vacation to Yellowstone. No one likes to go to their local park for a lunch break to find that they're stuck eating their burrito beside a pile of someone else's trash. No matter where you go, pay attention to posted signs and strive to leave the environment in better condition than you found it. That's a good overall goal for our time on the planet, and we can start by applying it to the time we spend in our parks and wilderness.

This Land Is Your Land, This Land Is Their Land

Congratulations! You are the proud co-owner of more than six hundred million acres of land. And that's just the federal lands, including national parks, national forests, wild and scenic rivers, national trails, wildlife refuges, and other wild areas that belong to all Americans—you have even more land that belongs to you, as a member of your community, in your state and local parks. Imagine all the incredible wild animals who live in your extended backyard of lush forests, rivers, grasslands, mountains, and deserts.

It's a lot of responsibility to take care of that much land, but don't worry, the government manages it for us. On second thought, the government's management style gives us, as animal lovers, a lot to worry about. Federal lands aren't just beautiful places to visit and preserve; they also provide sanctuary for endangered species from grizzly bears to greater sage grouse, protecting them from the development of cities, suburbs, agricultural fields, and the highways crisscrossing the country. The government, however, decided that some of these lands have profit potential, so they lease them out to industry for logging, cattle grazing, and fossil fuel development—all of which degrade the land and destroy wildlife habitat.

The fossil fuel industry alone already holds leases to an area of public lands and waters fifty-five times the size of Grand Canyon National Park.[4] The Keep It in the Ground movement is calling for an end to government fossil fuel leases to keep that carbon in the ground instead of emitting it into the atmosphere for the sake of our public lands, the wildlife who live there, and the future of our climate.

There's constant pressure to sell off public lands to industry or turn them over to states, so there's a constant threat to our remaining wildlife and wild places. The best thing we can do is keep our public lands out of private hands and make sure they're protected across the country by strong federal laws. If you're an American, you have a voice in how these public lands are cared for. Tell your representatives that you want your public lands protected, not sold to the highest bidder. Go ahead and give them a call now—at any given time, there are active threats against these lands and the wildlife who live there, so it's never a bad time to let your representatives know this is an issue that matters to you.

Speak up for your local parks, too. Those millages that show up on the ballot to fund park improvement are worth it—parks increase our quality of life, improve mental and physical health, and build community. But it takes money to maintain parks, even to install the trash, recycling, and dog pickup stations that help keep parks unpolluted. When you contribute to parks through taxes or donations, you're contributing to a future for wildlife.

Comment and Share

In 2015, President Obama started the Every Kid in a Park initiative. As the name implies, the idea was to get every kid in America away from their screens and out into nature to discover the amazing public lands they'll inherit. As part of the package, the government started offering free admission to national parks and other federal lands and waters to every fourth grader, and up to three accompanying adults, for an entire year. If you know anyone with kids, let them know about this incredible opportunity. If you're lucky, maybe they'll even bring you along.

State and local park services also have family-friendly and kid-oriented programs to get kids outside and teach them more about the world we live in and the wildlife we share it with. Spread the word about those, too. There might even be volunteer opportunities for you to share your love of wildlife with the next generation. If your local parks are lacking in outdoor education, ask your parks and recreation department to add programs. Raising kids who care about the wild benefits everyone (especially wild animals).

Sharing our parks also means making them more accessible while still maintaining their wild character and valuable habitat. Small changes like parking lots that can accommodate buses for school field trips and creating areas that are wheelchair accessible allow more people to visit parks, especially people who might not otherwise have the opportunity to experience nature.

But it takes more than simply having a program available to help people connect with the outdoors. Parks need to be inclusive—they should feel welcoming to everyone. To make that happen, diverse communities need to be included in conversations about how we protect parks and nature. Diverse representation and cultural sensitivity are important for many reasons, especially when it comes to kids seeing themselves in the outdoors. And it's critical that the education provided by our parks and historic sites recognize the history and people who suffered and were displaced in the name of environmental stewardship. Support diversity in parks, not just among staff, but in educational materials, signage, and outreach. Everyone should have the chance to enjoy nature and want to protect it—for our sake and for the animals.

The more we share the love and howl our support for our parks, the harder it will be for the government to sell them out from under us and all the animals who need these wild places to survive. However and wherever you choose to heed the call of the wild, share your experience with your friends to inspire them to get outdoors and enjoy it responsibly, too. You may not always be able to spot the animals among the trees or cacti or river rapids, but they're out there, and staying connected to the wild helps us remember how important it is to protect the wildlife who live there.

! Action Alert

THREE THINGS YOU CAN DO TODAY

1 • Spend some quality time outdoors.

2 • Know your park or wilderness rules and respect them.

3 • Invest in nature by utilizing parks department programs, volunteering, and advocating and voting for their protection.

ANIMALS YOU'LL HELP SAVE

The buffalo who roam, the deer and antelope who play, and all the other wildlife whose home is on the range, in the mountains, or in our backyards.

Get Personal

Be the person your dog thinks you are.

—J. W. Stephens

Dolphins are natural acrobats, jumping from the waves and sometimes turning complete flips before splashing back into the ocean. The aptly named spinner dolphins will spin in the air as they make their flying, above-water leaps. It's as much fun as it looks. Play has been well documented in wild dolphins—they like to chase each other, ride waves, surf in the wake of boats, and use random found objects as toys in group games or to amuse themselves. This playfulness—along with natural curiosity, intelligence, a need to socialize, and their happy-go-lucky appearance—has gotten dolphins in trouble. Unable to heed stranger-danger warnings, dolphins have been captured from the wild and their spirited natures exploited to perform tricks to delight humans since 1938. Those dolphin smiles, upbeat soundtracks, and effervescent trainers in wetsuits have been fooling crowds for decades, but just like circuses that use elephants or big cats in their acts, marine mammal shows are one-sided entertainment.

Dolphin-trainer-turned-activist Ric O'Barry frequently says, "The dolphin smile is nature's greatest deception. It creates the illusion that they're always happy." He should know. In the 1960s, O'Barry trained dolphins for the entertainment industry, including the ones who played the title character on the popular TV series *Flipper*. When one of the show's stars died in his arms, O'Barry had an epic change of heart. He could no longer be part of the abuse that went into training wild marine mammals for show business and dedicated himself to fighting the mistreatment and misery of the industry he left behind.[1]

In the wild, dolphins and other marine mammals have complex social lives and caring families and the vastness of the ocean at their fins. In captivity, they're often separated from their families (both when captured and if they give birth in the tank), live solitary existences or are thrown together with little to no regard for social dynamics, and are forced to live in what's basically the equivalent of a bathtub while a bunch of other creatures (a.k.a. humans) gawk and make them perform tricks. Although none of this may be news to dedicated animal lovers, movies like *The Cove* and *Blackfish* have been successful in exposing the cruel behind-the-tanks reality of marine mammal parks to a much broader audience, resulting in many of these shows starting to shut down.

Animals are fascinating and hilarious, and we should appreciate that. But it's one thing to capture your cat's ridiculous antics on video and share it online; it's another to force a tiger to leap through hoops of fire in an attempt to awe a ticket-buying audience. Presumably your cat was being ridiculous of her own free will, isn't forced to perform for profit, and lives a pretty cushy, happy existence. When animals are exploited to make money, denied their freedom, taken from their families, abused, or put in harm's way for the purpose of entertainment, we've crossed a line.

Unfortunately, we've been crossing that line for centuries, all around the world, in ways that range from bizarre to violent. Think of the lions forced to fight gladiators in ancient Rome and dogs pitted against bears, bulls, pigs, or each other in modern America. Flipper's fifteen minutes of fame may have come and gone—and even Shamu's star is rapidly fading—but wild animals are still regularly used and abused for live shows, television, and movies. Unless that grizzly bear standing on his hind legs and roaring at the hapless campers is computer-generated, you're watching an animal who certainly wouldn't have chosen an acting career over freedom.

In recent years, we've been holding the line against the cruelty of animal entertainment, with marine mammal shows and animal circuses struggling to fill their bleachers, CGI and other visual effects replacing live animals in movies and television, and stronger laws being passed to crack down on blood sports and competitions using wild or domestic animals. There's been a lot of progress, but we can't take our victory lap until we've stopped abusing animals for our own recreation. As animal lovers, our entertainment choices are one more way we can put our money where our hearts are.

Clown Car of Cruelty

They call it "family entertainment," and a lot people want to believe the advertising. Seeing elephants and big cats up close can be pretty amazing. Until you look at it from the other side—they were born for jungles and savannas, and instead are surrounded by concrete and chaos. It's tempting to believe that these massive, powerful animals wouldn't do anything they didn't want to just because a human asked. But we haven't been asking nicely—sharp tools, whips, starvation, and drugs aren't exactly a fair fight. We've broken these majestic animals.

Circuses pack a lot of animal misery into a small space. The most famous modern big top, Ringling Brothers, faced decades of relentless protests to its mistreatment of elephants. In 2016, they retired their elephants, and in 2017, the circus embarked on its final tour, much to the relief of animal activists and, one can assume, the lions, tigers, and other animals used in the show (at least those who were allowed to retire rather than being sold to other circuses). But there have been a string of lesser-known circus acts, sideshows, and publicity stunts that cast wild and domestic animals in bizarre performances. Tigers used in magic tricks. Boxing matches between kangaroos and men. Horses forced to dive from sixty-foot platforms into pools of water, or the Russian donkey who was forced to parasail over a beach for a promotional stunt.

That donkey didn't hook herself up to the parasail for a joyride. If an animal is doing something that strikes you as unnatural, your instinct is probably right, especially if there's a profit-gaining wizard behind the curtain. If an animal is on stage or screen in costume, it's safe to assume she didn't pick out her wardrobe. And if a real wild animal is featured in any show, live or recorded, unless you're watching a nature documentary, it wasn't her choice to be there and almost certainly required unpleasant tactics to get her to perform her part. In other words, if an animal is involved, it's not as family-friendly as the advertising.

The Dark Side of Creative Expression

Sometimes they call it "art," like the windowless room filled with live but-terflies at London's Tate Modern, which resulted in the deaths of nine thou-sand butterflies over the course of the twenty-three-week exhibit. Or the installation at a Danish museum that featured goldfish in blenders, which people were invited to turn on. From tattooed pigs to tossing cats up a flight of stairs or filming a dog being shot, art has taken its toll on animals. There are many who argue that art is meant to be *"controversial"* and *"thought-provoking."* I agree to a pretty large extent, but neither of those words are synonymous with causing physical harm without the consent of your subject.

Beyond instances of direct abuse and death, art and other forms of en-tertainment can have a ripple effect on animals. In 2014, three African sulcata tortoises, which are designated as a vulnerable species, had a pair of iPads stuck to each of their shells. First, they were set loose to wander around a ghost town to capture footage of the abandoned streets and buildings, then they were placed in the garden of the Aspen art museum to show off the images. The museum defended the use of the tortoises by cit-ing the lightweight features of the iPads and the ability of the tortoises to roam free in their enclosure. "Each unit, with iPads attached, weighs less than 3 pounds," the fact sheet for the exhibit explained. "By comparison, tortoises' thick, sturdy legs accommodate their own weight and upwards of 150 extra pounds during mating."[2] Is there really any comparison between the act of mating and being part of someone's art project?

But there was a bigger problem than the iPads, or even that the exhibit was originally supposed to run well into the fall, when the weather would've been too cold and wet for the desert dwellers. (It was canceled early and the tortoises sent to a sanctuary due to public outcry.) The exhibit was touted as "forgotten stories of the once prosperous ghost towns . . . retold from the tortoises' perspective." Except the tortoises' perspective is that they're disappearing from their natural habitat.[3] And while their treatment might have been four-star compared to Ringling Brothers elephants and Sea-World orcas, the use of wild animals in entertainment fuels the pet trade. People see cool-looking, seemingly docile animals in human environments and get the misguided notion that that's where they belong. Not only are most people poorly equipped to provide proper care for desert tortoises, but animals are taken from their wild homes in huge numbers to supply wannabe exotic pet owners. (Learn more about the exotic pet trade in chapter 10.)

Rigged Races and Unfair Fights

They call it "sport." From rodeos to horse racing, and bullfighting to dogfighting, there's a slew of legal and illegal competitions that are rigged against the animals. Thoroughbred horses and greyhounds may love to run, but they don't love running to the point of sheer physical exhaustion and injury (which often means the end of their careers and lives), or in the case of racing dogs, living in dark cages between training and competition. Rodeos rely on terrified cattle and horses. And bullfighting . . . well, no one wants to be taunted and speared to the cheers of a crowd.

Being an animal lover isn't a spectator sport. When in Kentucky, you don't have to go to the derby just to partake in lavish hats and mint juleps. Get together with friends with your ginormous hats and minty bourbon and plan a protest against the abuse in the horse racing industry. If you've been bit by the gambling bug, you have plenty of alternatives to test your luck at the casino or online that involve only you and a dealer or machine. Support laws that shut down greyhound tracks (if dog racing is still legal in your state), and urge your city council and local fairgrounds to refuse to host rodeos and other events where animals are mistreated. Dogfighting is a felony in all fifty states, and cockfighting is illegal in every state, so report any signs you see of these activities to your local law enforcement.

And remember that the animal athletes are the victims here. Greyhounds make great couch potatoes, and they need loving homes when tracks are shut down or when they're saved from the industry's final, lethal retirement plans. When dogfighting rings are busted, those dogs deserve a chance to recover from the violence they suffered and enjoy the pampered life. Even if you can't adopt a rescued victim of dog sports or an ex-racehorse yourself, support the rescue groups that find them homes and the laws that allow them to do so.

Box Office Boycott

For animal lovers, that "No Animals Were Harmed" line at the end of movie credits offers a warm blanket of reassurance that you can feel good about the feel-good (or not-so-feel-good) movie you just saw. Unfortunately, that line doesn't mean much. A shocking investigation by *The Hollywood Reporter* into the American Humane Association's disclaimer found that animal injuries and deaths on set were often underreported.[4] In response to the exposé, AHA said that "in many of the cases reported, [the injuries] had nothing to do with the animals' treatment on set, or occurred when the animals were not under our care."[5] But as an animal lover, the "if I didn't see it, it didn't happen" defense isn't good enough. If animals are used in entertainment, their treatment from training through retirement matters as much, if not more, as what happens during their brief time on set.

I'm not saying you should stop seeing all movies about animals. Animals have always been an important part of our lives and the stories we tell. But don't rely on the "No Animals Were Harmed" claim as your only assurance that no animals were, indeed, harmed. Consider what might be happening behind the scenes. As with live animal shows, wild animal "actors" are kept in captivity and forced to perform in unnatural situations. These days, especially when it comes to wild animals, there's no reason not to use computer-generated imagery. By the time a movie's previews are out, you can usually Google to find out if its wild animals are truly wild or the wild imaginings of visual effects artists. If you see something that concerns you, contact the studio and post on social media. While they can't undo what's already wrapped in production, they can commit to new standards going forward. And if the price of admission includes animal abuse, boycott the box office to drive the message home.

The lines can get a bit fuzzier when it comes to domestic animals in movies because messages and training methods vary widely, and our relationship with animals like dogs and cats means that they're generally more willing partners in the spotlight. Popular movies that focus on a particular dog breed—like *101 Dalmatians*—often cause a slew of irresponsible breeding and homeless animals as people rush out to get their own little star, only to learn the hard way that the script doesn't always match reality. Movies that feature dogs can use their movie promotions to help educate people about rescue and responsible pet care. Some movies do this really well—the 2009 movie *Hotel for Dogs* cast most of its stars from animal shelters around the country. Not only did the movie itself have a rescue message, but the cast and crew helped the canine stars find homes after filming.

Let the companies that use CGI and promote a better world for animals know that you support them by dropping them a message, sharing the story of their good works on social media, and seeing the movie with your friends and family. Box office buzz and ticket sales help determine what kinds of movies will continue to be made.

Comment and Share

Here's something not to share: If you see a video of animals being used in entertainment, such as chimpanzees acting like humans, don't share it. Viral videos showing people getting too cozy with wild animals can have a similar effect to big box office movies in spurring the exotic pet trade (not to mention being dangerous). And if you ever find yourself somewhere that you can have your photo taken with a lion or other large wild animal, walk away. Your new profile pic isn't worth the drugging and mistreatment that animal had to endure to be considered safe enough to pose with people.

Animal entertainment exists for one reason: to make money. Many of us have animal exploitation skeletons in our closet. When I was a kid, we went to SeaWorld on vacation. I didn't know better, and neither did my family. Don't let the dolphin shows, circuses, or rodeos of your childhood define you. Let whatever the last animal show you attended be your last. The best thing you can do for wild animals used in entertainment is to refuse to buy a ticket to their suffering and let the company (and the world) know why. Ringling Brothers and SeaWorld both retired their biggest animal shows due to lagging ticket sales caused by public outcry. The Aspen museum's iPad-toting tortoises were relocated from the art exhibit to a sanctuary after more than twelve thousand people signed an online petition and people called for a boycott of the museum.[6]

So make some noise. Tell your friends why you're skipping the show. Write a letter to the editor or an op-ed about why you're opposed to using animals in entertainment. If it's a circus or a rodeo in town, there might already be a protest you can join, or start your own. Let the arena or fairgrounds or whatever venue is hosting the animal show know that you won't be attending their events and that their support of animal abuse has harmed their reputation.

The saying that "there's no such thing as bad publicity" is often attributed to P. T. Barnum, of Barnum & Bailey Circus, which eventually became Ringling Brothers and Barnum & Bailey, which had its farewell tour in 2017 due to bad publicity. If Barnum did coin that phrase, he'd probably change his tune after seeing the outcome of persistent negative media and protests. The entertainment industry lives and dies on the audience's cheers and jeers, so help create the publicity that will create a better world for animals. You won't be missing out by supporting human-only entertainment; the feats of Cirque du Soleil put sad elephant tricks to shame every time.

! Action Alert

THREE THINGS YOU CAN DO TODAY

1 • Skip the animal circus—don't buy tickets for shows that use live wild animals.

2 • Protest venues that host animal entertainment online, in the media, and in person. Bad publicity is good for the animals.

3 • Save the CGI whale! Let production companies know you appreciate their investment in animal-saving technology.

ANIMALS YOU'LL HELP SAVE
Elephants, tigers, bears, chimpanzees, horses, and other animal athletes and actors that some shady animal talent agent promised would "be a star."

Clean Conscience

Rats laugh when they're tickled. That's probably not something you've had the occasion to experience. And it puts them in a good mood, making them more optimistic about getting treats. If you're not sure how to tell if a rat has a case of the giggles, you can tell if they're happy by their facial expressions and if the delicate skin on their ears turns pink. Gives new meaning to the phrase tickled pink. *Rats also demonstrate altruism and empathy, and they're wicked smart—so smart that they've outperformed college students in cognitive learning tests.[1] But instead of giving rats Ivy League scholarships, humans tend to persecute or experiment on them. Ninety-five percent of all animals used in laboratory experiments—as many as one hundred million every year—are rats and mice (who are similarly charming and intelligent) suffering not just in the name of modern medicine, but also for the latest trends in cosmetics and cleaning products.*

Most people agree that animals shouldn't die for lipstick or shampoo or toilet bowl cleaner. But even though we have stores full of cosmetics and cleaning products that have been deemed safe for every skin type and surface, chemicals are still routinely tested on small animals like rats, mice, rabbits, and guinea pigs. The global cosmetics industry alone—which includes makeup, hair care, skin care, deodorant, nail polish, toothpaste, mouthwash, body wash, and dozens of other personal care products—tests their products on an estimated one hundred thousand to two hundred thousand animals each year, according to Humane Society International.[2] And that's only the animals used in testing for products to clean you; when it comes to cleaning your house, even more animals are subjected to chemical tests. And these aren't written exams—chemicals are force-fed to animals, dripped directly in their eyes, and rubbed on shaved skin to test for irritation. The animals aren't given anything to relieve the pain and are killed once the tests are over, regardless of whether they pass or fail.

The harm to animals doesn't stop once the products hit the shelves. Despite all this animal testing, many products are filled with ingredients that are known carcinogens, endocrine disruptors, and other bad actors. The more products you use—25 percent of women use fifteen or more personal care products a day[3]—the more likely that you're exposing yourself, your family (human and nonhuman), and your environment to a toxic stew of chemicals.

Killer beauty shouldn't actually kill, and you should be able to clean your house with a clean conscience. Fortunately, animal testing for consumer products has been banned in several countries, isn't required in many others, and is a public relations nightmare thanks to animal lovers saying enough is enough: Our beauty and clean floors aren't worth their suffering.

Lather, Rinse, Don't Repeat

Animal testing for cosmetics has been banned in places around the world like India, South Korea, and the European Union. Yes, even in Paris, the fashion capital of the world, you can only buy cruelty-free beauty products.

In the United States, the Food and Drug Administration doesn't specifically require animal testing for cosmetics.[4] They just say manufacturers are responsible for showing that their products and ingredients are safe, which can be done through using already-verified ingredients and approved animal-free testing methods. Household products are regulated by the Federal Hazardous Substances Act through the Consumer Product Safety Commission—neither of which require animal testing for those hazardous warning labels.[5] Animal testing is listed as an option for determining the safety of products or need for cautionary labeling, but the commission's policy is to find alternatives to replace animal testing. Unfortunately, the lack of a requirement isn't the same as an outright ban on testing or selling products tested on animals, but there's a movement to pass a Humane Cosmetics Act in the United States that would put an end to cosmetic animal testing—and it's a good look to ask your legislators to support such a ban.

Animal tests are notoriously expensive and unpopular. They're also unreliable—after all, our bodies don't work quite the same way as a hamster's. So, if no one really likes animal testing for consumer products, why is it still happening?

We're obsessed with finding the next miracle cure to give us that airbrushed magazine glow or eradicate shower scum. We think if we just had the right cleanser, lotion, or scrub, we could defeat genetics, discover the fountain of youth, and keep our homes clean without having to put so much effort into cleaning. Products that introduce new ingredients have to prove that they're safe. So, if there's some newly developed chemical that has the potential to defy the natural laws of time and aging, the company has to show that their time-travel-in-a-bottle won't inadvertently harm you—so they harm animals first. There are alternative testing methods for many potential irritations and other side effects, but not all of them, so new products often mean new animal tests.

The second big reason animal testing persists, when it comes to cosmetics, is that companies want a piece of the Chinese market pie. There's a lot of money to be made in China, but Chinese law requires premarket animal testing for imported beauty products and can require additional animal tests on ingredients that are new to the country. Many companies that have stopped testing on animals for their products sold in the United States, Europe, and other countries leave the door open to allow animal testing if places like China require it. This is a problem for animal lovers, since it means purchasing your favorite conditioner that's not tested on animals in the United States could be supporting animal suffering overseas.

But just like companies have the choice whether or not to test on animals in the first place, they have the choice whether to break their cruelty-free code by entering markets where animal testing is required. When the makeup brand Urban Decay, a cruelty-free favorite, announced that it was changing its policy on animal testing so it could expand to China, it didn't go over well with its core customers. The outcry prompted the company to cancel its expansion plans. Urban Decay turned its back on a big opportunity—showing that brands are vulnerable to protest, but also that they need our support when they do the right thing.

An astonishing number of chemicals are allowed on the market in the U.S. without knowing how they might affect our health, but there are some eleven thousand ingredients used in personal care products that have already been proven safe in Europe.[6] The shelves are full of beauty products with these verified ingredients, as well as other products that are effective in cutting grease, eliminating window streaks, getting rid of funky smells, and making your floors and counters shine without the need for additional animal testing. If we stopped looking for solutions to problems that really don't exist, we could stop a lot of animal suffering.

The list of already-verified ingredients makes nationwide bans on products tested on animals possible. However, those verified ingredients and products exist, in large part, because of a legacy of animal testing. Even the "cruelty-free" products you purchase may stand on the shoulders of previous generations of lab animals. We can't erase that dark past any more than you can really erase the process of aging. But that doesn't mean we should keep repeating the pattern of cruelty. We can choose to honor the sacrifice those animals made by keeping household products and cosmetics free of the ugliness of any more animal testing.

Toxic Scrub

Animals aren't just harmed by beauty and cleaning products in the lab. We allow so many persistent chemicals in products that go down the drain, thwart wastewater treatment efforts, and are returned to water sources that our rivers, lakes, and other waterways have become one giant test on wildlife. And in many cases, we don't know the results yet. Chemicals from laundry detergents were found in more than two-thirds of U.S. streams tested by the U.S. Geological Survey, with nearly as many containing disinfectants.[7] Phosphates in cleaners that wind up in waterways can cause an algae growth spurt, which threatens fish and other freshwater species. Phthalates and other endocrine disruptors commonly found in cosmetics and cleaners have been found in fish, which studies show may harm their reproductive processes. Some of these chemicals can also accumulate up the food chain and back into the bellies of humans.

Once upon a time, there were more than one hundred facial scrubs, body washes, and other personal care products on the market with exfoliating plastic microbeads. It was estimated that 808 trillion of these tiny plastic pellets were rinsed away every day,[8] so it was no surprise that researchers found high concentrations of microbeads polluting the Great Lakes and accumulating in fish. The microbeads are bad enough on their own, but they also act like sponges, soaking up and concentrating other pollutants around them. In 2015, after public outcry prompted several companies to promise a phaseout, Congress banned microbeads, forcing manufacturers to find formulas to scrub your skin without contributing to plastic pollution in lakes and rivers.

The chemicals in products we use don't just affect wild animals on the other end of the drain—our product choices also affect the animals who share our homes. Our dogs and cats have a higher exposure to these chemicals than we do because they're closer to the surfaces we're cleaning and they have a tendency to sniff and lick things that we don't. Household cleaners are the second-most common poison cats are exposed to, according to the calls received by the Pet Poison Helpline.[9] So, when choosing products, keep the other members of your household in mind and store all cosmetics and cleaning products (as well as medications and pesticides) well out of reach of your four-legged family members. If you're not sure what products or foods might be poisonous, check out the Pet Poison Helpline website at www.petpoisonhelpline.com. And if you suspect your animals got into something they shouldn't have, call your vet or the help line as soon as possible.

Humane Makeover

You should be able to feel good about yourself and your home without having to feel bad about animal cruelty in your routine. Look for the Leaping Bunny label on cosmetic and household products certifying that the ingredients and the final formula weren't tested on animals. Leaping Bunny has an online database you can search before you leave the house, and there are several apps that use the Leaping Bunny data and other lists of animal-friendly companies to help you once you're at the store. You can find cruelty-free products just about anywhere once you know what to look for.

Limit exposing yourself, your animals, and wildlife by choosing household products with safer ingredients. Check out the Environmental

Working Group's Skin Deep online database and Guide to Healthy Cleaning, or download their Healthy Living app complete with a handy bar code scanner to discover what's in your favorite products. It can be a bit a disturbing at first, like letting a toxic genie out of the bottle, but the app can also help you choose new, less scary favorites. When it comes to cleaning, the same rules apply: Look for the Leaping Bunny label and look up the ingredients. You can also make your own cleaning products with simple, safe ingredients you probably already have in a cupboard somewhere. A little soap, water, lemon juice, baking soda, and vinegar go a long way, even in my houseful of animals. Just like with food, don't rely on the "natural" label to be your guide. "Nontoxic" and "eco-friendly" also aren't regulated. But many known toxic chemicals are, so if you see hazard, caution, "may cause irritation," or similar labels, it's a good bet that you're not looking at the safest, most sustainable choice.

Speaking of sustainability, the basics of reducing unnecessary waste apply here, too. The whole "lather, rinse, repeat" instruction isn't because hair needs to be double or triple washed—for the most part, all that repeat accomplishes is making you use more product so you have to buy more. People who sell cosmetics are masters of the upsell. If you go into the store looking for one product, they'll sell you five. Those bottles, tubes, compacts, and jars add up—not just at the cash register, but in the environment. Even cruelty-free products often come in plastic or nonrecyclable packaging and require water, energy, and other resources taken from wildlife in the manufacturing process.

It's okay to spoil yourself now and then, but stay strong when you go cosmetic shopping. Think about what you need ahead of time to avoid overpurchasing products you might not ever use. And if it is a household product you use frequently, consider buying the bigger size so you're buying less packaging.

Comment and Share

You're beautiful just as you are. But whether you buy personal care products to feel good, to impress your loved ones, to recapture your youth, or just for basic hygiene, you can accomplish all of that with ingredients and products that are already on the market and cruelty-free. There's no fountain of youth, but there is a deep pool of compassion. Support those companies that don't do any animal testing at all, even if it means they're shut out of international markets. If your current favorite cosmetics aren't on the Leaping Bunny list, contact customer service to find out why. If they test on animals, even if they say it's only where required by law, it's time to find new favorites and let the old cosmetic company know why you broke up with them. Wherever you buy your cosmetics, ask those stores to stock only cruelty-free products, especially if they're trying to build a reputation as an animal-friendly or sustainable business.

Your house is also lovely without needing that chemical sparkle. Choose natural cleaning methods and premade cleaners that haven't been tested on animals. Whether you're shopping for personal care or household products, spend a little extra time researching your options and reading labels. When you find something you love—whether it's a cruelty-free product or way to simplify your routine, brag about it. Your word of mouth can help others ditch products tested on animals and give rats a reason to giggle.

! Action Alert
THREE THINGS YOU CAN DO TODAY

1 • Look for the Leaping Bunny label for cruelty-free products.

2 • Clean up your act: Try paring down your beauty and cleaning routines and buy only what you really need.

3 • Contact the companies whose cosmetic and household products you use. If they aren't certified cruelty-free, ask them to take a stand against animal testing. If they're already on Team Humane, let them know it's an important part of why they have your business.

ANIMALS YOU'LL HELP SAVE
Literal guinea pigs, plus rabbits, hamsters, rats, and mice.

20   What Not to Wear

Foxes are expert navigators and hunters. Like other members of the dog family, they have impressive senses of hearing and smell. Unlike your family dog, they have whiskers on their faces and their legs to help them feel their way around. They also use the earth's magnetic field to find prey.[1] They're not the only animals paying attention to the poles—one study determined that domestic dogs prefer to align themselves with the north-south axis when defecating[2] (bet you're tempted to get out the compass next time you take your pup for a walk)—but foxes are believed to be unique in using magnetic fields to judge both direction and distance, allowing them to successfully leap on prey, even when their prey is out of sight. Yet this impressive set of skills can't get foxes out of cruel leghold traps and fur farm cages. They need our help for that.

As an animal lover, you probably aren't modeling your wardrobe after Cruella de Vil. But even without resorting to Dalmatian puppy coats, clothing stores and runways are full of jackets, sweaters, hats, shoes, purses, and other garments and accessories made from farmed and wild animals. There are a lot of misconceptions about the fur and leather industry—it's frequently romanticized as a "sustainable" way not to let any animal parts go to waste. The fur industry often refers to the millions of animals it kills each year as a "renewable resource." Leather has a reputation as a by-product of the meat industry, implying that it's an afterthought rather than its own lucrative product that can be more profitable than the animal's meat (especially when it comes to "specialty" leathers like ostrich, alligator, and snakeskin).

Fur and leather, as well as materials like wool and down that are taken from live animals, come from animals who live on factory farms. Yet many people who have reduced or eliminated meat and dairy from their diets for the animals' sake don't always think about the animals used for their shoes, purses, or the trim on their winter jacket. If you're concerned about how cows, pigs, and sheep are treated for their meat, shouldn't that same concern apply to your clothing? After all, calfskin leather is nothing if not honest: If the idea of eating veal makes you squeamish, that soft calfskin jacket should be off the table, too.

Back in the day, hides and furs were necessary to keep warm. These days, technology has given us a lot more fabric and insulation options that weren't made at the expense of animals. Even snow bunnies can avoid hypothermia without harming any actual bunnies. There are plenty of ways to minimize the impact of your wardrobe on animals and a growing number of top designers to help you do it in style.

Return of the Undead Fur Trend

You may not see many floor-length mink coats at the local grocery store these days, but fur clothing is far from extinct. Unfortunately, it's making a zombie-worthy comeback with a resurgence of animal pelts in fashion, led by younger designers and trendsetters who missed the whole *"Fur Is Dead"* era of the 1990s and 2000s.

For a while, it seemed that fur really was dead thanks to the relentless protesting of animal lovers. Coats made from mink, foxes, lynx, bobcats, beavers, coyotes, baby seals, and other cute, fuzzy animals started to fall out of fashion. People realized that these animals, many of whom were close relatives of our dogs and cats, were raised in horrible conditions and died even more horrible deaths—poisoned, gassed, drowned, or electrocuted to preserve their pelts. They decided that fur really looks better on the animals anyway. The number of fur farms in the United States plummeted from more than a thousand to fewer than three hundred.[3] Around the world, fur production continues to shed its popularity, with the number of mink stuck in fur farms dropping 25 percent between 2015 and 2016.[4] Farming animals for their fur is now illegal in the United Kingdom, Austria, and a handful of Eastern European countries. The Netherlands banned fox and chinchilla farming, and Japan's last mink farm closed in 2016. Thirty-five countries, including the United States, have taken a stand against clubbing baby seals for their fur by banning seal fur products that come from commercial hunts.

Eighty-five percent of fur comes from farm-raised animals, according to the International Fur Federation. Mink, the most popular animals used for fur, are relatives of otters and ferrets, who like to hang out by water and establish their territory in the wild. Fur Europe, an industry group based in Brussels, has decided that mink on fur farms are fine living their entire lives in small wire cages and that access to swimming water and large territories aren't really "essential" for captive animals.[5]

The other 15 percent of fur products comes from animals trapped in the wild; not only do those animals suffer, but the brutal traps set for them harm nontargeted animals who wander into the wrong patch of brush, including endangered species and family dogs.

If fur can return from its fashion grave, the voices of animal lovers can rise again, too. It's going to take more than simply not buying fur, since that's already a niche market—designers aren't expecting you to impulse buy a mink vest when you're at the mall with friends or to have a fur hat on your back-to-school shopping list. No matter how the animals are raised, fur is sold in stores as a luxury item with an unjustifiable cost of cruelty. Boycotting a few fur coats, hats, key chains, and trimmed gloves and hooded jackets won't be enough to get a designer's attention; if they use fur on anything, boycott their entire line and let them know why. If your favorite store carries fur, ask them to discontinue the department or lose your business. Instead, choose companies and brands that have made a commitment to go fur-free.

If you love the look of fur, go faux. Product labels can't always be trusted—fur is supposed to be labeled with the type of animal and country of origin, but fur-trimmed clothing that's been labeled as man-made or not labeled at all has been found to contain real animal fur in investigations by the Humane Society of the United States.[6] You can often tell the difference between fake fur and real fur by taking a closer look. The base of real fur will be attached to real animal skin, while if you part faux fur, the base is often attached to a fabric backing. The tips of real fur taper to a point, where fake fur generally has a blunt end. However, advances in fake fur manufacturing to make it a more appealing alternative may make it more difficult to know for sure if you're looking at animal or textile. If you find fur that you suspect might be mislabeled as fake, contact the Humane Society of the United States. Stick with the companies that have made fur-free commitments, and when in doubt, you can always leave the furry look on the rack.

If you happen to find yourself with a fur coat that you inherited or purchased before adopting an animal-friendly lifestyle, donate it to a wildlife rehabilitation center where it will be used to help keep injured and orphaned wildlife cozy.

Saving Their Hides

Factory farmers try to use every part of the animals to maximize profits—their skin for leather, and their bones and unmarketable organs rendered for pet food, farmed animal feed, soap, cosmetics, and other products. Purchasing leather isn't preventing a slaughtered animal's life from going to waste so much as it's making industrial animal agriculture more money.

As inadequate as labeling regulations are on meat and dairy, there aren't any labeling requirements for leather to indicate how the animals were treated before they became coats, belts, handbags, and shoes. And because there's such a high demand for cheap leather, much of it comes from countries with negligent or nonexistent animal welfare regulations.

While there are environmental concerns with PVC, still commonly used as a nonanimal leather substitute, leather has its own pollution problem, since the typical tanning process creates toxic waste from the chemicals used to prepare the hides. Non-leather alternatives have come a long way—some companies are using recycled materials or a combination of materials that cuts down on the PVC content and creates softer, more versatile products. Even better, keep an eye out for up-and-coming plant-based leather substitutes, such as those made from by-products of the pineapple and wine industries. If you're uneasy about supporting the mistreatment of farmed animals—including alligators, ostriches, snakes, and others farmed for fashion—but can't bring yourself to give up leather accessories, buy recycled or secondhand leather so you're not lining the calfskin wallets of industrial meat producers or exotic animal farmers.

While some animal products don't require slaughter, that doesn't mean the animals fared any better than their skinned counterparts. Sheep, like other farmed animals, are regularly castrated without pain relief and are frequently abused in the shearing process. Merino sheep, known for their extra-soft wool, have been bred to have more skin folds to produce more wool, but those extra skin folds collect moisture and attract flies, which like to lay their eggs in the folds near the sheep's derriere. This condition, known as fly-strike, is very painful, and in Australia, it's commonly treated by "mulesing," which is carving away chunks of skin without any pain relief to create smoother skin that's less attractive to flies.

In the United States, wildlife are regularly killed to protect grazing sheep (and the wool they produce). As with leather, there are no labeling standards to know if any wolves or other wild animals were shot for the sake of your wool sweater. Nor are there labels on down coats or bedding to know if the feathers were plucked from live birds or if they came from the foie gras industry (which creates the fatty liver "delicacy" by force-feeding geese and ducks). The only way to know that no animals were harmed in the making of your outfit is to avoid materials that come from animals. There are lots of options out there, including warm, weather-resistant synthetic alternatives to down insulation and wool clothing in winter.

Polyester Dreams

If you're trying to keep animal products out of your closet, there's a good likelihood that you'll wind up with polyester in your wardrobe. In fact, no matter what your style, there's a good chance polyester is involved. It's no longer just the fabric of stiff uniforms—it's also in yoga pants, running gear, hiking clothes, Halloween costumes, jerseys, dresses, sweaters, and that groovy 1970s retro suit. Polyester is the fastest-growing type of fabric in the world, accounting for 60 percent of fabric produced in 2014.[7]

In addition to environmental concerns about polyester as a petroleum-based, never-goes-away plastic product, when polyester clothes are washed, tiny fibers are rinsed down the drain. And when they are, they join the waves of microplastics in the ocean that are being eaten by fish and shorebirds, slowly starving them to death. (For more on the impact of plastic on wildlife, see chapter 13.) One study found that a single washing machine cycle could wash away more than 700,000 microfibers in the environment.[8] That adds up fast—it's estimated there are more than 1.4 trillion microfibers in the ocean.[9]

By now, you might be wondering if the only way to have an animal-friendly wardrobe is to not have a wardrobe at all. Before you show up to work in your birthday suit, know that this is one of those problems that's bigger than any single individual. While there are a growing number of after-market gadgets you can buy to help capture microfibers in your spin cycle, we need clothing manufacturers to be part of the solution—to use the creativity that came up with these nonanimal alternatives in the first place to continue innovating to find a solution that doesn't harm animals or the environment. We need them to commit to solving the problem and to be transparent about their efforts and the effects of their current clothing lines on our oceans and wildlife.

Put the Brakes on Fast Fashion

As individuals, there's one key step we can take to minimize the impact of our clothing on animals: Buy less. The clothing industry has shifted toward a disposable culture, where we're expected to jump on the latest trends, then toss them by next season. And the seasons are no longer restricted to the old standbys of winter, spring, summer, and fall—there can be fifteen or more seasons a year in the fashion world. No matter your style, the materials and resources that go into producing "fast fashion" and their impact on the environment when they're discarded will never be in vogue as far as animals are concerned.

You've probably heard of the slow food movement, and now we're in need of slow fashion. Because of rapidly revolving trends, an astonishing amount of clothing winds up in landfills. More than eighty pounds of clothing is tossed per person in the United States every year, and only about 15 percent of that gets donated or recycled.[10] A lot went into producing that clothing, whether it's cheap leather, wool, or fur-trimmed garments, or plastic-based fabrics contributing to ocean pollution. The average cotton T-shirt was grown using seventeen teaspoons of chemical fertilizers and about a teaspoon of pesticides.[11] So those piles of imprinted T-shirts with clever-but-fleeting sayings given away as festival swag played a role in poisoning amphibians and other wild animals and used land that was former wildlife habitat converted to cotton fields.

Clothing waste has been growing about 40 percent per decade over the past twenty years.[12] And while those metal donation bins have been sprouting like weeds on street corners and in parking lots, they're not a real solution. Oftentimes, the clothing that's dropped in those big metal boxes is shipped overseas. Used clothing has become a major export for the United States, and the billion pounds of clothes we're passing on to other countries can flood local markets, threatening the cultural and economic viability of traditional textile industries.[13]

Fast fashion has turned clothing donation charities into dumping grounds. They're receiving more than they can handle, and whatever they can't sell usually winds up in the trash. Charities like Goodwill are typically only able to use less than 20 percent of the mountains of clothes they receive;[14] some call textile recyclers to salvage what they can to be repurposed into insulation, carpet padding, and industrial rags, but for a lot of last season's looks, these charities are just a detour to the dump.

Take your wardrobe out of the fast lane. If you need new clothes, it's worth paying more for higher quality and timeless staples. For animal lovers, secondhand shopping is always fashionable. If you need special gear for skiing, camping, or other outdoor activities, try a used sporting goods store. If you're feeling frumpy without a revolving wardrobe, start a clothing swap with friends to trade styles every few months, join a clothing swap website, or sign up for a subscription box that allows you to send back what you no longer want to wear for others to try out. Some of my favorite clothes are the pieces I've adopted from friends' closets over the years (with their permission, of course).

When you clean out your own closet, it's still better to donate than to throw your clothes in the garbage, but skip the metal drop-off bins and donate directly to local charities. Churches, shelters for victims of domestic violence, and programs like Dress for Success (which empowers women to achieve economic independence by giving them the tools—including professional clothing—to help them be successful in their careers) are more likely to match your donations with local people in need, helping your community and reducing the carbon footprint of your old clothes on their way to their new life.

Comment and Share

Check out the Humane Society of the United States' list of fur-free designers. Thank the brands and companies that are on the list, and reach out to the ones that aren't, to ask if they have a fur-free policy. If not, it's time to let the virtual fur fly: Show them animal-friendly commitments matter by sending letters, posting on their social media pages, calling customer service, and urging your friends and local stores to join the boycott until the clothing company leaves the fur where it belongs—on the animals.

While some designers grab attention with controversial fur on the runways, others are making headlines for choosing compassionate fashion. Stella McCartney, daughter of Linda and Paul McCartney, inherited her parents' love of animals and chooses not to use fur or leather in her designs. John Bartlett was once known for leather and fur until learning about the cruelty behind the industry gave him a change of heart. There are several others, from up-and-coming trendsetters to mainstream brand names, that design clothes for a more animal-friendly world. When you find a cruelty-free company you like, let others know. Similar to the effect of Instagram culture on food, fashion photos can help influence the perception of what's trendy in your network.

! Action Alert

THREE THINGS YOU CAN DO TODAY

1 • Dress compassionately: Avoid purchasing clothes made from animals and, when possible, buy secondhand.

2 • Dress loudly: Let companies and your friends know which designers and stores you support, which you don't, and why.

3 • Dress slowly: Don't give in to fast fashion. Embrace the trend of smaller wardrobes, classic pieces, and trading clothes with friends.

ANIMALS YOU'LL HELP SAVE

Foxes, mink, beavers, lynx, bobcats, sheep, and other animals who want to keep their beautiful coats to themselves, plus cows, alligators, ostriches, and snakes who want to save their own skin.

Old MacDonald Lost His Farm

Cows are some of the most Zen animals out there, spending their days hanging out in the sun, chewing their cud, lying around, and hanging with their BFFs. No, really—if you hang out with the herd, you'll notice that cows form friendships. Like all animals, they each have their own personalities. They're known to frolic and play. They like music and respond differently to different types of music, often preferring slower jams to dance beats.[1] Cows are more socially complex, intelligent, and emotional than they usually get credit for. Unfortunately, the cow utopia of lazy days in open pastures is reserved for the 1 percenters of the bovine world; the majority of cows are stuck in veal crates, dairy sheds, or feedlots. And for all their natural calm and charm when left to their own devices, cows stress out and suffer when they're confined and abused by the factory farm system. The best way to be a friend to cows and other farmed animals is to start taking them off your plate.

If you ask someone about their most recent animal encounter, they'll probably tell you about their dog or cat, or maybe the bird who whitewashed their windshield. You aren't likely to hear about their last meal, even though every time we sit down to eat (or stand over the sink—I don't judge), our food choices impact animals. Food is one of the most common ways we interact with other species. You are either eating animals or products taken from animals . . . or you're not.

Most people dealing in health these days recognize the benefits of plant-based diets. After all, more than eight million Americans identify as vegetarian or vegan, with another eighty-two million choosing to eat vegetarian meals on a regular basis.[2] And it's not just a popularity contest: The Academy of Nutrition and Dietetics (formerly the American Dietetic Association) says that vegetarian or vegan diets are "healthful, nutritionally adequate, and may provide health benefits in the prevention and treatment of certain diseases."[3] From heart disease to diabetes, doctors are turning to prescriptions of plant-based diets as part of their patients' health plan. The academy also gives well-planned vegetarian diets the thumbs-up for all life stages, whether you're an infant, an athlete, or a senior citizen.

But even as being vegetarian or veg-curious becomes more mainstream, billions of animals are killed each year for food. That's hundreds of animals per second in the United States alone; an estimated 97 percent of the animals killed in this country die for the food industry.[4] You know that picture-book image of happy cows, pigs, and chickens grazing sunny pastures in front of charming red barns with a friendly guy in overalls standing at the ready with fresh hay until the day they peacefully pass away? For the vast majority of food produced in the United States, that's pure fairy tale—today's factory farms make your average dungeon look like a five-star hotel.

New MacDonald's Farm

A few years ago, a farmer in Russia installed LED televisions in his barn. He hoped showing his cows the lush fields of the Swiss Alps would make them happier so they'd produce more milk.[5] As opposed to, you know, letting the cows out into real fields. I can only imagine he came up with this idea because he crunched some numbers and the televisions came out cheaper than the costs of letting his grazing animals actually touch grass and breathe a little fresh air.

Cows don't get much out of watching TV; baby calves aren't exactly raised on *Sesame Street* and *Dora the Explorer*. Also, they're red-green color blind, so even if they're given the latest high-def flat screens and know what to make of the two-dimensional pictures, a lot would get lost in translation. On the other hand, cows are able to detect odors as far as five miles away. Imagine having that sense of smell and living with a few dozen people in a studio apartment where the windows don't open and the one bathroom doesn't work. I doubt a new TV would be much cause for celebration. But that's factory farm logic for you.

Getting more nuggets out of every chicken means breeding them so their bodies are so big their legs can no longer support them. Meeting the Thanksgiving demand for turkeys means accelerated growth spurts that can lead to heart problems and crippling deformities. Feeding the bacon craze means sows spend their lives in tiny cages, locked in a cycle of pregnancy, birth, nursing, and more pregnancy until their bodies give up. The milk needed for lattes comes from cows spending their lives indoors, hooked up to milking machines, which can cause painful swelling in their udders. They're also caught in an endless cycle of pregnancies to produce the milk that, instead of going to their calves, goes to grocery stores and coffee shops. (This chapter focuses on land animals; for information on the toll of seafood on marine animals, see chapter 15.)

No matter how they're bred and treated, animals raised for food are destined to die. That's the reality of eating animals, and one that many animal lovers struggle with. But even if you don't support the system with your own diet, the other reality is that animal agriculture isn't going away anytime soon, and farmed animals shouldn't have to suffer cruel and unusual punishment just because they're on death row. Yet these practices— and more—are all considered the acceptable, standard way of doing things on New MacDonald's farm. The fact that the animals are living creatures with their own sets of needs—like the maternal drive to raise their young, or even the basic desire for a life free of pain—may be irrelevant to the producers trying to maximize profits at any cost, but it's very relevant to the people buying animal products. Most people, even those who wouldn't call themselves animal lovers, want to believe the animals they're eating were raised humanely.

The majority of animal abuse statutes explicitly leave farmed animals out, but in recent years, there's been a wave of laws to ban some of the worst forms of confinement, like battery cages for egg-laying hens, gestation crates for sows, and veal crates for baby calves, as people learn the truth about how these animals are treated. Rather than responding by reforming cruel practices industry-wide, the animal agriculture industry has been trying to get new laws passed that make it illegal to share images of factory farm cruelty and make it harder to hold meat, dairy, and egg producers responsible for animal abuse on their farms. This legal tug-of-war can feel frustrating and slow, but it is a sign of progress and an important step toward ultimately ending the nightmare of factory farming.

Thanks to undercover investigations by animal protection groups, people are starting to realize just how far we've strayed from Old MacDonald, and they're demanding better laws and transformation in the market. From high-end bistros to fast-food drive-throughs, restaurants are changing how they source animal products to meet customer demand. You can help increase that demand through your food choices, asking your favorite restaurants to rethink their menus, supporting laws to end factory farm abuse, and educating others on the harsh reality of New MacDonald's farm.

What's in a Name?

Free range. Cage-free. Crate-free. Grass-fed. Natural. Organic. Farm fresh. It's easy to get confused—and fooled—because there are more labels in the meat, egg, and dairy aisles than there are regulations. Many of these labels mean more for the price tag than the animals' welfare.

Let's start with the egg before the chicken. A world without battery cages is a good thing. But *cage-free* does not automatically mean cruelty-free. It literally only means that the birds are not kept in cages; they can still be housed in overcrowded conditions without access to the outdoors. *Free range* means the hens are cage-free and have access to the outdoors. It's a step up, but a small one—"free range" could be an overcrowded warehouse with a little side door to a patch of dirt most of the birds never see, and that counts as "access." Labels like *natural* and *farm fresh* are just advertising copy.

Similar to their egg-laying relatives, chickens and turkeys raised under the "free range" meat label are supposed to have some kind of access to the outdoors, but there's no guarantee that they get to stretch their wings or that they won't be subjected to debeaking and other painful procedures. Here's more bad news for chickens and turkeys: No matter how they're raised and labeled, they've been left out of the Humane Methods of

Slaughter Act, so there's nothing protecting them in their final moments from pain and suffering.

Labels don't provide much more reassurance to other animals either. *Pasture-raised*, *sustainably raised*, *humanely raised*, *natural*, and *free range* aren't government regulated for cows or pigs. Grass-fed animals fare somewhat better: Instead of getting feed that contains anything from plastic (used as a fiber substitute) to gummy worms (when corn prices rise, candy is always cheap!), they're supposed to be fed a forage-only diet, including delicacies such as grass, hay, and alfalfa. They usually even get to graze and hang out in pastures, though that's not guaranteed unless the operation is certified by an independent group that requires pasture time as part of granting its seal of approval. But grass-fed cattle and other animals can still be subject to painful procedures like castration, dehorning, and tail docking without pain relief. In addition, grazing cattle and sheep pose a threat to wildlife (see chapter 15). And, in 2016, the USDA withdrew its grass-fed marketing standard, so this label isn't officially regulated by the government.[6]

Although cows and pigs are covered under the Humane Methods of Slaughter Act, Sir Paul McCartney said it best: "If slaughterhouses had glass walls, everyone would be vegetarian." And this doesn't even get into the mistreatment endured by animals during long, uncomfortable, terrifying transports from the factory farm to the slaughterhouse. Animals can be crammed in those metal trucks for hundreds of miles, in all kinds of weather, without food, water, or rest. Some of them never make it to their final destination.

Unless we curb the demand for meat and dairy and insist on animal protection laws from birth through death, plus meaningful labels so people can make informed decisions, producers will continue to look for ways to cut corners while trying to convince us that their animals are happy.

The Burger of the Future

Maybe you can't imagine a summer without burgers and hot dogs. Or the holidays without ham. Maybe it's your mom's homemade mac and cheese, or even the boxed kind. We all have our guilty pleasures. The concept of not eating animals may be straightforward, but for many people the decision can feel more complicated than "to meat or not to meat." Our cultural ties with food can be hard to untangle. Allergies, gluten intolerance, and other personal health considerations can narrow down menus pretty quickly. Fast-food burgers are often more readily available, cheaper, and more tantalizing than salads. Although we might like to think we're immune to the hypnotic influence of advertising, the food industry spends billions of dollars and employs every psychological trick in the book to influence our eating decisions for a reason. And it's usually not spinach starring in their commercials.

Personally, I like tofu. It's like the chameleon of foods (without harming any actual chameleons). Tofu picks up whatever flavors you surround it with—it can blend in just as well in Asian cuisine as it can at American-style cookouts. You can grill it or fry it or use it in smoothies. But you don't have to be pro-tofu to eat an animal-friendly diet. Believe it or not, there are a lot of vegetarians and vegans out there who believe the humble block of soybean curd deserves its bad name. (Poor tofu.) You don't have to give up the flavors you love. From cupcakes to soul food, pretty much everything is being veganized in cookbooks and restaurants. But you don't have to be a gourmet chef. In fact, I hate to cook. Yet I manage to eat healthily (for me and the animals) by enjoying the already-vegan options in ethnic cuisine and relying on a handful of go-to meals that require minimal ingredients and preparation. I could eat avocado toast with Sriracha every day, a recipe with only four ingredients, counting the chili sauce and salt.

You may not even have to give up meat to eat an animal-friendly diet. Companies are sprouting up with the mission of providing meat alternatives that can satisfy the hungriest carnivores without harming animals or the environment. The newest innovations in veggie burgers are experimenting with different types of plant-powered protein to create patties that look, cook, and feel more like meat on your taste buds—some even use beet juice to make their veggie burgers "bleed" like a medium-rare patty. And ever since the first beef burger created from a handful of bovine cells (instead of a slaughtered animal) debuted in 2013 for the price of $325,000, the race has been on to perfect the technology into a new generation of cruelty-free hamburgers for grocery store shelves. The price has already dropped 96 percent since then,[7] so even though the cost is still steep compared ground chuck, it won't be long until "clean" burgers made from meat without the butcher will be hitting grills near you.

Some people question whether meat that started in a lab instead of a barn can ever really catch on, or whether it's too "unnatural." Considering the annual sales of foods like Twinkies and Hot Pockets, people aren't too married to understanding the intricacies of how their food is produced as long as it tastes good. And when it comes to animal products, studies have shown that people dissociate from their food—their subconscious kicks into gear and, with the help of terms like *bacon* and *steak*, turns off any association with the cute, innocent animals they intellectually know the meat on their plate came from. If people can ignore factory farms when digging into a Big Mac, they ultimately won't have a problem setting aside any uncertainty about laboratories and petri dishes when chowing down on a "clean meat" burger.

You don't have to be into high-tech hamburgers to embrace eating better for animals. Familiar favorites in nonanimal versions help a lot of people make the leap to a diet that's healthier for farmed animals, wild animals, and human animals. But you can also simply eat less meat and rediscover the tasty, colorful palate of fresh fruits, vegetables, beans, and whole grains available in the world. Of course, there are plenty of ways to eat plant-based and unhealthy: Oreos and french fries are vegan, but you won't impress your doctor with that diet.

Whatever your style, tastes, or cooking skills, you can work it into an animal-friendly diet. The best part is, you may not be giving up as much as you think. Vegans like good food, too. Really. You might be surprised how good cruelty-free tastes. Maybe you'll even like tofu.

Should My Dog or Cat Go Veg, Too?

At this point, you might be sneaking glances at your dog's or cat's bowl and wondering what you should do about their meat consumption.

When it comes to dogs, they'll eat just about anything, from roadkill to your socks. Not to say these are recommended parts of a healthy diet, but as omnivores and scavengers, dogs are built to digest a variety of foods. So a vegetarian or vegan diet can meet all their health needs. There are a number of quality dog foods on the market with meat-free formulas. However, soy and corn are often used as cheap sources of protein in dog food, and a lot of dogs are allergic to those ingredients. So, if you are going to change your dog's diet, make the transition slowly to allow your dog's stomach to get used to its new contents and to give you a chance to watch out for any other health effects. And, of course, check with your vet about your dog's individual needs.

Where dogs are nature's garbage disposals, cats are meat eaters through and through. They're what's known as an *obligate carnivore*, which means they're designed to eat other animals. In order to survive, your cat needs a diet high in protein and the amino acid taurine. Without it, she can go blind or suffer from heart disease. And, despite her catnip addiction, her digestive system is actually too short to fully digest veggies and other plants as a primary source of nutrients.

You can find vegetarian and vegan cat foods, some of which have the stamp of approval from the association charged with making sure pet foods meet basic dietary needs. But it takes a lot of processing and additives to turn plants into something that will be accepted by a digestive system designed for meat. Many veterinarians will tell you these foods are still risky. Continuing to feed your cat meat can be a difficult decision for an animal lover, especially if you've committed to a vegan lifestyle for yourself, but it's worth thinking twice about what's best for your cat. Don't risk your cat's health just to have a meat-free kitchen—you might be able to check off a box, but it misses the point of striving to make choices that make animals' lives better.

If you decide to make any changes to your animal's diet, it's always a good idea to talk to your veterinarian first.

Friends, Not Food

There's no way to sugarcoat it: Eating animals undermines your animal-friendly lifestyle.

Most Americans are appalled by the idea of eating dog meat, yet pigs are just as smart and social (some argue more so) than dogs. Cows and birds also have their own personalities and social structures and the ability to suffer. Studies have shown that even fish exhibit complex means of communication and have shown signs of fear in the face of pain.

As an animal lover, it becomes harder to justify the difference between being okay with eating one species but not another, especially as we learn more about the lives of different animals. Even more difficult is accepting the mistreatment of animals that's an unavoidable part of mass-producing them in order to keep cheap meat in supermarket coolers. As long as we continue to eat the huge amounts of animal products consumed in the United States, animal abuse will continue to be a staple of our food system. And the meat and dairy industries will do everything in their power to keep you from thinking too hard about the animals who wind up on your plate.

There's a decent chance you've never met a real, live farm animal, except maybe that one time at a fair when you were a little kid or if you took a field trip to a farm. Sure, cows are photogenic and there are some pretty cute pig personalities on social media, but I recommend heading offline for this one. Take a field trip to visit a farm animal sanctuary near you (check out www.sanctuaries.org for a list by state). Get to know the animals. There are billions of these guys living in cruel conditions for our food system, and most of us haven't given them the time of day. Not only will you get to play with adorable critters who get to live out their lives free from suffering, but it will help you connect with the real-world impact of your food choices. Even if you decide to continue eating animal products (though hopefully not as much as before), at least you'll be doing it with your eyes open. We've come a long way from the days when we all had to raise our own food, and it's easy to forget where the stuff in the supermarket came from.

Dinner Table Confrontation

Many of us have been in the position where we're minding our own meat-free business at the dinner table and someone asks why there's no steak, chicken, or fish on our plates. Sometimes speaking honestly about what moved you to order your veg meal (The animals! The planet! My health! Um, it just looked better?) leads to a shared moment of understanding and others nod along, saying they feel the same and maybe they'll think twice next time they order. But sometimes things start to get confrontational, and suddenly you're being interrogated about protein, amino acids, the statistics of corn used for feed versus biofuel, the life cycle breakdown of greenhouse gas emissions, the comparative nervous systems of people to pigs to plants, and world hunger, and you're wondering how the conversation went awry.

Chances are that it's not you. Most people, even those who don't see themselves as animal lovers, don't like causing animals pain. But most people still enjoy eating meat. Researchers call this the *meat paradox* and have actually started to study the ways that we dissociate from the food on our plates. And when people feel forced to confront that paradox, they often get defensive. It's not personal; it's psychology. There's a lot of pressure in our society when it comes to food. What we eat is tied into our cultures, traditions, and social expectations. As a result, changing what you eat—or even talking about it—can be challenging.

This doesn't mean you have to give up dinner with meat-eating friends. Or that you can't start changing your own diet until you've earned a few more master's degrees. People eat more vegetarian foods than they think; many have switched to almond or soy milk without marking the occasion as a big moral decision. Next time the topic comes up when you're out with friends, invite them over for a vegan or vegetarian potluck—they'll get the chance to try new recipes, you'll get the chance to feel more prepared to answer their questions, and you can talk about it without the awkwardness of anyone feeling judged for what they've already ordered.

How to Talk to Your Loved Ones About Vegetables

When you choose to eat fewer or no animal products, every meal can feel like an intervention—either you're being grilled on everything from philosophy to nutrition, or your meat-loving companions feel the need to justify every bite. Dinner shouldn't be this hard. Here are a few tips to get you through the meal without losing any friends.

1 • **Don't pick a fight.** Your friends aren't hanging out with you for a lecture on the evils of their eating habits. Guilt and shame rarely motivate people to change their ways (but are effective in ruining relationships). The goal is to show how your animal-friendly diet is an all-around win. If people see that you can still eat good food and have normal

conversations, all while helping animals and the environment, they're more likely to follow your lead (and still be your friend). If your food choices become a hot conversation topic, make it about you—why *you* chose to change your diet, what *you* enjoy eating, and why *you* love cows, chickens, and pigs. Don't worry about what they are or aren't doing—you're not going to change a lifestyle of dietary habits and beliefs by dessert, but you can get them thinking about their choices by the time the check comes.

2 • **Forget the all-or-nothing attitude.** One of the most common things vegetarians and vegans hear is "But I could never give up bacon/cheese/schnitzel/other-random-favorite-meaty-dish." Instead of shrugging or judging, tell them they don't have to. They can start by eating smaller portions or saving it for special occasions, and substituting the things that don't trigger feelings of deprivation or lost childhood. If they don't feel strongly about the creamer in their coffee coming from cows, that could be a good place to try out nondairy alternatives. Celebrate baby steps rather than making favorite foods an irreconcilable difference and they're more likely to come around. Or not—they may never want to give up that dish, but if they ultimately cut some of the other meat and dairy from their diet, that still helps a lot of animals.

3 • **Prepare for a pop quiz.** You don't have to be a dietary expert, nor are you required to justify your food choices to your friends, but people learn through asking questions, and the more prepared you feel to answer them, the more likely you are to have a deeper conversation with the potential to change minds. Here are three common conversation starters you'll likely encounter:

Where do you get your protein?

While it may be tempting to ask your meat-loving friends where they get their vitamins or fiber, resist the urge to answer this most frequent of FAQs with a challenge. It's often an innocent question from people who've been told their whole lives that no one gets enough protein (false) and that beef is what's for dinner (also false). There are lots of great nonanimal sources of protein. In case you missed the #LovePulses hashtag, 2016 was the International Year of the Pulse to celebrate beans, peas, chickpeas, lentils, and other legumes (or pulses) as an important, sustainable source of protein, vitamins, and fiber. Protein can also be found in many vegetables, as well as grains like quinoa or wild rice, nuts and seeds, and meat and dairy substitutes. By eating a variety of plant-based foods, you can meet all your body's nutritional needs. (But if you have any concerns, talk to your doctor or nutritionist.)

Why are you doing this?

Because you love animals. Because you're worried about global warming. Because you want to eat healthier. Because you just felt like it. Whatever motivated you, don't be afraid to tell people. You don't need to have a reason that feels profound to others any more than they need to explain their food choices to you. Again, assume the best of your friends and family—they're often just curious about what's new in your life.

Do you ever miss meat?

It's okay to be honest. If your mouth waters at barbecues or sometimes you crave a bagel with lox and cream cheese but choose not to eat it because your reasons for being vegetarian or vegan matter more to you, admit it. If you miss your favorite hamburger—or even let yourself have it every once in a while—it's not the worst confession in the world. In fact, these stories humanize your journey, making it easier for others to see the path they might take toward an animal-friendlier diet.

Comment and Share

Share animal-friendly foods with your friends, family, and coworkers to show them that nixing meat and dairy doesn't mean nixing taste. Take a delicious plant-based dish to your next barbecue. Bring vegan cupcakes to the office party. (Baked goods can be very convincing—my dad is a dedicated meat-eater and chocoholic, but thanks to the right baker, his favorite birthday cake is now animal-free.)

Social media is your ally here, too. When people see celebrities or their friends choosing plant-based diets, they pay attention—and posting about the hot new vegetarian restaurant doesn't put people on the defensive like having a conversation over their plate of chicken wings. It's no secret that social media loves food photos. Posting your delicious recipes or favorite low-prep snacks can inspire people to give them a try and help bust myths about boring plant-based meals. In 2016, *The Guardian* published an article about "the rise of the vegan teenager," crediting online resources, communities, and particularly Instagram for making veganism more attractive.[8] And if you're not sure what you can eat or your compassionate diet is feeling uninspired, check out what others are posting under hashtags like #vegan, #whatveganseat, and #meatlessmonday.

Every meal matters. So don't worry if you're not sure you're ready to jump into the deep end of the vegan pool—test the waters by trying more plant-based meals and reducing your meat portion sizes. Of all the personal choices you can make to help animals, this is one of the most impactful. According to Compassion Over Killing, cutting meat from your diet one day a week saves 28 land animals and 175 aquatic animals each year.[9] From there, the lifesaving math is pretty simple: The more you fill your plate with plant-based choices, the more lives you save. (Plus, extra credit for environmental and health benefits.)

There are far too many apps, recipe websites, cookbooks, and other online and offline resources dedicated to plant-based eating to name here (though you'll find a few in the appendix)—and new ones are surfacing all the time. So, wherever you hang out and whatever level of motivation you need, a quick search will give you plenty of options, from recipe banks to apps that help you find the closest veg-friendly takeout.

Last but not least, keep sharing those videos of goats in sweaters and baby chicks hanging out with dogs. Bring your friends to the farm sanctuary with you. Endless images of cruelty in your newsfeed can be hard to swallow, but cuteness can be a powerful way to convince others to eat compassionately.

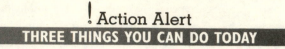

! Action Alert

THREE THINGS YOU CAN DO TODAY

1 • Start changing one meal, one day, or one ingredient at a time. It's not about perfection; it's about saving animals.

2 • Share your favorite animal-friendly foods with your friends, online and offline.

3 • Go hang out with some farm animals.

ANIMALS YOU'LL HELP SAVE
Cows, chickens, pigs, turkeys, bison, goats, sheep, and fish.

Holiday Hangover

Turkeys are curious explorers who can distinguish one another by voice and are known to have at least twenty to thirty different vocalizations. Makes that whole "gobble-gobble" bit seem rather insulting. Sure, gobbling is one variation, but wild turkeys also cluck, yelp, cackle, and purr, among other sounds to express excitement and contentment, as well as sounding the alarm, finding each other, and looking for a good time with a mate. They're not just chatty; they're also intelligent and playful. And, according to Benjamin Franklin, the turkey is a "bird of courage" who is a "much more respectable bird" than the bald eagle, "though a little vain and silly."[1] Despite all this charisma, the bald eagle gets all the respect while turkeys have gained an unfair reputation for being dim-witted and have been relegated to the role of dinner in American culture.

It's a long-standing Thanksgiving tradition for the president of the United States to publicly grant a pardon to a turkey. Unfortunately, some forty-six million of that lucky bird's relatives aren't so lucky that day.[2] Within weeks of Easter, real-life bunnies, chicks, and ducks aren't feeling so blessed when they find themselves homeless after the pastel baskets and plastic eggs are put away. On July 5, animal shelters across the country are filled with firework-phobic dogs sent running from their yards by the previous night's blasts.

Holidays can be a hazardous time for animals. Celebrations, decorations, and a festive break in routine for us can be confusing and even life-threatening for the animals in our lives. No matter how many times you watch *A Christmas Story*, your dog or cat doesn't understand the miracle of Christmas. At best, they understand extra treats and more time with their families at home. At worst, they get into deadly foods and are terrified by the sudden wave of guests and noisy parties.

No matter what the occasion, remember that your companion animals rely on you every day. Make sure they don't get lost in the party shuffle. Make sure you make it home safely from your Saint Patrick's Day night out. We can't explain to them why their world was turned upside down for a day, so the least we can do is always come back home to them and protect them from hidden dangers.

Holidays don't have to be all doom and gloom for animal lovers—they're also an opportunity to do good. The season of giving can be a time to give back to animals by donating your time and money to causes that help other creatures. And holiday traditions that may be dangerous for your four-legged family members, for farmed animals, or for wildlife aren't carved in stone. There's no better time than now to create new traditions with animals in mind.

Pet Party Fouls

Your dog or cat may not feel the same way you do about hosting parties, whether it's Thanksgiving dinner with family or a New Year's Eve blowout. It's a lot harder to keep an eye on your animals when you're busy getting the door, refilling food trays, opening bottles, collecting dishes, and schmoozing, and the sudden influx of people and noise in their living space can be stressful.

While most cats are pretty adept at hiding when the situation calls for it, it's still a good idea to set your cat up with treats and water in a favorite cozy spot behind a closed door to ensure that he doesn't have a chance to make a run for it if the front door is accidentally left open. If your dog is a party animal who likes to mingle, make sure she's wearing a collar with up-to-date identification in case she devises an escape plan as guests are coming and going. And make sure everyone is clear on the list of party fouls:

- Don't share leftovers. Too much fatty food can lead to acute pancreatitis and other gastric distress, and poisonous perils like chocolate and grapes are never worth the risk.

- Keep plates and glasses out of reach. Unintentional scraps left at nose level can be even more dangerous than intentionally giving in to begging.

- The dog is not a toy. If you want to show off your dog's party tricks, that's one thing, but unsanctioned attempts at stupid pet tricks—especially after the alcohol has been flowing—are rarely amusing for your dog.

Add your own depending on your animal's personality, fears, bad habits, allergies, or other health or behavior concerns. And don't forget the year-round rules of the house. If you don't let your dog on the couch, allowing or encouraging her to embrace her inner lapdog during the party will only be confusing for her when the party's over and the rules are reinforced.

Even outgoing animals can feel overwhelmed by party guests, especially if it's a lot of people they don't know well. Nervousness and stress aren't just hard on your dog or cat; they can be a bite waiting to happen. If you have any doubts about how your animals will handle a party—or how the party will handle your animals—there's no shame in playing it better safe than sorry. Give both of you less to worry about by putting her in a bedroom with the TV or radio on to keep her company.

These tips don't just apply during the holiday season. Halloween (plastic masks can be terrifying), Super Bowl Sunday (common staples like chicken wings and guacamole are both on the danger list for dogs), kids' birthdays (lots of small people running around can be overstimulating, especially when the guest list includes kids who aren't used to being around animals), and other celebrations all have their own hazards. Watching out for your nonhuman family members doesn't mean being the fun police or giving up your Hostess of the Year aspirations—just keep them in mind when party planning, even if that means keeping them off the guest list for their own safety.

Keep your animals in mind when you decorate, too. Dogs and cats can easily choke on tinsel and other garlands if they get their mouths on them. If you have a live tree for Christmas, make sure they can't get at the water, and clean up pine needles to avoid stomach problems. And, of course, make sure your tree and other decorations are secure; if you have a cat who likes to climb or a rambunctious dog with a tendency to knock things over, you might have to rethink where you place your tree and what type of ornaments to hang. Don't leave candles unattended around animals, and beware of plants like holly, mistletoe, poinsettia, and lilies that can be highly toxic for dogs or cats.

Don't forget the animals outside your home, either: Holiday light displays can create disorienting light pollution for nocturnal wildlife while sucking up enough energy annually to power nearly five hundred thousand homes for a year.[3] Find ways to reduce your electricity use during the holidays and choose decorations that don't put anyone in danger.

Cook Up New Traditions

Holidays are all about traditions, and we often carry on the same ones that we grew up with and our parents grew up with and on down the line. Tradition is what connects us to the meaning of the holiday and the warm memories of holidays past. But sometimes traditions hit their expiration date. Maybe your taste in decorations changed and those honeycombed tissue pumpkins aren't doing it for you anymore. Maybe you grew up and decided that Jell-O salad served at every Memorial Day barbecue really wasn't as exciting as you thought it was when you were five. Or maybe you meshed your customs with your partner's into something new and representative of your life together.

It's okay to let go of old traditions. Starting new traditions can be an empowering part of defining your life and how you want to live it. If letting go of a tradition feels like letting go of something bigger, such as family or culture, take a step back to think about why it's important to you and whether you can come up with an alternative that honors those feelings without sacrificing the values you've grown into. For example, some Jews practice the ritual of kaporos, where a live chicken is passed over one's head as a way of symbolically transferring the person's sins to the bird, then the chicken is slaughtered and donated to the poor. There's a growing movement to take the chickens out of the equation and perform the same rite using money, which maintains the purpose of ritual, atonement, and charity without harming any animals (and also happens to be a suitable alternative, according to Jewish law).

There are traditions around the world that call for ritual animal sacrifice and are often met with outrage and horror. Meanwhile, the traditions of the most common holidays celebrated in the United States call for an enormous amount of animal sacrifice, except it all happens behind the scenes. The centerpiece of most holiday meals is meat—in addition to the turkeys slaughtered for Thanksgiving, about 318 million pounds of ham is served during the holiday season.[4] Memorial Day, Fourth of July, and Labor Day are the biggest meat-eating days of the year. During barbecue season, Americans eat an average of 818 hot dogs per second.[5]

One of the best ways you can make your holidays more animal-friendly is to mix up the menu. Thanksgiving dinner is already at least as much about the side dishes as it is about the turkey—at least in my family. We've turned everyone's favorite sides into the main course. By veganizing all the classic sides and adding a few new ones every year, there's plenty for everyone to eat. Use barbecue holidays to try meat-free grilling and enjoy creative salads with seasonal fresh fruits and vegetables. Spread some Christmas cheer to pigs by leaving ham off the table and dishing up new, meat-free comfort foods.

Use the holidays to try something a little different, such as a vegan recipe you've bookmarked or volunteering at your local animal shelter. Get the whole family involved to create new compassionate traditions for the next generation.

Guilt-Free Gifting

The tradition of giving gifts has gotten out of control. Wrapping paper alone during the holiday season uses the equivalent of more than thirty million trees.[6] Imagine all the wild animals who lost their homes for those ten seconds of tearing open presents—many of which will be returned or forgotten about within a matter of weeks. Instead of things that people don't really want or need—and which take resources from wild animals and pollute their homes when tossed—commit to giving meaningful gifts. Crafts, collages, or photo albums will be treasured more and longer than the scented candle set or hilariously ugly sweater (unless you knit the sweater for them yourself, making it ugly *and* sentimental).

If you're not the crafting type, give experiences like a special night out or an opportunity to learn a new skill. Take it one step further and give experiences that help animals, such as meat-free cooking lessons, a national park pass to reconnect with wildlife, a visit to an animal sanctuary, or a craft party to make dog blankets or homemade cat toys or whatever is on your local shelter's wish list. And, of course, you can always donate to an animal protection charity in their name. Or give coupons to clean their house or walk their dogs for a month. For kids, get out of the rut of cheap plastic toys and give games that the family can enjoy together, take them camping or to a museum, share books to teach them about bugs or birds or whatever their favorite animal is. Whatever you wind up wrapping, save habitat by giving gifts in reusable bags or using newspaper, comics, magazines, or paper bags from the recycling bin decorated with your own designs.

When it comes to giving live animals as gifts, there are several cautionary tales to keep in mind. Never use animals as novelty gifts or props, as bunnies, chicks, and ducks often are in Easter baskets. Don't gift animals to anyone who isn't expecting an animal or prepared for one. If someone isn't in the market for a new puppy, it's not much of a gift for them to unexpectedly change their lives to care for a dog. If people aren't ready to commit to caring for an animal, the animal could wind up at the shelter or on the side of the road. Giving frogs, turtles, or fish to kids without parental consent will more than likely lead to a dead or abandoned frog, turtle, or fish.

Even if someone is desperate for a dog or cat in their lives, it can be tricky to pick out an animal for another person. Most people want to form a bond when they first meet their animals, and they might have preconceived notions of what age, size, breed, or temperament they're most likely to fall in love with. Since this is a lifetime commitment, the moment of surprise often isn't worth the risk of it being a wrong match. Instead of putting the animal under the tree or in a gift box, put together a gift basket of toys, treats, leashes, beds, and other supplies, along with a gift certificate to go to the local shelter. That way, they get the surprise and the joy of choosing their new best friend when the time is right.

Comment and Share

While holidays should be a time of good cheer, they're often a time of high stress and family tension. It doesn't help if you go to a family dinner and there's nothing there for you to eat. Don't be shy about your dietary preferences—politely tell your host that you're trying to eat less meat and dairy, and offer to bring a dish. Share animal-friendly recipes with everyone you'll be celebrating with to give them ideas for potlucks and office parties. Be forthcoming with your gift list, too. Whether it's the holiday season or your birthday, you can always ask for no gifts, a donation in your name, or exactly what you want to ensure that you'll get something you'll actually use. Most people are relieved when the mystery is taken out of gift shopping.

You can even create an online gift registry to help people get you what you really want or need. You can do this the traditional way if there are things you need from a particular store—they don't really care if you're getting hitched or having a baby when you create your wish list, and many stores now have "other" options for registries to cover all occasions. Or even better, with tools like the SoKind gift registry you can include non-material gifts, like donations to your favorite charities, family recipes to help you create a friends-and-family cookbook, skills you want to learn from your friends, and cash requests for specific purposes, such as campground fees and organic trail mix or whatever else you need to get you through your big birthday camping trip.

Instead of making New Year's resolutions or birthday wishes, challenge your friends and family to join you in changing the world for animals. Turn over your new leaf by picking an issue or a set of actions and getting to work. You don't even have to wait for January or the next convenient Monday to start your new life.

! Action Alert

THREE THINGS YOU CAN DO TODAY

1 • Plan parties with your nonhuman family members' safety in mind.

2 • Mix up your holiday meal plan to celebrate with fewer animals on the menu.

3 • Revamp your gift list to give and receive meaningful, lasting experiences that minimize waste and help animals.

ANIMALS YOU'LL HELP SAVE
Dogs, cats, turkeys, pigs, cows, and wildlife saved from waste.

Don't Get Catfished

Catfish, named for the whisker-like sensory organs near their mouths, have complex ways of communicating with each other, producing a variety of sounds from different body parts, including calls to indicate if they're threatened or if they are the threat. Most catfish are bottom feeders with a reputation for being difficult to spot. Human catfish can also be difficult to spot, hiding behind the anonymity of the internet, though thanks to increased exposure of people using fake online profiles to lure someone into a relationship (and internet users getting savvier about Googling contacts they don't know), it's becoming harder to pull off. The term catfish *comes from a story told in the 2010 documentary by the same name about catfish being used to keep cod caught for the seafood industry active during shipment, supposedly the same way people using fake profiles keep the rest of us on our toes. The legitimacy of this tale is questionable, but the name stuck. While catfishing usually refers to seducing people, the anonymity of the internet can also be used to scam people into opening their hearts and wallets in the hope of finding puppy love.*

If there are two things Americans love, they are our animals and our internet. When those loves collide, amazing things can happen, like viral cat videos, the ability to instantly share and rack up likes on every cute moment in your furry best friend's life, and the transformation of homeless dogs from passed-over kennel waifs to online superstars with people lining up to adopt them. Unfortunately, terrible things can happen, too, like untraceable videos of animal cruelty, puppy mills masquerading as "family-owned" breeders, and people forgetting every stranger-danger lesson they've ever heard to send their animals off to an unknown fate with someone they know nothing about other than a screen name.

Most days, it seems that the Web was invented for animal lovers. And it's become a powerful tool for the rescue community. But like the chat room creeps your mother warned you about, online anonymity has provided new ways for animal abusers and scammers to deceive people, especially those looking for a new family member to love. As we all (hopefully) know by now, you can't believe everything you see on the internet.

It's probably safe to assume that anyone reading this book views their dog or cat as family, with a unique personality and wants and needs. You know your cat's go-to furniture for shredding and how he acts on a catnip buzz. You know what toys your dog will ignore and which she'll drop in the hall for you to step on in the middle of the night. You know whether they prefer tummy rubs or scratches behind the ear, and that they'll always be waiting for you at the end of a bad day or a good one.

You're not alone. The majority of Americans view their companion animals as part of the family. But just as it's becoming more common for people to meet their future spouses online, people are turning to online profiles to choose their next four-legged family member. But how do you avoid getting catfished into buying a dog or cat who's nothing like what you thought you were getting? How do you know you're not doing business with an animal abuser?

Step 1: Don't Buy an Animal Online

Getting a dog or cat shouldn't be like buying a book from Amazon. You can't just retape the box and send it back if it's not exactly what you wanted. When you're about to make a lifetime commitment to a living, loving creature, it shouldn't be about one-click ordering and prime shipping discounts. Your dog or cat is family, not a product. But to online pet retailers—just like the brick-and-mortar stores that sell puppies and kittens—they're merchandise. Products that require food and water, and if they're not sold quickly, they could get sick and become a profit loss. But when they do sell, they can be very profitable, even leading to additional sales of bowls and treats and squeaky rubber alligators. You might even be able to find a deal with free shipping or financing for your new puppy, like a new car.

This isn't just a technicality. When puppies are treated like products, the only real winners are puppy mills. If you're envisioning a plush maternity ward for those mama dogs (since commercial breeders haven't figured out a way around the basic biological inconvenience of how puppies are created), remember that this is all about the bottom line and keeping puppies in stock, so it's the bare minimum for these puppy-making machines. They're kept in small wire cages, often with little protection from the elements and even less attention to basic sanitation. They're not petted or given treats, or even allowed to bond with their puppies or let their bodies recover before the next pregnancy. Forget vet care—if one falls sick, it's usually cheaper to replace her with a younger model. And since people will pay hundreds of dollars for a puppy, commercial dog breeding is a lucrative business for someone with an extra barn and a lack of compassion.

Pet store owners have noticed that the truth about puppy mills is spreading. Some have stopped selling puppies and kittens from commercial breeders and started showcasing rescued dogs and cats in their cages instead or inviting local rescue groups and shelters to bring animals into their stores for adoption days. That's the ideal outcome (and one that you can help along using some of the tips in chapter 2). Others, however, have decided to go into damage control mode with slick advertising to make you believe their puppies were "family-raised." Many will use American Kennel Club registration as a selling point, though kennels that have been cited for Animal Welfare Act violations have been known to continue selling "AKC registered" puppies.

As pet stores get an increasingly bad rap, puppy peddlers are turning to the internet. There are entire websites dedicated to selling puppies and kittens. Others advertise on sites like Craigslist, masking the size and condition of their kennels behind word count limits. And, unlike pet stores where customers might spot runny eyes, lethargic puppies, and dirty cages, online retailers never have to change their profile pictures, making it even easier to dupe well-meaning customers.

The hardest part about seeing those adorable puppies for sale online and knowing the truth behind the photos is that, just like when dealing with pet stores, the best thing to do is *not* to buy them. Puppy sales work the same way as any other "product" sold online or offline. It's a supply and demand business. If you buy one of those puppies because you know you can give him a good life, you may save that one dog from an uncertain fate, but you'll keep the puppy mills churning. Even if you tell the store owner that you're only buying the puppy to save him from their evil ways, they don't care. They're too busy counting big, gold cartoon dollar signs because you just freed up a cage for them to sell another.

In fact, don't buy anything from a store or site that sells puppies or kittens. There are plenty of wonderful pet supply retailers that refuse to be a part of the puppy and kitten mill industry by sticking to selling products that don't have feelings and by supporting animal adoptions. Give the good guys your money. It's the only way to show the puppy peddlers that a cruel business model doesn't pay.

Note: While this chapter is mostly focused on puppy mills—the most notorious and well-documented type of commercial breeders—all animals sold for profit in pet stores are part of an industry that's out to make money, not to make the world a better place.

Step 2: Adopt, Don't Shop

The best way to make sure you're not being fooled into lining the pockets of puppy millers is to adopt your next companion. Across the country, millions of dogs and cats are in need of loving homes. Tragically, as many as three million of them will never find new families and will die in animal shelters.[1] Every adoption helps reduce that number. (Along with spaying and neutering—until we figure out how to teach sex ed to other species, it's up to us to break the cycle of unintended pet pregnancy.)

If you're not sure you can handle cage after cage of puppy-dog eyes at your local shelter, or you just want a preview of what kind of animals are available, the internet is a dog's best friend. More than ten thousand organizations list animals on Petfinder.com, from tiny rescue groups to large animal shelters, so it's a great way not only to find potential companion animals in your area, but also to search for specific characteristics, like size or whether they're known to be good with kids. And it's not just dogs and cats—you can also find rabbits, pigs, hamsters, snakes, birds, and a menagerie of other rescued animals in need of homes. There are a number of online listing services, and many shelters and rescue groups feature their adoptable animals on their own websites and social media pages.

It's also possible to walk into a pet supply store and pay for a dog or cat without supporting commercial breeders—more and more pet stores are inviting local shelters and rescue groups to adopt out animals from their storefronts. The common theme (and major difference from online pet retailers) is that even if you start out browsing online, you'll get to know your prospective new family member and will have to prove you're a real person before the deal is done.

Whether you've already adopted or are considering adopting a new family member, never underestimate the impact of this decision. When you adopt, you've saved more than one life—both the one you're bringing into your home and the one that you just made room for in the shelter or rescue group. Plus, you're one less customer keeping puppy mills in business.

Puppy mills have already gotten more creative by posing as "family kennels" online and avoiding commercial regulation by shipping dogs directly to people from their websites. They'll continue to adapt as technology changes, but no matter how slick their puppy-choosing app seems or if they're able to someday project a hologram puppy into your living room, remember that no one who cares about their animals would ship you a family member without getting to know you and knowing you're prepared for what you're getting into.

Step 3: Always Meet IRL

It is possible to find your true love online, but at some point, the relationship has to move IRL. When it comes to choosing your next family member, that point should be before you make any financial or emotional commitments. This is also the most effective way to make sure the animal you think you're getting actually exists. The Humane Society of the United

States warns of several variations of a scam where innocent people pay to have a puppy shipped to them, then the dog gets "lost" at the airport and the seller disappears. Sometimes they seem legitimate, claiming that you have to meet certain requirements to get the dog or by saying the imaginary dog has papers. If you're not the type of person who would send your bank account details to a Nigerian prince who emails you about a financial transaction, then don't be the type of person who would send money to purchase an animal you haven't actually met.

Like a bad made-for-TV movie plot, online forums can be a dangerous place for innocent animals. In other words, apply the same common sense and healthy dose of suspicion that you would to any other online interaction. No responsible breeder, shelter, or rescue would place an animal through an impersonal click-and-ship method or by sending out a mass email asking for money.

This logic also applies if you ever have to rehome your companion animal. Hopefully, this will never be the case because bringing a dog or cat into your family is a lifetime commitment. But sometimes things happen—life changes in drastic, unforeseen ways, such as a new baby with a deadly cat allergy, Grandma has to go into assisted living and her four chihuahuas can't come with her, or an unexpected turn in health or wealth that leaves you without the ability to continue providing proper care. If this does ever happen to you, the first step is to contact the shelter, rescue, or breeder where you originally got the animal—the responsible ones will take them back or help you with placement. If you're on your own for finding your dog or cat a new home, start by using your social networks. A friend of a friend will be far less stressful than putting your beloved animal in the hands of a stranger, and you may be surprised by who's willing to help once you ask. If you do go the online classifieds route, never list your animal as "free to good home"—charging something, anything, can help deter animal abusers. And always make sure you meet the prospective adopter, visit where they'll be living, and ask for references.

With hundreds of thousands of animals available for adoption at any given time, where do you start when you're looking to grow your family? Even once you narrow it down to local shelters and rescues, and filter out goats and chickens and whatever other species are not the ones you're looking for, you could still have hundreds of options. While some people can go into a shelter and immediately meet their match, it can be a harder process for others. And even once you've fallen in love, how do you really know what life will be like when you get home?

Well, you don't. Even with purebred dogs, genetics has its limits. I don't know about you, but even though my siblings and I share the same parents, we're all very different people. The same is true of animals. I've met retrievers who ignore tennis balls and scent hounds whose noses couldn't lead them to a barbecue pit. While knowing the breed can help us guess their personalities and needs, every animal is unique. That's why we love them.

But there are a few things you can do to set yourself up for a successful adoption:

1. **Make sure you're ready**—and everyone in the family is ready—for the new addition. The last thing you want to do is rescue a dog from the shelter, then realize no one really wanted the responsibility.

2. **Before you start looking,** make a list of what you want in a dog or cat. Think about your expectations, and be realistic about your lifestyle. Are you really going to take your dog jogging every morning, or are you looking for more of a Netflix couch-surfing companion? Are you willing to put the time into a long-haired cat's beauty routine or to train a puppy who doesn't know the difference between boots and bones? Have you considered what the other animals in your house might think about their new sibling/interloper?

3. **Ask questions.** Some shelters and rescue groups will describe the ideal home for each animal, but don't be afraid to bring up your list. The shelter employees and rescue group volunteers will know a lot more about the animals than they could fit on a cage card or online description.

4. **Spend time with the animals.** You're about to make a commitment that will last a decade or more, depending on the age and health of the dog or cat, so it's worth giving the decision more than five minutes.

5. **Keep an open mind.** With millions of animals going in and out of the adoption system, you never know who you might find. Also, keep that mind open and your patience flowing after you bring your new critter home—they'll need some time to adjust, learn the rules, and get to know you.

6. **Trust your gut.** There may be a cat who's a fan favorite of the shelter staff but doesn't steal your heart. Or it might be love from the first time you saw their online profile picture and it only got better when you finally met in person. If you have a strong feeling one way or the other, go with it. After all, this is a family member you actually get to choose.

What If You Really, Really Want a Specific Breed?

We all like to pretend that looks don't matter, but I know of very few instances where someone's decision to adopt or keep a stray wasn't influenced at least to some degree by factors like the animal's size or gender or type of fur. Even the most diehard rescuers I know have their favorite breeds and even colors within those breeds. That's okay. (At least, to a reasonable degree. Don't be that person who dumped her cat at the animal shelter because she redecorated and the cat's fur no longer matched her furniture. True story.)

Just because you have your heart set on a particular breed, it doesn't mean you have to sacrifice your morals. It's estimated that one in four shelter dogs are purebred.[2] There are rescue groups dedicated to only taking in specific breeds, and many of them are networked nationwide to help match their dogs with the right families, no matter where they live. Thanks to the internet, you can find dogs of all sizes, breeds, and ages who need homes without resorting to puppy mills.

What if you've searched for months with no luck, or you really want to meet the parents of your future family member? If you're intent on purchasing from a breeder, remember that a breeder who cares about their dogs will be open about how they raise their litters, and they'll carefully choose each puppy's new family. Breeders who see their puppies and kittens as future family members instead of four-legged walking dollar signs would never leave a litter at the pet store or ship them sight unseen to a complete stranger.

And you don't have to take their word for it. Responsible breeders will not only carefully screen potential buyers, but they're happy to let you meet the puppy's parents and see where they live. They're dedicated to their dogs as individuals and as a breed—they breed a limited number of litters from their healthiest, stablest dogs. You'll likely have multiple conversations with the whole family before you and the breeder mutually agree that it's a good match. The best breeders are active in breed rescue groups or support their local shelter.

Buying from a backyard breeder is as bad as buying from a pet store. Although this particular breed of breeders may not have a warehouse of dogs, they're still breeding carelessly, with little regard for the welfare or future of their dogs. They're selling litters to make a little cash or because they wanted their kids to "witness the miracle of birth" (even though their kids have probably already seen it all on YouTube). Once the puppy or kitten is off their property, it's no longer their problem as far they're concerned. If they don't find homes fast enough, they often drop the aging litters at animal shelters and start all over again.

So, if you've scoured animal shelters and rescue groups for your favorite breed (and you've at least considered adopting a mixed breed) and your heart is still set on going to a breeder, choose wisely. The internet is a good place to start doing your research, but always meet the breeder and their animals in person before making a final decision.

Comment and Share

If you're dealing with a brick-and-mortar pet store, you can check up on the animals. If they appear sick or poorly cared for, take notes (and photos, if you can, but you'll likely get kicked out if any employees notice what you're up to), then report what you've seen. Report them to the

USDA, but also give the local humane society or animal control officer a call. It's their job to investigate animal cruelty, and they often rely on customer reports to crack down on shady pet store operations. They can work with state or federal officials and seize the animals, when appropriate, then find them good homes without perpetuating the cruel business of pet sales.

Tell everyone you know not to shop at that store. Most pet stores are on Facebook or Yelp or other online business directories where you can let other potential customers know what you've seen. Public pressure has convinced many pet stores to change their ways and has forced others to close their doors for good. Only support pet supply stores that love animals as much as you do.

It can be harder to shut down shady online businesses, but some of the same rules apply. Don't buy anything from those sites and tell your friends to steer clear, too. Report suspicious business dealings to the FBI's Internet Crime Complaint Center (IC3). If you see ads for online puppy sales on another site—such as your favorite pet blog or online catalog—drop them an email and ask them not to take advertising money from potential puppy mills.

If you've spent any time looking at adoptable animals online, you know that photos and video matter. Sure, just like people, some are more naturally photogenic than others—they can be making a weird face and it still looks adorable. But for others, particularly older animals, a breed that's common in the area, or black dogs and cats who are harder to photograph, it can be a challenge to attract attention. If you're a good photographer or you're the one all your friends ask to write their online dating profiles, see if your local shelter or rescue group needs help posting animals online. A cute photo and charming life story can make all the difference.

Now that you know the pitfalls of online animal relationships, tell your friends. Even if you're not in the market for a new family member, you may know someone who is. While your friends may be enlightened, compassionate people, it's hard not to fall for those puppy photos or kittens playing in a pet store window. Plus, if you get involved, you could get to live vicariously through their experience of adopting and loving an animal in need of a home. And once you've adopted, brag about it. When people see the photos of your rescue dog or cat, it helps them picture taking in a rescue animal of their own.

! Action Alert

THREE THINGS YOU CAN DO TODAY

1 • Never buy an animal over the internet or from a pet shop.

2 • Don't buy anything from a retailer that sells puppies, kittens, or other animals for profit.

3 • Adopt your next four-legged family member, and take advantage of those well-earned bragging rights.

ANIMALS YOU'LL HELP SAVE
Dogs, cats, and other critters sold as pets online and offline.

24   If You See Something, Say Something

If you ever could've sworn you knew what kind of mood a horse was in just by looking at his face, you were probably right, since many horse facial expressions are similar to those in dogs, cats, and primates. And the feeling is mutual; horses can recognize our emotions from one look at our mugs, too, even just from photos.[1] Humans and horses understand each other, which is no surprise considering we've been living with one another for more than six thousand years. That hasn't always been a good deal for horses, though—as we've domesticated them, we've put them to work, we've used them in sports and war, and we don't always provide them with the best care. Like other companion animals, horses can suffer from neglect and outright cruelty, and when that happens, they need animal lovers to look out for them and gallop to the rescue.

On January 24, 2013, temperatures in Newark, New Jersey, had dropped below zero, and local news stations and officials had taken to Twitter to advise people without heat on how to stay warm. One reporter noticed a dog left outside in the freezing cold and tweeted about it. The weather could have been life-threatening for an animal without shelter. Then mayor Cory Booker saw the tweet and went to scope out the situation himself. He picked up the dog, put her in a police car, cranked the heat, and called the owners. They were out of town and said they didn't know the dog had gotten outside; it was lucky for them and their dog that Booker was on the case. Five months later, Booker responded to another tweet from a concerned citizen about a dog reportedly left in a crate for days. Booker worked with the humane society to rescue her.

Most cities don't have a mayor who will rush to the rescue of mistreated animals on the basis of 140 characters or fewer. But every city does have law enforcement, and animal cruelty is against the law everywhere. Although animals are still considered property under the law, pets do have more protections than your grandmother's china. If you break an heirloom teapot or gravy boat, it's between you and your nostalgia, and possibly your family, depending who else was attached to the set. If you break your dog, it's between you and the law. You've committed a crime. (Unfortunately, animals used by industries—such as meat and dairy production or cosmetic testing—enjoy far fewer legal protections than the animals in our homes, despite the fact that they feel pain the same way.)

Since companion animal abuse and neglect tends to happen on private property, much of it flies under the radar. That's why the cops charged with stopping animal cruelty—and the animals suffering from it—need you to be their eyes and ears.

Not-So-Cruel Intentions

In order to be on the lookout for animal cruelty, you need to know what it looks like. If someone is directly, physically harming an animal by inflicting violence on them, that's a pretty obvious form of abuse. But a lot of companion animal abuse takes the form of neglect. That can be a dog left outside in freezing weather without shelter. Or a dog chained outside without human contact and no access to fresh food or water. Signs of cruelty could be a cat who's emaciated, a flea- or tick-infested dog, a horse with untreated skin conditions, or an animal showing signs of illness or abuse like lethargy or limping. Sometimes it's a hoarding situation, where someone has far more animals than they can care for and all the animals are showing signs of neglect. It could be an animal left in a car in the summer, where even on a seventy-degree day, temperatures inside the car can hit one hundred degrees in less than half an hour; on an eighty-five-degree day, it only takes about ten minutes for the car to get that hot.[2] (This is one of the most preventable forms of accidental death. Show your dog you love her by leaving her home in the summer. It's not worth gambling her life on whether it will really only take two minutes for you to run into a store with her in the car on a hot day.)

The specifics of how animal abuse and neglect are legally defined vary state by state and, in some cases, community by community. But when an animal's life is at stake, you don't need to be a legal scholar to call for help. If an animal appears to be in imminent danger, your first move should be to call 911. But what if you suspect that an animal isn't receiving the care that he should, though he doesn't seem to be in an immediately life-threatening situation?

If you feel comfortable doing so, you may want to try talking to your neighbor before you call the cops on them. If it feels dangerous to approach the person—for example, if they're violently abusing their animal, they may turn those violent tendencies on you—skip this step and go straight to law enforcement. But sometimes the dog who's limping or seems too skinny may already be undergoing veterinary treatment, and you can save yourself unnecessary neighborhood hostility by simply asking if their dog is okay instead of raining down a SWAT team on someone who's taking their dog in for surgery the next day. Sometimes the dog may need veterinary care but his family can't afford it, and you may be able to help out with a neighborhood fund-raiser or by helping them research options, such as clinics with sliding fee scales or funds that provide financial aid for vet bills.

It's important to note that keeping animals outside is not illegal as long as they have food, shelter, and basic vet care. However, keeping dogs tethered 24-7 is illegal in thirteen states and some cities, and in others, the length and type of chain allowed is spelled out. Dogs who spend their lives on a chain tend to be lonely, bored, and anxious. It's no wonder that so many dog bites happen with chained dogs—if I spent my life tied up, I'd probably have a short temper, too. And it can be a vicious downward spiral; dogs are banished to the yard because they never learned how to behave in the house, but the longer they're kept in the yard spending less time around their families, the worse their behavior becomes.

If your neighbor has an outdoor or chained dog who seems otherwise healthy and well fed, get to know them and their dog. You may find out that they want to stop tethering their dog, but aren't sure they can afford a fence. You may be able to help them build one or fund-raise for one—you may even be able to get a local company to donate a fence. Maybe the dog doesn't have shelter because they didn't know what to get to make him comfortable. Or they might just need some training help to bring him back inside. Maybe they were always raised with outdoor dogs and never really thought about how much better their lives and their dog's life would be if he came indoors. If they plan to keep the dog outside and are providing shelter and fresh food and water, you can offer to walk the dog or play with him a few days a week to help keep him happy.

In some cases, people simply don't know how to provide better care for their animals. Having their animals taken away isn't how they'll learn. Animal neglect cases can be hard to prosecute, but even if they get a stiff sentence that includes a prohibition on getting more animals, they'll usually get more animals anyway and repeat the cycle. But if they're willing to learn how to be a better caregiver, it could change the world for their families and any future animals they take in.

Showing compassion toward our own species is often the first step toward improving the lives of animals. I tend to be an introverted, reclusive neighbor, but I always keep an eye out for my neighbors' animals, whether it's helping them get to the vet when they don't have transportation or chatting about the benefits of spaying and neutering and where to get it done for a discount. And neighbors I've never talked to before have knocked on my door if they've spotted a stray dog who looks like one of mine. (It never is, but they know I'll get the dog to safety.) Animal lovers have to stick together. I may not have a cup of sugar to lend, but if you ever need a cup of dog food, I'm happy to help, no questions asked.

Justice League

There are certainly cases of animal abuse and neglect where no amount of benefit of the doubt will change the situation. When faced with this reality, it's not only about saving the animal who's been hurt, but also getting justice to prevent future abuse. When you report animal cruelty, it's important to have the facts to help law enforcement make their case. Note the exact location, date, and time when you witnessed the abuse, whether it was a specific act of violence or when you noticed the neglected or abandoned animal, as well as any observations. Try to stick with what you're seeing, not opinions (for example "cat seemed weak and unable or unwilling to move" is more helpful than "cat was depressed as she pondered the hopelessness of her existence"). If you can safely do so, capture some photos and video. When you file the report, note the date and time of your report so you can follow up. And if you're comfortable doing so, being a willing witness instead of reporting anonymously can help with prosecution.

Download a crime watch or digital witness app, such as ICE BlackBox or LiveSafe, that allows you to record incidents and easily report them to your local law enforcement with all the basic details they need. This not only makes it easier to report animal abuse, but it gives officers on-the-scene information to prepare them when they arrive. It could also become valuable evidence if the case goes to court. Hopefully you're not stumbling upon animal cruelty so often that this will become one of your most-used apps, but downloading an app today can help you be prepared if it does happen.

It can be tempting to save an animal at any cost, but breaking the law for rescue heroics usually isn't all that helpful. For one thing, if you have animals, they need you at home, not in jail. But it can also backfire for the animal you're trying to save. If you see an animal who appears to be neglected and you trespass to get really compelling footage, that footage might wind up being useless and jeopardizing the case because it was obtained illegally. Stealing an animal from someone's yard—even if the animal is in distress—is still stealing. You could end up arrested and the animal returned to her neglectful or abusive owner.

It's important to go through the right channels to get justice. Those channels can be slow as a sloth crossing the road. They can also be frustrating—animal abuse cases can be difficult to prosecute and many anticruelty laws are inadequate for the suffering the animal endured. But the solution isn't to go vigilante and put yourself and the animals at risk. If you're going to get out your cape, use it to urge your elected officials to make the laws stronger. Use your superpowers to pay attention to what's happening with the animals in your neighborhood so you can get them help as quickly as possible.

Who You Gonna Call?

When you want to report animal abuse, your first call should be 911. Depending on where you live, you may have a separate animal control department or humane officers associated with the animal shelter. After you've called the cops, let your local animal shelter or humane society know that there's an animal in distress. If your local law enforcement is lacking when it comes to animals, contact the Humane Society of the United States—they may have regional offices or additional resources that can help get the animals the assistance and justice they need.

If you see a dog or other animal in a hot car, call 911, then go into the nearest store and ask them to make an announcement. Even if the police are on the way, the animal could get help faster if the person with the keys is nearby and responds to the call. A handful of states have laws that allow people to break a window to save an animal in distress, but in most states, you'll still be liable for destruction of property. Make sure you know your local laws before you go throwing any bricks. (To find out the law in your state, visit www.animallaw.info and search "dogs in hot cars.")

If you witness animal cruelty at a business, such as a pet store or petting zoo, report it locally, but also contact the U.S. Department of Agriculture, since those situations typically fall under their jurisdiction. If it's an online business that appears to be abusing animals (such as puppy mills), contact the FBI's Internet Crime Complaint Center (IC3).

Comment and Share

Social media can be a helpful tool—as it's been for the animals in Cory Booker's neighborhood—but it shouldn't replace filing an official report. However, once you've made the call, tagging local officials via social media can help get their attention. In some cases, such as when there's particularly compelling video footage or if it's a business or animal shelter that's neglecting the animals in its care, spreading the word on social media and contacting local TV and other news outlets can help get the story the attention it needs to spur animal-saving action. But be careful about hitting Send if it might interfere with an investigation or if you're less certain about the abuse or neglect that you're witnessing, especially if there's a chance that you could improve the situation through education. Animal lovers tend to react strongly to these stories online, and internet bullying won't help the cause if you're hoping to talk to your neighbors about how to better care for their animals.

Not all animals are created equal in the eyes of the law. Dogs tend to have more protections than backyard chickens. But all the animals living in your community—dogs, chickens, cats, horses, rabbits, pigs, hamsters— deserve justice if they suffer cruelty. Advocate for stronger anticruelty laws. Start at your city council—there are a lot of laws that local communities can pass to protect their animals before needing your state legislators to get involved.

Help educate others on what to look for when it comes to animal cruelty. There are a lot of great, shareable memes and other resources out there to remind people to leave their dogs at home when running summer errands. Give your friends the tools they need to help chained dogs in their own neighborhoods and to keep an eye out for other signs of abuse or neglect. And while judges aren't supposed to be influenced by online petitions asking for strong sentencing of animal abusers, when those cases become high profile, it can help lead to stronger animal protection laws being passed.

! Action Alert

THREE THINGS YOU CAN DO TODAY

1 • Be a nosy neighbor—get to know your neighbors and their animals, and pay attention to what's going on in the animal world around you.

2 • Install a crime watch or digital witness app on your phone so you're ready to quickly report animal abuse or neglect.

3 • Ask your city council to pass ordinances that help prevent and punish animal cruelty, such as banning continuous dog tethering or making it illegal to leave animals in hot cars.

ANIMALS YOU'LL HELP SAVE
Dogs, cats, horses, rabbits, birds, and other animals who are part of your community.

The Ambassador of Dogville

Dogs essentially domesticated us as much as we domesticated them, and we've been together ever since. The road from wolves to dogs wasn't just a happy accident or a one-way street. It was not only mutually beneficial for our species to stick together, but our brains, metabolism, and digestion evolved side by side.[1] They've shaped human development and history and influenced our art, science, and politics. We might feed and shelter them, but they also save our lives in countless ways. They alert their families to danger and can detect medical crises from oncoming seizures to cancer. Their uncanny ability to know how we're feeling and provide comfort has given them an important role in our mental and emotional health. The relationship between humans and canines is so mutually beneficial that it's not hard to imagine an alternate universe where a dog has created a guide on how to be a good ambassador for your person.

Even if you don't have a dog, there are dogs all around you—in the homes of people you love, in the homes of people you tolerate, in the homes of people you don't even know, and in the streets or shelters, waiting for a home. Dogs are a big part of the community, and those of us with canine companions need you, as a fellow animal lover, to be our ally as we navigate local politics to protect our loved ones and create a town where dog people and non–dog people can peacefully coexist.

If you have a dog, there's a good chance that much of your life revolves around his or her comfort and happiness. We make sure they're fed and walked. That they have comfy places to sleep and things to chew on. We give them treats and snuggles and playtime . . . and all of that makes for a pretty sweet life. I've had a number of people tell me they want to be reincarnated as one of my future dogs, usually after I've done something to rearrange my life to keep my dogs happy. However, ensuring our dogs' happiness also means ensuring their safety.

Safety is rarely the fun and glamorous side of anything, and that includes puppies. No one really wants to think about what happens if your dog runs out the door, escapes the yard, or gets loose on a walk. No one really wants to think about your city council passing laws that require certain dog breeds to be muzzled or euthanized. No one really wants to think about the fate of dogs who get lost or abandoned by their families. But our canine companions need us to think about these things. It's up to us to make sure there are places where they're welcomed, to respect the places where they're not, and to help them be model ambassadors for their species wherever they go.

Canine-Friendly Communities

Every year, magazines and websites rank the top cities for dog people. Top rankings go to pet paradises with dog parks, dog treat bakeries, and restaurants with water bowls on their patios. There's quality vet care, including specialists, and probably some swanky pet boutiques. On the other end of the spectrum, you'll find cities where basic pet supply stores and vet care are scarce, and grassy parks taunt you and your pup with No Dogs Allowed signs. Some of these cities probably ban dogs who look a certain way. With canine culture varying so much from city to city, how do you make sure your town gets the best puppy perks and doesn't become a doggy dystopia?

Not only do our dogs need to be good ambassadors, but we need to be good ambassadors for them. More likely than not, it wasn't your dog's decision to drive to a park that doesn't allow dogs, or has strict leash rules, and let him run loose through somebody's family reunion to scare all the small children and elderly relatives. It's important to respect rules and local laws for our dogs. If we ignore signs to pick up after them and leave their waste for people to stumble upon (and into), it's going to be hard to convince anyone that there should be more dog-friendly parks for us to pollute. And if you don't like the rules that have been set for your dog, don't break them—change them.

While some dog rules may be set by local businesses, the vast majority that you'll run into are set by your town or county. That includes leash laws, establishing dog parks, and whether dogs are allowed to dine with you at restaurants. As with any campaign, if you want to change a local ordinance, you want to make sure you present your case in a clear and compelling way. Start by contacting your city council members, mayor, and/or county commissioners. You can contact them all, or start with the ones who pose with their own dogs on social media. Send an email with your request, along with examples of other towns that have the law you want to see passed, so they know exactly what you're asking for and what it looks like in practice. Follow up with a phone call. Gather letters of support from others in the community, and present them at the next public meeting. Politely let them know that you and your well-behaved dog are not going away and you're not alone in wanting to make your town more dog-friendly. You may have sympathetic elected officials who see the light pretty quickly, or you might be in this for the long haul, eventually joining your parks commission to convince others from the inside that your town needs an off-leash dog park or poop bag stations.

(A quick note on dog parks: They can be great places to provide off-leash exercise and socialization, but they're not for everyone. Know your dog—if he's likely to be stressed out, tends to inexplicably be picked on, or is the bully on the playground, skip the dog park. Your dog will be just as happy with leashed walks, off-leash solo play in your yard, or one-on-one supervised playdates with the dogs he's accepted into his social circle.)

Fight Breed Discrimination

One of the most insidious kind of local dog laws are those that target dogs based on how they look. Known as *breed-specific legislation* or *breed-discriminatory laws*, these laws are driven by misinformation about certain breeds of dogs and false ideas about preventing dog bites. Some of these laws outright ban the targeted breeds, while others create special requirements for them, such as keeping them muzzled in public and making their owners carry extra insurance. When these laws pass, all dogs lose.

Some cities have gone so far as to take dogs from their homes to kill them, and in other places, owners panic at being unable to meet the requirements of a new law, and shelters fill with dogs who can no longer be placed locally. Families are broken apart, innocent dogs lose their lives, and the breed ban has done nothing to prevent dog bites in the community.

It's usually pit bull–type dogs targeted by these laws, but lists of banned breeds are often broadened to include whatever dogs the city council happens to irrationally fear, any breeds responsible for dog bites in recent memory, or vague criteria for determining breed that can apply to dozens of breeds and the majority of mixed-breed dogs. At one point, Italy's list of restricted breeds swelled to ninety-two breeds of dog, including border collies and schnauzers; it was eventually narrowed down to seventeen breeds before, thankfully, being replaced in 2009 with a law that targeted irresponsible dog owners. In other words: First they came for the pit bulls . . . so anyone who loves dogs should be concerned about breed-specific legislation.

At the first whiff of breed discrimination, speak up for the dogs in your community. Dog bites can be traumatic, and it's understandable why people want to prevent them—and they can do so effectively and humanely with laws that target the people responsible for their dogs' behavior rather than going after dogs who haven't done anything more than being born with short fur and big heads. Lobby your city council to reject breed-specific legislation and pass dangerous dog ordinances that focus on the other end of the leash. Support neighbors with pit bulls by rallying behind them and helping them tell the stories of their happy, loving family dogs at council meetings, to the local news, and on social media.

You're not alone in this. Whether it's breed-specific legislation or ordinances to allow dogs to eat on restaurant patios, you'll find examples online from other towns that you can model your advocacy after. People all over the country have had similar fights, and many of them are more than happy to share their wisdom to improve the lives of dogs everywhere.

Sit, Stay, Train

If you have a dog, odds are that you have the most adorable, amazing dog on the planet—quirks and all—and the rest of the world just needs to realize this fact. It's up to you to help your dog get the respect and recognition she deserves. This isn't just about building your dog's fan club—all the non–dog people in your neighborhood have votes that count the same as yours. The only one who doesn't get a say is your dog.

Plus, your dog's behavior reflects on all the dogs in the community. It only takes that one poorly behaved off-leash dog crashing someone's family reunion for all dogs to get permanently kicked out of a park. And when a dog bite happens (most commonly by a dog who is not spayed or neutered, is kept as a backyard dog instead of a family companion, and to someone who is not known by the dog and/or an unsupervised child),[2] it could bring down restrictions—including breed-specific legislation—with far-reaching fallout. As someone who lives with rescued pit bulls, the breed most likely to be targeted by anti-dog regulations, I'm far more afraid of a single irresponsible dog owner in my community who has the power to put my dogs' lives at risk than I've ever been of any dog.

I also respect that cynophobia—the fear of dogs—is real. And I make sure that I don't give people a reason to fear my dogs. To a cynophobe, one of my dogs happily bounding over to say hi could be a terrifying experience. But if that same person is assured that my dog is only off-leash in designated off-leash areas, he or she could become an ally to create more off-leash dog parks in the community. I have friends who used to be afraid of pit bulls and now have their own rescued pitties. I have friends who will always be afraid of dogs, but will also fight to protect my dogs' rights because they know my dogs are family. This is why having good canine ambassadors is important.

Your dog doesn't have to be an obedience champion to be a good ambassador. Mine sure aren't. They know a few basic commands, they have some boundaries, and when I know they'll be around people who might be bafflingly immune to their charms, I manage their behavior to prevent negative experiences on either side. I don't want people to feel unsafe around my dogs—and I never want my dogs to feel unsafe either.

It's tempting, as humans, to equate pure, unfettered freedom with happiness. But if that freedom means that they're sometimes rewarded for being on the couch and sometimes punished for it, that only creates confusion. If that freedom means that they don't know what's expected of them or how you'll react in a new situation, it quickly becomes stressful. And if that freedom means putting themselves or others in danger, that's definitely not the way to happiness.

When it comes to commands, it's a good idea to teach the five basics: sit, down, come, leave it, and drop it. The first two are invaluable, touchstone commands. They help you get your dog's attention and gain control if he's overexcited by physically forcing him to chill out for a second. It's impossible to both sit and jump up at the same time. The next three commands are lifesavers. If your dog ever gets loose and is running toward traffic, being able to call him back to you is essential. And dogs find all kinds of things to get into, from harassing the cat (leave it!) to picking up chicken bones left by someone's picnic at the park (drop it!).

Dog training doesn't have to be a chore and shouldn't be painful for either of you. Put away the choke chains and electric collars and get out the treats, toys, and praise. Using positive, reward-based training turns it into a game and strengthens your bond. So don't stop with those five essential commands. Teaching your dog tricks keeps him from getting bored and makes it even easier for everyone else to fall in love with him.

The greatest training tool of all to have up your sleeve is consistency. Dogs learn from us every day, whether or not we realize we're teaching them. Think about how your dog acts when you get your shoes on. Or when you're cooking dinner, does your dog hover at your feet, or go lie down in the next room? Either way, you probably inadvertently trained your dog to do it by dropping scraps or giving her attention, or by ignoring her to focus on your task. Set the rules of your house—and the behavior you expect from your dog—and stick with it. Bending the rules (*"Okay, you can leap on the bed on my birthday and Valentine's Day, but not the other 363 days"*) only makes it harder to get them back in shape.

And this is where you decide what behaviors are most important to you. It's important to my mom not to have paw prints all over the house, so every dog she's ever had knows to wait by the door to get their feet wiped before coming back inside. Some people would add heel to the list of must-have commands, but I personally don't need my dog to walk beside me as long as he knows he's not allowed to drag me down the street. My hiking companion is seventy-pound pit bull who takes up a lot of space on the trail—he's free to sniff at the end of the leash until we see other hikers, but he knows when I tell him to "share the trail" that he has to come stand beside me to let them pass. I didn't teach him this through training sessions, just by building the habit out of necessity for safety on the trails.

Don't get me wrong: I'm not saying dog training is always a breeze. It takes time and focus (from both you and your dog). Plus, our dogs have their own minds—some aren't as willing as others to learn new tricks. Some seem to come into our lives knowing exactly what we want from them while others seem to only know the exact opposite of what we want. And most of the time, minimal dog training is fine. Your dog doesn't have to trot in perfect heeling position if you're just strolling through the neighborhood, but you should be able to control her if the neighbor's kids come racing by on their bikes. If you don't have a good "leave it" command to keep her from yanking your arm out of the socket, at least have a good no-pull harness to slow her down.

Sometimes dog ambassadorship comes down to managing the situation rather than solving it. If you have a dog who knows the five essential commands but just can't help wanting to leap up to greet guests no matter how hard you try to break the habit, you may need a work-around like having your dog on a leash or in another room when people first arrive until she calms down. Even as they've evolved alongside us, the ways of our world are often weird to our canine companions. You know your dog better than anyone—pay attention when she's telling you that she's stressed out or too excited to listen, and do what you need to do to keep her, and everyone around her, safe.

Who Let the Dogs Out?

In his book *The Dogs Who Found Me*, Ken Foster wrote, "People ignore stray dogs the same way they ignore stray people, the way your friends in the city insist that they have never seen any homeless people or, when pressed, offer the opinion that these people choose to be on the street and wouldn't want a home if they had one."[3] Some communities have more stray dogs than they can handle, so many that they've formed packs and seem like part of the scenery. Others only have the occasional runaway whose family is out looking for them. Dogs, like people, prefer to have homes where they are warm, dry, fed, and loved. So, when you see stray dogs, what's the best way to help them?

Saving strays isn't always a leash-less walk in the park. Sometimes all you need to do is fling open your car door and the stray dog leaps in. I've even had stray dogs come up to my front door and start barking to let me know their adventure was over and could I please give their families a call to let them know where to pick them up? But some stray dogs are wary and scared, running away when you're only trying to help. Or you may be more of a cat person, and while you never want to see a dog go hungry or get hit by a car, you're also not entirely comfortable with leaping out onto the highway to try to catch one you've never met before. That's okay. Rule number one when it comes to strays: Trust your gut. If you're not comfortable with the situation, you don't need to be the one to don a superhero cape. In some cases—such as strays spotted near a busy highway—chasing the dog may only put you both in danger. If you approach a stray dog and start to get an uncomfortable vibe from him, walk away. Don't get bitten. Don't get run over. Don't chase him closer to danger.

If you see a stray dog and you're unable to catch him yourself, call animal control. Whether they're picked up by animal control officers or you give the dogs a lift, the local animal shelter is often the best hope they have of getting back home. If they're running scared, their families may have no idea where they are; the shelter provides a central place for people to look for their lost animals, and it's better than leaving them at risk of running into traffic or worse. If they still have their tags or have microchip identification, they can be kept safe while their families are contacted. Even if they don't have ID, they're a lot more likely to be found in a shelter than by random search parties. And, if their families never show up, they have a shot at finding new families.

However, some shelters have better adoption rates than others, are able to keep animals for longer, and work harder to get them adopted, so do your research to learn about your local shelter and what's likely to happen to the dog if you bring him in. If you're able to pick up the dog yourself and decide to let him hang out at your house while you search for his family, it's a good idea to call the shelter anyway so they can try to match any lost reports they may have received to the dog you found. If you can't hang on to the dog and your local shelter is overcrowded or has a poor adoption record, contact rescue groups in the area (you should be able to find them with a quick internet search or by looking on Petfinder.com) to see if they can assist, then start a campaign to improve conditions for the homeless animals in your community.

Try to get a good picture of the stray. Whether the dog goes to the shelter or bunks at your place, you want to start spreading the word to get him home as quickly as possible. You never know who the people in your network know, so post the dog's info on social media, along with where you found him and who to contact if someone thinks this may be their lost pup. (If you've kept the dog instead of bringing him to the shelter, use common sense when people contact you; ask for proof that the dog is theirs and meet in a public place instead of inviting strangers who found your number on the internet over to your house.) Your town has a "stray hold," which is the legal number of days that people have to claim their dogs (usually three to five days). After that, the dog can be put up for adoption, sent to a rescue group, or euthanized. So, if the stray dog's family doesn't show up, your photo can come in handy to help him find a new home.

Once you start seeing stray dogs, you may see them everywhere. Helping strays is such a rewarding, visible way to change a life that it may become addictive. If you're thinking about starting a rescue group of your own, do your research and talk to other local rescuers before you get started so you can do the most good without getting in over your head.

Comment and Share

It might be tempting to fill your social media feed with every shelter dog profile you can find, especially for dogs in shelters that set specific euthanasia dates. While well intentioned, this is more effective as a way to get your posts muted than to save lives. A better way to help animals find homes is to work with your local shelter—ask about volunteering to take better photos of adoptable dogs and write clever, informative descriptions for their online profiles that will grab potential adopters' attention. Most shelters also use volunteers to help walk, train, and play with the dogs in their care, all of which keeps the dogs happier and makes them more likely to get adopted. (If your shelter doesn't do these things, ask about starting a program.) Spread the word about local adoption events to encourage people with room in their hearts and homes to find the right match for their families. Promote adoption opportunities and happy endings with hashtags like #AdoptDontShop.

If a special dog comes along who has been at the shelter a long time or seems like she may have a harder time getting adopted, start a social media campaign to spread the word, using upbeat descriptions and providing as much info as you can about the perfect home for her. If she might be purebred, let breed rescue groups know about her. Talk to your shelter about contacting local media to feature her story—most local papers and news stations love a good dog tale.

Help dog-friendly businesses and parks thrive in your community. Dog people are a vocal, loyal bunch, so if you find a business or other dog-friendly hot spot, tell your friends. Leave positive reviews online. The more successful dog-friendly businesses and dog parks are, the more likely others will follow and you can be on your way to living in—or maintaining your status as—a top destination for dog lovers. Plus, if you ever want or need to change local laws for your dog's benefit, local businesses can be powerful allies.

Spread the gospel of being a responsible dog parent. Share tips and resources to help other dog families with training and canine politics. And, yes, show off your dog. Happy, well-behaved dogs are an asset to a community. The more people fall in love with your dog, the more likely they are to help you make the world a better place for her.

! Action Alert
THREE THINGS YOU CAN DO TODAY

1 • Go on, show off your pup. Teach her a new trick, capture it on video, and share the love.

2 • Judge the deed, not the breed. Protest any laws that target dogs based on the way they look and advocate for laws that target irresponsible dog owners instead.

3 • Help get strays off the streets and into homes by seeing the stray dogs in your community, getting them to safety, and supporting adoption.

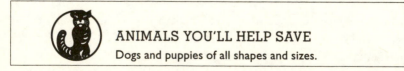

ANIMALS YOU'LL HELP SAVE
Dogs and puppies of all shapes and sizes.

Unconditional Love

Cats were so beloved by ancient Egyptians that killing a cat was punishable by death. They were seen as the earthly representatives of gods—possibly even as demigods themselves—and, as such, were spoiled while alive and mourned after they passed. It didn't hurt that cats helped protect food supplies and control disease through their hunting. In many ways, the legacy of cats hasn't changed much. We worship our feline companions with gourmet treats, a vast array of toys, and their own furnishings, like multistory indoor cat trees and custom catio outdoor enclosures. Back in the day, cats were given a legacy through mummification; today, they've been immortalized in internet memes, gifs, and videos. But they're benevolent deities on earth. After all, they bring us dead things—not so much out of love, but because they've taken pity on our sad hunting skills. Still, they wouldn't try to help us out if we didn't matter to them. And there's no question that they matter to us.

For most of us, cats and dogs are family members. They can be with us for ten to twenty years, so we go through a lot with them by our sides. They see relationships come and go, kids growing up, our schedules and stress levels changing with our careers. And when we fall on hard times, so do they. When the breadwinner loses his or her job and there's not enough bread to go around, the family dog or cat suddenly becomes one more mouth to feed. A bag of kibble may not seem like much, but when the budget is tight, every purchase counts.

You may be thinking, *I'd never, ever give up my animals.* I'm right there with you—I couldn't imagine anything more devastating than choosing between my home and my four-legged family, and I hope I never have to. But I also know that it's coming from a place of privilege because I haven't had to face that terrible decision. Instead of judging people for the choices they make in times of struggle, such as homelessness or domestic violence, animal lovers need to band together to make sure companion animals can stay with the people who love them. We need to fight against the idea that you must meet a certain income level to share your life with animals. After all, we know that when everything else in the world is bleak, our animals keep light in our lives.

There are a lot of people who put themselves at risk for the sake of their nonhuman families. Most domestic violence and homeless shelters don't allow animals, which means people stay in dangerous situations, facing physical harm or exposure to the elements, to stay by their animal's side. Nearly half of domestic violence victims report that they delayed leaving their abuser out of concern for their animals. It's estimated that 5–10 percent of homeless people have companion animals, with that number jumping as high as 24 percent in some parts of the country.[1]

Social issues are hard enough to tackle on their own, and it's even more challenging when animals are involved. But we're a society of animal lovers, and as the human-animal bond has gained the credibility it deserves, communities are finding ways to help families in crisis stay together.

Homeward Bound

Unless animals are being abused, the best homes for them are their current homes. Odds are, their families love them—and they love their families—even if the humans don't have the resources or knowledge to spoil them or even meet their basic needs without assistance. Shelters are full of animals who don't have loving homes, and one of the best things we can do to fight dog and cat homelessness is to help people keep their dogs and cats. Increasing fines when people bring their animals to the shelter will only result in more animals being abandoned or stuck in homes that can't properly care for them. On the other hand, starting a program to donate food and pet supplies to people in need can help keep families together and animals who are loved out of shelters. Free and low-cost spay/neuter services and vaccine clinics in low-income neighborhoods, as well as transportation assistance to veterinary hospitals, can help people care for their animals even if they're not able to drive them to appointments. Volunteer animal behavior and training services can help people trouble-shoot problems, such as housebreaking or separation anxiety, before the landlord or less tolerant family members reach their breaking point.

We should do everything we can to address the root of these problems to prevent animals from unnecessarily losing their loving homes. That means helping our fellow human animals in need. We know what social services look like for people, and we can use those models to provide assistance and services for companion animals. More animal shelters are starting to work with local food banks or creating their own system to distribute dog and cat food to families with hungry animals. When the housing bubble burst, many shelters experienced an increase in animals being given up as people lost their homes. Shelters were able to reduce that number by working with families to find pet-friendly housing and support for helping their animals adjust to their changing circumstances.

Some shelters also provide temporary housing for animals, such as when a family loses their home and doesn't have a pet-friendly place to stay while they look for a new residence. Organizations like Dogs on Deployment help members of the military network with volunteers willing to care for their animals during their service. Temporary changes or setbacks shouldn't be a permanent loss.

Domestic Violence Against Animals

There's a well-known link between animal abuse and violent crimes, which-ever way you look at it: Animal abusers commonly have records for other crimes, and violent criminals often have a history of animal cruelty. The National Sheriffs' Association has created an app to help law enforcement officers recognize signs of animal abuse, document it, and make the con-nection between cruelty and other crimes. Sometimes, simply asking whether the family dog or cat has been hurt can open doors in an investi-gation. One study found that when a crisis hotline added a question about animal cruelty, it resulted in an 80 percent decrease in domestic violence homicides.[2]

More than 70 percent of abused women report that animals have been threatened, harmed, or killed by their partners.[3] And when kids witness violence at home, they're more likely to repeat it, creating a cycle of abuse.[4] In addition to abused animals being an indication that other members of the household might be in danger, pets are often used as a form of intimidation and control. The threat of harm against a vulnerable animal can be a frighteningly effective way to convince someone to stay in a dangerous relationship and stay silent about the abuse. That's just one more reason why animals need a way out of abusive situations, too.

Unfortunately, most women's shelters don't allow companion animals, but there's a growing movement to change that. Some now allow on-site housing for animals, while others have arrangements with local animal shelters to provide safe harbor. Check with the domestic violence protection organizations in your community to find out their policies. The American Kennel Club and RedRover offer grants to help shelters set up space for animal victims of domestic abuse.

In thirty-two states, animals are allowed on temporary restraining orders, providing further protection for people who want to know that their entire family will be safe if they leave a violent situation. The federal Pet and Women Safety (PAWS) Act of 2017 would provide nationwide protection for victims of domestic violence by including threats toward animals in the definition of stalking and in interstate protection orders, ordering domestic violence restitution to include vet bills, directing the USDA to provide grants for housing and services for victims with companion animals, and urging all states to allow animals on protection orders. Urge your representatives to support policies that protect the entire family.

Shelter from the Storm

When Hurricane Katrina slammed into the Gulf Coast in 2005, it breached the levees, adding catastrophic flooding on top of the storm's damage. It displaced hundreds of thousands of people, resulted in more than 1,800 human deaths, and cost more than $100 billion in damage and losses.[5] It was also a turning point for how animals were treated during emergencies. As people were evacuated, their animals' fates were uncertain. Nearly half of the people who refused to leave stayed for their animals,[6] and some lost their lives as a result. Some people didn't realize they wouldn't be able to take their dogs or cats with them until after they were already in the rescue boats. Others thought they'd be back in a couple of days and were kept out of their neighborhoods for weeks. The internet and news media were swamped with dramatic photos of forlorn animals on porches and rooftops, surrounded by murky water, or trying to swim to safety.

A Herculean rescue effort saved an estimated fifteen thousand animals.[7] But because so many people had to leave their homes for so long, matching displaced dogs and cats to displaced people proved nearly impossible; only 10–15 percent of the rescued animals were reunited with their families.[8] The rest were dispersed around the country for foster care and adoption. Attempts to reunite people and their animals lasted for months. For many who had lost everything to the hurricane, they'd also lost their nonhuman family members. Hundreds of thousands of animals had been left behind, and despite the incredible efforts of rescuers, most of the animals in New Orleans and the other communities hit hard by Katrina were left fending for themselves.

After witnessing the tragedy of animals left behind and families torn apart, the Pets Evacuation and Transportation Standards Act was passed, which requires state and local agencies to include companion animals in evacuation planning and provides federal funding for animal-friendly emergency shelters. Several states passed their own laws, too, to include animals in emergency plans.

Hopefully we've learned our lesson from Hurricane Katrina, but you can't just count on local authorities to save your nonhuman family members in an emergency. Include your animals in your own disaster preparedness planning. Even though communities have to plan for animals, that doesn't mean they have to keep you and your animals together—you could end up at an emergency shelter while your dog or cat is sent to an animal shelter. Keep a list of pet-friendly hotels and motels in case your local emergency shelter doesn't allow them to stay with you. Make an emergency kit for your animals, too, including food, water, dishes, medication, vet records, kitty litter, toys, treats, towel or blanket, and first aid supplies. Keep leashes and carriers or crates handy since you may need to confine your animal, and make sure everyone's identification is up to date in case you get separated. And remember that they'll likely be scared—keep them close by and keep a close eye on their behavior. Most of all, make a plan; know who is responsible for evacuating your animals, who can help if you can't get back to your house, where you'll stay, and what you'll need to bring with you.

Don't leave your animals behind. They need you more than ever during an emergency to care for them and comfort them. That goes for small animals, too—your hamster may only have a life span of a year or two, but he's counting on you to care for him every day and he won't fare well if left on his own in a crisis.

Comment and Share

Find out what programs are available in your community to help keep animals in their homes, such as pet food banks, training resources, temporary housing, and low-cost or no-cost vaccine clinics and spay/neuter programs, and spread the word. It's hard to ask for help, and oftentimes people don't advertise when they're struggling, so you never know whose life you can save by sharing these resources with your network. If your community doesn't have these kinds of social service programs for animals, talk to your local animal shelter about getting some started. If you can, support these programs with time or money—volunteers are often invaluable in getting local pet supply stores to become collection sites and helping pick up and deliver donations. If you have room in your home, consider becoming a foster for military families or local safe harbor programs.

Make sure your city or county has an emergency plan that includes animals. If they don't, tell them it's time for an update. When you make your own emergency kit, share photos and an item list on social media to inspire your friends and family to include their own animals in their disaster preparedness plans. Don't wait for disaster or devastation to strike to figure out how you'll afford it. Start budgeting today and create an animal emergency fund so you'll have what you need to pay for pet-friendly hotels during a disaster or cover vet bills if times get unexpectedly tight.

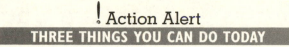

! Action Alert

THREE THINGS YOU CAN DO TODAY

1 • Help the hungry by donating to a pet food bank. If there isn't one in your community, contact your local human food bank or animal shelter about starting one.

2 • Support low-cost spay/neuter and vet care clinics. In addition to financial support, many clinics can use volunteers for transportation and assistance during neighborhood vaccination events.

3 • Make an emergency kit for your animals, including a plan for how you'll evacuate them if needed.

ANIMALS YOU'LL HELP SAVE
Dogs, cats, and everyone else in the family.

Be the Change

Elephants take care of each other, and not just when everything is rosy for the herd. They'll surround vulnerable family members to keep them safe. They'll slow down if one is injured or sick. They'll try to lift each other up—sometimes literally if a herd member is ailing. Their mourning rituals are complex and well documented, and they're known to weep in times of distress. They try to console one another, and they try to save one another. They've also been known to save other animals in trouble, such as a baby rhinoceros or a dog. Elephants live in a world rich with emotion and empathy, where they know their actions affect those around them. We should all be more like elephants.

By now, you know that your personal choices affect the lives of animals—what you do or don't buy and how you live your life can influence individuals, industries, and policies to make the world a gentler or a harder place for animals. Your lifestyle can inspire others to change their lives and start a movement. You get to define what matters to you and choose what kind of world you want to live in.

Animal advocacy isn't what it used to be. Knowledge is more available, decision-makers are more accessible, and brands are more vulnerable. Your social media and email can help you reach more people faster than activists could've dreamed of a few decades ago. The world is a smaller place, and your voice echoes further in the halls of power.

Still, in some ways, it hasn't gotten any easier. With awareness comes a sense of responsibility, and with the internet waiting for us to log in from our phones, tablets, and computers anytime from anywhere, we're nothing if not aware. And with hyperawareness comes a sense of being overwhelmed, sometimes to the point of confusion or paralysis or both. As an animal lover trying to change the world, you'll likely go through an elephant-sized range of emotions. It's important to acknowledge those feelings and move through them so you can continue to be an effective voice for animals.

It's Okay to Start Small

Some people will know exactly where they want to start—whatever will save their favorite species, or speaks to them as an exciting way to help animals. Or maybe there's something they've been thinking about for a while and now have even more reason to do it. Maybe one of these issues coincides with recent news in their community. If this is you, that's fantastic. Jump in with both feet.

But maybe you find this all a bit overwhelming. Animals need our help whether we're at the ballot box or in the bedroom. Everything you do—and don't do—can have an impact. Then there's the Sophie's Choice of it all: If you spend your time helping cows, what about all the chimpanzees who need help, too?

If you're feeling paralyzed by the breadth of challenges animals face in the world today, start small. Do something that you're pretty confident you can stick with. Small changes are often more lasting than trying to do everything at once. And although there are big, systemic problems that animals face, sometimes starting with transforming our personal lives to align with our values can bring us closer to the problems we're trying to solve, help us take responsibility for our role in animal suffering, and allow us to speak with more authority on issues. Eventually, that can snowball into more effective, bigger change.

So take a deep breath. You don't have to do it all. Doing something—anything—for animals is better than doing nothing. That first step is often the hardest, but once you've taken it, it's a lot easier to keep moving.

It's Okay to Take a Break

Take another deep breath. Is that the first time you've stopped to breathe lately? Because breathing is important. Animal lovers have a tendency to get so wrapped up in caring for other species that we forget to care for ourselves.

There will be days when the news is too much or things become more difficult than you think you can bear. No one ever said changing the world was easy.

When you start to pay attention to what animals are up against in this world, you start seeing animal mistreatment everywhere. You could spend all day signing online petitions, scrolling through photos of homeless dogs and cats, reading stories of animal abuse and news about animal industries getting away with murder (often literally). It's basically a nonstop shock-and-awe campaign out there for animal lovers. If you don't get discouraged, you'll probably find yourself getting increasingly frustrated and angry. You may become tempted to post every story and every petition and every dog in every shelter across North America who's slated for euthanasia with an all-caps rant about how horrible humanity is . . .

Stop.

Step away from the internet. Breathe. (And if you're not sure you remember how, there's an app for that. Meditation and mindfulness apps will walk you through breathing exercises to relax and refocus.)

Social change rarely happens overnight. Habits can be hard to break, and the process of creating new policies or undoing old ones is slower than free hotel Wi-Fi. It's important to know your limits, physically and emotionally. You can't save all the animals by yourself by the end of the workday. Changing the world is a long-term commitment. So settle in and be patient with yourself. That means accepting the fact that even when you commit to making better choices for animals, you'll make mistakes because you're tired or because you didn't realize what you were doing or because you found yourself in a situation with limited options. Or because of a thousand other factors life throws at you. Don't give up on your efforts to live an animal-friendlier life just because you can't do it all.

And when it starts to feel like it's all too much, give yourself a break. You won't be much help to the animals if you're burned out.

Burnout is a little different for everyone, but we all have internal alarms that tell us when we're in the danger zone. We just need to learn to listen to them. Signs can include exhaustion, inability to focus, lack of creativity, lack of empathy, difficulty sleeping, apathy, cynicism, mood swings, unhappiness, guilt, hopelessness, loss of purpose, and questioning whether you're really doing any good in the world. You may have an increase in headaches or stomachaches or find that you're getting sick more frequently. If that happens, your body may not give you a choice when it's time to slow down. If you're just generally not feeling like yourself, you may be experiencing burnout.

Not only do people experience burnout differently, but the timing can vary, too, connected to all the other stressors in your life. Maybe there was a time when you were single-handedly running a greyhound rescue and feeling perfectly fine, and then a few years later, a basic letter-writing campaign to shut down a dog racing track has you feeling like you've been the one chasing a mechanical rabbit. Maybe work has gotten more stressful, or you've recently married or divorced or had a child. Maybe you've gone back to school or moved, or you're anxious about money or politics. Maybe you can't pinpoint a reason why your fuse is so much shorter than it used to be. And you don't have to—it doesn't matter why you're feeling burned out. You don't need to justify it; you just need to take care of yourself.

Self-care is entirely personal. There are people who just need a little meditation and yoga to recharge. For others, that may sound like a circle of hell, and what they need is a night out with friends at the local brewery or dance club. Only you can decide what will make you feel like yourself again—and there's likely not one magic formula that will work every time. When I'm feeling burned out, sometimes I need to go for a long hike and sit by a waterfall to think about nothing. Sometimes I need to unplug and curl up with a book. Sometimes I need to plug in for a mindless Netflix binge. Self-care doesn't have to be an epic getaway or lifestyle reboot—sometimes reclaiming the small, simple moments of normality that got left behind is exactly what you need.

The only universal rule when it comes to self-care is to make sure you're at least hitting the basics of what your body needs to function: food, water, exercise, and sleep. Beyond that, it's up to you.

Here are a few ideas that might help you get your groove back:

- Hang out with your dog or cat, or a friend's dog or cat, to enjoy the simple things that make her happy, or check out a farm sanctuary or wildlife refuge to reconnect with animals in a positive way.

- Hang out with other animal lovers who understand why this matters to you so much and how frustrating trying to change the world can be.

- Hang out with other humans doing something that has nothing to do with animals or activism. See a movie, go to a winery, play mini golf, go bowling, have a craft night.

- Take up a new hobby. Try knitting or crocheting or scrapbooking. Learn to play the guitar or the accordion. Become a master chef.

- Take up a different cause. Give your activism a change of scenery by focusing on a different species or something that's not animal related at all.

- Write down all the things you've accomplished to see what a difference you've made. (See chapter 1 for ideas on how to track your impact.)

- Reorganize yourself. Physically rearranging your space or mentally reorganizing through task lists, journals, or productivity apps can help you regain focus.

- Take a vacation. You deserve it.

Don't wait until you're deep in a rut to take care of yourself. Pay attention to your basic biological needs and know your limits—you're not a bad person if you choose not to watch every graphic abuse video or take on every issue. It's okay to turn off the news, log out of social media, and take a break. The animals will still need you tomorrow.

When Good Intentions Go Bad

Even among animal lovers, we don't agree on everything. Debates between cat lovers and bird lovers can make ultimate fighting matches seem like hugging fests. Some people approach diet from a "vegan or bust" perspective. There are wildly disparate views about zoos and pets, whether they should exist and under what circumstances. These are complex issues, tangled up in history and culture, knowledge and morality, priorities and privileges. Give people the benefit of the doubt, especially when interacting online, where you rarely know the full story and often lack the context of tone and personality. Be open to engaging in dialogue to better understand other points of view. This also happens to be the best way to educate people and start changing minds.

Don't let your good intentions pave over your basic human decency. I've seen the social media mob turn on people who gave up their dogs when they lost their jobs and homes or were unexpectedly deployed overseas. When these families who turn to the internet hoping for solutions during a time of crisis receive only criticism and threats, how does that help their animals or change the outcomes for others who may be facing similar situations? All too often, entire groups of people are attacked because of an obscure cultural tradition involving animals, or animal lovers respond to violence against animals by calling for violence against the perpetrators. In their horror, outrage, and sadness, sometimes animal lovers forget that humans are animals, too.

Be compassionate toward all species, including our own. Make space for whatever emotional response you need to have to animal mistreatment, then channel those feelings into productive action. Taking your anger out on someone who turns his or her dog over to a shelter won't solve the problem, prevent history repeating itself, or find that dog a new home. Vigilante justice against a single animal abuser will never be as effective as pushing for stronger anticruelty laws and better-educated law enforcement to implement them. Use the ideas in this book, connect with animal protection organizations, and network with other like-minded animal lovers to seek resolution, not retaliation.

Comment and Share

Don't be afraid to ask for help, whether you need people to join a campaign or you need emotional support. People generally want to help but aren't always sure how. And if you're up against a challenging situation in your community, your advocacy, or reaching your personal goals, the internet hive mind is full of ideas, knowledge, experience, resources, and contacts that can help you find a solution.

While you're being patient with yourself and with strangers, be patient with your friends and family, too. Everyone, even people you know, comes at these issues from different places. Bombarding your social networks with guilt and horror may not be the most effective way to convince your friends to learn more about an issue or join you in creating change. Even for animal lovers, images of animal abuse filling up their feeds can be traumatic, causing them to shut down and block you instead of taking action. Sharing positive stories, cute photos that remind people who they're saving, the reasons why the issue is important to you, and practical ways to help can reach people in ways that shame and shock often cannot.

When you've found self-care tactics that help you become a healthier, better advocate, share those with your friends. Too often, we present ourselves on social media as überproductive cyborgs living our best lives. But we're all in this together, and showing the ways you're taking care of yourself *and* changing the world for animals can help others learn to take better care of themselves, too. Sharing the small victories in your journey to an animal-friendlier life can help others start down their own path of saving animals.

There will always be more work to do and more animals who need to be saved, but as an animal lover, you've already taken the first step. You've shared your compassion and your passion with those around you. You've decided that how your life affects other animals matters. Now let's go change the world.

! Action Alert
THREE THINGS YOU CAN DO TODAY

1 • Give people the benefit of the doubt. There's enough cruelty in the world without those trying to do the right thing turning on each other.

2 • Take care of yourself. You can't help the animals if you're suffering from burnout.

3 • Do something today, anything, that helps an animal. Use that momentum to keep going.

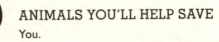

ANIMALS YOU'LL HELP SAVE
You.

APPENDIX: ADDITIONAL RESOURCES

There are books, apps, websites, and organizations mentioned throughout this guide to help you make animal-friendly choices, increase your impact, connect with other animal lovers, and stay up to date on the latest campaigns and issues affecting animals. But it's not easy changing the world, so here are a few dozen more.

Disclaimer: Websites and apps have a way of changing and disappearing, so some of these links may become outdated. Hopefully they'll be replaced by new-and-improved tools for animal lovers, but use your judgment if any of these resources don't appear as described.

There are far too many amazing links, stories, documentaries, and books about animals to include in these pages, so even more resources and recommendations are available on my website at www.stephaniefeldstein.com, and I hope you'll share your favorites with me on social media.

Part I • Get Political

Chapter 1: The Animals Need You

The Human-Animal Bond

The Dodo curates and creates shareable videos, stories, and other digital content to tap into our emotional connection with animals and our growing concern over their welfare. www.thedodo.com

When Elephants Weep by Jeffrey Moussaieff Masson and Susan McCarthy (New York: Delta, 1996) is an exploration into the emotional lives of animals that's become a classic among animal lovers.

Beyond Words: What Animals Think and Feel by Carl Safina (New York: Henry Holt, 2015) explores what animals experience through stories of behavior that challenge the boundary between human and nonhuman animals to discover why we feel so close to them.

The Ten Trusts: What We Must Do to Care for the Animals We Love by Jane Goodall and Marc Bekoff (New York: HarperOne, 2003) outlines ten lessons humans must embrace to create a safer, more peaceful, and loving world for animals and ourselves.

Measuring Change

Penzu makes it easy to journal your actions and progress with the ability to upload photos and search your entries to track your impact by type of activity, animals you helped save, or any other category or key word you choose. www.penzu.com *App available for iOS and Android.*

HabitBull is a simple habit-tracking app that you can set up to track how many days you take action for animals, eat meat-free, avoid using plastic, or whatever goals you want to set for yourself. www.habitbull.com *App available for iOS and Android.*

Vegetarian Calculator is a simple online tool that helps you calculate the monthly and yearly impact on farmed animals and the climate based on how many months you've been vegetarian. www.vegetariancalculator.com *App available for iOS and Android.*

The Vegan Calculator calculates the total farmed animals, gallons of water, square feet of forest, pounds of grain, and greenhouse gas emissions you've saved over the months or years that you've been vegan. www.thevegancalculator.com

    Hint: If you've reduced your meat and dairy consumption, but haven't adopted a vegetarian or vegan diet, track each of your meatless meals (counting one day for every three meals) and input the total to discover your impact.

Chapter 2: Animal Advocacy 101

Campaign Tools

Care2 is an online community where you can get news, take action, and start your own petition. www.care2.com

Check out Care2's Petitions 101 series to learn more about online petitions: www.thepetitionsite.com /petition/

Change.org is a petition platform that helps you create your online campaign with a simple step-by-step process, complete with tips and examples. www.change.org

Faunalytics conducts research on animal issues and trends to help animal lovers be more effective advocates. www.faunalytics.org

Humane Society of the United States' Toolkit is a one-stop shop for tips on talking to your representatives, passing local laws, writing letters to the editor, lobbying, and more. www.humanesoci ety.org/action/toolkit/

PETA's Guide to Becoming an Activist has lots of great tips for putting your love of animals into action, with a focus on talking to others about the issues you care about and how to answer tough question you may face (with a focus on veganism). www.peta.org/action/activism-guide/

Puppy Mill Awareness of Southeast Michigan has been successful in protesting pet stores in southeast Michigan and has shared their secret sauce online. Check out "Launching Pet Store Campaigns" under the webinars archive for a step-by-step guide to protesting pet stores that sell puppy mill dogs. www.michiganpuppymills.com

Chapter 3: Share the Love

Get to Know Other Causes

DoSomething.org lets you explore campaigns and actions you can take across a range of causes, whether you have five minutes or five hours to get involved. www.dosomething.org

Meetup makes it easy to find social justice groups and actions near you to get involved with other causes. www.meetup.com/topics/social-justice/ *App available for iOS and Android.*

A Is for Activist by Innosanto Nagara (New York: Triangle Square, 2016) is a picture book that encourages children to take a stand against injustice, inequality, and threats to the environment. This introduction to activism will get your family talking about social justice while reminding all of us that we don't have to choose just one cause to care about.

Chapter 4: The Political Beast

Don't Miss an Election

Vote.org provides online tools for all things voting related: register to vote, check your registration status, get your absentee ballot, find your polling place, sign up for election reminders, and learn about Voter ID laws. www.vote.org

Rock the Vote has been turning out millions of voters since 1990 with a campaign and resources geared toward young adults. www.rockthevote.com

Talk to Your Representatives

Countable is a user-friendly online database and app to make it easy to understand federal bills, see what others think, track how your representatives are voting, and let them know how you feel about the issues. www.countable.us *App available for iOS and Android.*

Town Hall Project helps you find local public events with your members of Congress so you can show up and speak out when they're home during recesses. www.townhallproject.com

Humane Lobby Days are an opportunity to speak with your state legislators about the animal issues you care about most. www.humanesociety.org/about/events/humane-lobby-days.html

Humane Society Legislative Fund works on state and federal animal protection laws, and their handy website lets you read their positions on the latest bills, take action, and check out your federal legislators' record in their Humane Scorecard. www.hslf.org

Run for Office

How to Run for Office is a no-frills website with a list of things to consider, a step-by-step guide, and resources that can help you if you're thinking about running for public office. www.howtorunforoffice.org

She Should Run works to inspire women and girls to get more involved in political leadership by encouraging women to run for office and supporting those considering public service. www.sheshouldrun.org

Run for Something is an aptly named organization that helps progressive millennials run for political office. While animal protection isn't among the group's priority issues, if you're also passionate about social justice, this can be a great resource. www.runforsomething.net

Animals in the Courts

Animal Legal Defense Fund files lawsuits to protect animals, provides legal assistance and training, advocates for stronger animal protection laws, and supports animal-loving law students and the emerging field of animal law. www.aldf.org

Earthjustice helps wildlife and the environment fight pollution, habitat destruction, and climate change in the courts to advance a healthy world for all. www.earthjustice.org

Animal Law Resource Center has model laws to improve animal welfare in agriculture, education, shelters, and more, as well as a searchable database of existing and pending legislation by state. www.animallaw.com

Several other nonprofit organizations mentioned throughout the appendix also have legal teams working for animal clients, including Center for Biological Diversity and the Humane Society of the United States.

Chapter 5: Money Talks

Challenge Business as Usual

The Humane Economy by Wayne Pacelle (New York: William Morrow, 2016) explores how animal lovers and non–animal lovers alike can help transform business practices using innovation and compassion to create a better world.

Consumerist is a source of news and information published by the not-for-profit subsidiary of *Consumer Reports* to help people engage with the marketplace (search for *animals* to see the latest animal-related issues). www.consumerist.com

Better Business Bureau has been around a lot longer than Yelp and other review sites, and is still trusted by customers and business owners for its standards for ethical business behavior and ratings. Customers can search business profiles and file complaints about negative experiences online. www.bbb.org

Invest Wisely

Animal Charity Evaluators is like GuideStar or Charity Navigator specifically for animal protection organizations, researching and reviewing animal advocacy groups to help you decide where to contribute your time and money. www.animalcharityevaluators.org

The Forum for Sustainable and Responsible Investment works to shift investment practices toward investing for positive social and environmental impacts. www.ussif.org

See chapter 19 for additional resources on cruelty-free shopping.

Chapter 6: Compassion in the Classroom

Cut Out Dissection

Animalearn is the educational arm of the American Anti-Vivisection Society, working to end the use of animals in education and providing resources for educators, students, and parents to help them object to dissection. www.animalearn.org

The Science Bank is a free online lending library (and a program of Animalearn) that offers more than 650 humane science education products for classrooms to borrow, including a variety of animal dissection models and software programs. www.thesciencebank.org

Save the Frogs is a leader in amphibian conservation, providing information and actions you can take against dissection and other threats to frogs. www.savethefrogs.com

Beyond the Science Lab

E-books for Empathy is an interactive e-book app geared toward kids ages seven to eleven, based off the RedRover Readers curriculum, to teach empathy through exploring the bond between people and animals. www.redrover.org/e-book *App available for iOS and Android.*

TeachKind is PETA's humane education division with lesson plans and other classroom tools for schools and educators on a range of animal issues. www.peta.org/teachkind/

Meatless Monday is the global movement with hundreds of schools, cities, restaurants, and other institutions participating to cut meat out of our diets once a week. Their website has a toolkit and free cookbook to help schools get started. www.meatlessmonday.com/meatless-monday-k-12/

Vegetarian and Vegan Youth provides resources for kids interested in becoming vegetarian or vegan, starting a veg club at school, or getting more meatless meals in the cafeteria. www.vegyouth.com

Chapter 7: The Power of Words

Animal Talk

Animology is a podcast by author and advocate Colleen Patrick-Goudreau about animal-related words and expressions, where they came from, and how they affect the way we interact with animals. www.colleenpatrickgoudreau.com/animalogy-podcast/

The Animal Museum preserves and shares the history of animal protection with exhibits online and in their Los Angeles museum to educate and empower visitors to create a more compassionate world. www.theanimalmuseum.com

Compassionate Celebrity Sites

Ian Somerhalder Foundation was founded by actor Ian Somerhalder to support, educate, and empower people to advocate for animals and the planet, with an emphasis on youth and grassroots projects. www.isfoundation.com

The Kind Life is an online hub for tips on living a greener, more humane, more meat-free life, started by actress Alicia Silverstone. www.thekindlife.com

The Jason Debus Heigl Foundation was founded by actress Katherine Heigl and her mom to end animal cruelty and abuse by supporting dog and cat rescue and spay/neuter programs. www.jasonheigl.foundation

Chapter 8: Find Your Pack

Get Involved

VolunteerMatch makes it easy to find volunteer opportunities where you can connect with other animal lovers in your community for a good cause. www.volunteermatch.org

Idealist helps you find jobs, internships, volunteer opportunities, events, and organizations to connect with people who care about changing the world. www.idealist.org

Get Together

Meet My Dog is a playdate app for your dog where you can set up a profile with your dog's photos and interests and search for other dogs in the area to connect with in the app and at the park. www.meetmydogapp.com *App available for iOS and Android.*

VeggieDate is an online dating site just for vegan, vegetarian, and veg-curious singles. www.veggiedate.org

Part II • Get Wild

Chapter 9: Green Is the New Black

Ecological Footprint

Global Footprint Network's interactive calculator will help you discover your ecological shoe size and how you can shrink it. www.footprintnetwork.org/resources/footprint-calculator/

CoolClimate Network is a program of the University of California–Berkeley with a detailed carbon footprint calculator and a list of actions you can take to reduce your greenhouse gas emissions and save money. coolclimate.berkeley.edu/carboncalculator

Oroeco calculates your carbon footprint based on your lifestyle and purchases and allows you to compare and compete with your friends and neighbors to become climate champions. www.oroeco.com *App available for iOS and Android.*

JouleBug turns sustainability into a game by awarding points for your daily eco-friendly actions and creating challenges to see who's racking up the greenest habits. www.joulebug.com *App available for iOS and Android.*

Buy Less

New Dream is dedicated to reducing consumption and redefining the American Dream to cultivate community, sustainability, and nonmaterial values. www.newdream.org

iFixIt is a free community-driven online repair manual with information on fixing products from old Atari game systems to stubborn zippers—and if the thing you need to fix doesn't have a manual, just ask the handy hive-mind for answers. www.ifixit.com

The Repair Association advocates for the right to repair cars, smartphones, and other electronics to give people more options to extend the life of their products rather having to go back to the manufacturers. www.repair.org

NeighborGoods is an online network for borrowing, renting, and selling stuff in your community, because not everyone needs their own set of power tools or party supplies. www.neighborgoods.net

Green Pet Products

Green Little Cat is a blog dedicated to eco-friendly tips to reduce your cat's environmental pawprint. www.greenlittlecat.com

Wet Noses dog treats are certified organic and verified non-GMO; they're not the only quality organic dog treats on the market, but they have been thoroughly taste-tested and approved by my pack. www.wet-noses.com

Molly Mutt makes bamboo collars and leashes and their signature dog bed duvet covers that allow you to upcycle old clothes, pillows, towels, or blankets that you're no longer using (or that your dog destroyed) into comfy sleeping spots. www.mollymutt.com

Doggie Dooley is a mini septic system that composts your dog's waste to save on plastic and pollution. www.doggiedooley.com

Chapter 10: Conservation Uncaged

Saving Wild in the Wild

Center for Biological Diversity fights to protect wildlife of all species great and small and the wildlands they need to survive. www.biologicaldiversity.org

The Jane Goodall Institute puts the vision of conservation legend Jane Goodall into action with an emphasis on inspiring people of all ages to create a better world for people, animals, and the environment. www.janegoodall.org

Half-Earth: Our Planet's Fight for Life by Edward O. Wilson (New York: Liveright, 2016) argues that if we're going to save biodiversity, we need to keep half of the earth wild.

Born Free USA advocates to end the suffering of wild animals in captivity, protect wildlife in the wild, and encourage compassionate conservation. www.bornfreeusa.org

Wild Experiences

    Planet Earth and Planet Earth II are BBC-produced documentary series narrated by superstar naturalist David Attenborough that bring you all the stunning beauty and drama of wildlife's wild lives. www.bbcamerica.com/shows/planet-earth and www.bbcearth.com/planetearth2/

    Joel Sartore's Photo Ark gets up close and personal with studio portraits of more than 6,500 species (and counting) to help people connect with endangered species and inspire them to save these amazing animals from extinction. www.joelsartore.com

    The International Ecotourism Society develops standards, training, technical assistance, and educational resources for travelers and travel companies exploring the ecotourism experience. www.ecotourism.org

    Wildlife Witness gives tourists and locals the tools to help stop the illegal wildlife trade with tips on what to watch out for and the ability to report incidents. www.wildlifewitness.net *App available for iOS and Android.*

Chapter 11: Neighborhood Bird-Watch

Resources for the Birds and Birders

    Audubon has been a leading voice for birds for over a hundred years, with nearly five hundred local chapters and resources for bird lovers of all feathers. www.audubon.org *Audubon Bird Guide App available for iOS, Android, and Amazon Kindle.*

    Peterson Field Guides can help you identify and learn more about the birds, plants, mammals, reptiles, amphibians, insects, and other creatures and features of the natural world around you. Peterson also has a birding podcast and field guide apps for birds and mammals to help you identify animals and update your life list on the go. www.petersononline.com *Apps available for iOS and Android.*

    Merlin Bird ID is the perfect app for beginning birders, brought to you by the Cornell Lab of Ornithology. By uploading a photo or answering questions about the bird's size, color, and where it was seen, this app helps you figure out what kind of bird you've spotted. merlin.allaboutbirds.org *App available for iOS and Android.*

Caring for Backyard Wildlife

    Beyond Pesticides advocates for a world free of toxic pesticides and provides resources for companies, communities, and individuals, including a pollinator-friendly plant and seed directory and the searchable ManageSafe database of the safest ways to deal with unwelcome guests in your home and garden. www.beyondpesticides.org

    Xerces Society looks out for the littlest guys by working to protect invertebrates like butterflies and bees and providing information from regional lists of native pollinator plants to a field guide to identify migratory dragonflies. www.xerces.org

    National Wildlife Federation's Garden for Wildlife can help you create a Certified Wildlife Habitat in your backyard by using sustainable practices and providing food, water, cover, and suitable places for wildlife to raise their young. www.nwf.org/garden-for-wildlife.aspx

Chapter 12: Unplug Climate Change

Go Solar

    Wild Energy is the Center for Biological Diversity's campaign to advance wildlife-friendly energy solutions. www.choosewildenergy.org

    Vote Solar works across the United States to advance state policies and programs that promote solar energy. www.votesolar.org

    Geostellar helps you estimate your roof's solar potential (similar to Google's Project Sunroof and Mapdwell), while also making it easy for you to explore financing options for solar panel installation. www.geostellar.com

Reduce Energy Waste

    Energy Star is a program of the Environmental Protection Agency to promote energy efficiency with tools to perform a home energy audit, DIY energy-saving tips, and a searchable database of products, builders, and financial incentive programs for increasing your home's efficiency. www.energystar.gov

Get more energy-saving information and ideas from the Department of Energy at www.hes.lbl.gov

Energy Cost Calculator allows you to calculate the annual energy use, cost per kilowatt, and carbon emissions for different devices in your home. *App available for iOS; other similar apps available for iOS and Android.*

Nest Thermostat learns your habits at different times of day and in different seasons to help you save energy with a personalized heating and cooling schedule and an app that allows you to track your energy use and adjust your home temperature from anywhere. www.nest.com/thermostat/ *Product app available for iOS and Android.*

Smappee (short for *Smart App for Energy Efficiency*) sells products that help you monitor the energy use and costs of your appliances, gas, and water, and turn devices on and off from your smartphone. www.smappee.com *Product app available for iOS and Android.*

Sense is a monitor that allows you to track your power use in real time, set alerts for specific devices, and watch for trends in energy use. www.sense.com *App available for iOS and Android.*

Drive Green

Waze Carpool helps you arrange ride shares for your commute or other local road trips. (Also check out the original **Waze** app, which crowdsources the fastest route in real time so you don't spend as much time sitting in traffic.) www.waze.com *Apps available for iOS and Android.*

Dash connects to your car to track your driving habits and vehicle maintenance to improve your fuel efficiency and help you drive greener. www.dash.by *App available for iOS and Android.*

Spinlister is a global bike-sharing app that allows you to find a bike for rent (or list your own) for a zero-carbon commute. www.spinlister.com *App available for iOS and Android.*

Chapter 13: Plastic Detox

Ditch the Plastic

The 5 Gyres Institute empowers action against plastic pollution and has a Plastic-Free Shopping Guide to help you get unnecessary plastic out of your life. www.5gyres.org

Plastic Pollution Coalition is an alliance of organizations, businesses, and individuals working to end plastic pollution, with useful online guides to plastic-free schools, eateries, events, and towns. www.plasticpollutioncoalition.org

The Story of Stuff takes on plastic bags, bottled water, microbeads, and microfibers with creative videos and opportunities to take action (check out their other resources on overconsumption, too). www.storyofstuff.org

Ban the Bottle advocates to eliminate single-use plastic water bottles in schools, offices, and public areas, promotes efforts to pass bottle bans, and provides tips to start your own campaign. www.banthebottle.net

OneLessStraw is a campaign created by One More Generation, a kid-founded conservation and animal protection organization, to urge individuals and businesses to use fewer straws. OMG also offers a plastic and recycling curriculum for schools. www.onelessstraw.org

Chapter 14: Down the Drain

Save Water, Save Lives

Water Footprint Calculator is an interactive online tool to help you estimate your water use, including water consumed indirectly through your diet and energy use. www.watercalculator.org

WaterSense is the Environmental Protection Agency's hub of information and water-saving ideas for homes, yards, and businesses, including water-efficient product recommendations. www.epa.gov/watersense

Don't Be a Drip is the Center for Biological Diversity's campaign to raise awareness about the connection between individual water use and wildlife impacts, highlighting the top water hog cities in the country and shareable graphics on how to save water at home. www.dontbeadrip.org

Your Daily Dose of Water is an interactive infographic that walks you through how much water you're using each day from your morning bathroom routine until bedtime. www.good.is/infographics /interactive-infographic-your-daily-dose-of-water

Unbottle Water

Food & Water Watch works to protect our food and water supplies, including the Public Water for All campaign that supports communities fighting against privatization of their water supply and the Take Back the Tap campaign that promotes tap water over bottled water on campuses. www.foodandwaterwatch.org

The Pacific Institute is a water-focused think tank that supports sustainable water policies. www.pacinst.org

The Story of Stuff not only fights against wasteful overconsumption, it also fights to protect public water sources from privatization as part of the #UnbottleWater movement. www.storyofstuff.org /unbottle-water/

Chapter 15: Take Extinction Off Your Plate

Eat Less Meat, Save More Wildlife

Take Extinction Off Your Plate is the Center for Biological Diversity's campaign to highlight the connections between meat and dairy production and threats to wildlife, and to help wildlife-lovers choose a more earth-friendly diet. www.takeextinctionoffyourplate.com

Food Monster by One Green Planet has more than eight thousand planet-friendly recipes, with more added every day, including seasonal ideas and the ability to browse by meal type or featured ingredients. www.onegreenplanet.org/foodmonster *App available for iOS and Android.*

Food for Thought encourages wildlife and other animal protection organizations to adopt animal-friendly meal policies, providing sample policies, event-planning resources, and information to help advocates talk to their favorite groups about joining the campaign. www.foodforthoughtcampaign.org

Under the Sea

Greenpeace Sustainable Seafood Consumer Hub tests your sustainable seafood smarts with an online quiz and lets you take action to demand more sustainable practices from your local grocery stores. seafood.greenpeaceusa.org

Seafood Watch by Monterey Bay Aquarium has a searchable online database, app, and printable guides with recommendations on which fish are the most sustainable choices, alternatives with some concerns, and those to avoid. www.seafoodwatch.org/seafood-recommendations *App available for iOS and Android.*

Bluefin Boycott is a campaign to reduce demand for bluefin tuna by calling on restaurants to take it off the menu before it's too late for this incredible imperiled fish. www.bluefinboycott.com

Fight Food Waste

Love Food Hate Waste helps you create meal plans, shopping lists, and recipes to buy what you need and use what you buy. www.lovefoodhatewaste.com *App available for iOS and Android.*

Save the Food is an interactive website and campaign by NRDC where you can learn more about the food waste problem and what you can do to prevent it. www.savethefood.com

EatBy helps you track the food in your house and reminds you to reduce overpurchasing and to eat the oldest items before they go bad. www.eatbyapp.com *App available for iOS and Android.*

The Ugly Fruit and Veg Campaign advocates to end strict cosmetic standards for fruits and vegetables by urging grocery stores to stock imperfect produce and through fun social media campaigns highlighting fruits and vegetables with character. www.uglyfruitandveg.org

See chapter 21 for additional resources to reduce your meat and dairy consumption.

Chapter 16: Let's Talk About Sex

Population Information

The Endangered Species Condoms Project gets people talking about population by giving away free condoms wrapped in packages with colorful wildlife art, humorous slogans, and accessible information on how population growth affects wildlife and what we can do about it. www.endangered speciescondoms.com

Countdown by Alan Weisman (New York: Little, Brown, 2013) investigates the dynamics of population growth around the world, including the effects of population pressure in different regions, the influence of different cultures, and whether it's possible to limit our growth in time to save ourselves.

Transition Earth provides resources and advocacy to empower women, educate youth, and advance programs that simultaneously address health care, family planning, and conservation to promote human rights and nature's rights. www.transition-earth.org

Reproductive Rights

Guttmacher Institute conducts research and policy analysis to advance sexual and reproductive rights and health in the United States and around the world. www.guttmacher.org

Bedsider is an online birth control support network that provides information about different types of contraception along with straight talk about having a healthy sex life without the fear of unplanned pregnancy and an entertaining app to remind you to keep up with your birth control. www.bedsider.org *App available for iOS and Android.*

Planned Parenthood is a leading health care provider, educator, and advocacy organization promoting the fundamental right of every person worldwide to manage their own fertility. www.plannedparenthood.org

Sustain Natural condoms and other products were created with the health of women and the environment in mind, and the company regularly blogs on reproductive rights and women's health issues. www.sustainnatural.com

Chapter 17: The Call of the Wild

Explore the Outdoors

National Park Service cares for our national parks and their website makes it easy for you to learn about the beauty and heritage of our park system and plan your visit to any of the sites across the country. www.nps.gov

The Outbound helps you explore the outdoors in your area with community submitted and rated trail suggestions, interactive maps, curated product kits for different types of activities, and the ability to save a list of the adventures you can't wait to check out. www.theoutbound.com *App available for iOS only.*

AllTrails has more than fifty thousand trails that you can sort by difficulty rating and whether they're dog-friendly, kid-friendly, or wheelchair-friendly, along with maps, photos, and reviews. www.alltrails.com *App available for iOS and Android.*

REI isn't always the cheapest option for outdoor gear, but they do carry quality products and offer classes and trips to help you learn to safely enjoy new activities; plus they earned bonus points with their #OptOutside campaign that started by encouraging people to get outdoors instead of shopping on Black Friday and their Force of Nature campaign to promote gender equity in the outdoors. www.rei.com

Inclusive Conservation

Next 100 Coalition advocates for more inclusive public lands that reflect the diversity of the American people, respect all cultures, and engage diverse communities. www.next100coalition.org

Outdoor Afro connects African Americans to outdoor experiences and celebrates African American leadership and inclusion in outdoor recreation and conservation. www.outdoorafro.com

Green Latinos works with a coalition of Latino leaders to address conservation issues that affect the health and welfare of the Latino community in the United States, including amplifying voices of minority, low-income, and tribal communities and mentoring the next generation of Latino environmental leaders. www.greenlatinos.org

Save Wild Places

Protect Our Public Lands is a campaign by Outdoor Alliance that provides information on the threats to public lands and opportunities to take action to keep our public lands public. www.protectourpublicland.org

The **Wilderness Society** works to protect America's wild places, advocate for conservation funding, and promote outdoor recreation. www.wilderness.org

Part III • Get Personal

Chapter 18: The Animals Aren't Amused

Marine Mammals in Captivity

Ric O'Barry's Dolphin Project was founded on the first Earth Day to raise awareness about dolphins in captivity, rehabilitate captive dolphins, and work to end dolphin exploitation and slaughter. www.dolphinproject.net

Death at SeaWorld by David Kirby (New York: St. Martin's Press, 2012) exposes the dark side of SeaWorld and the decades-long fight against keeping killer whales in captivity.

Animal Actors and Athletes

Performing Animal Welfare Society (PAWS) provides a retirement home and sanctuary for victims of the exotic pet and performing animal trades and other captive wildlife, including former Detroit Zoo elephants, Winky and Wanda. www.pawsweb.org

GREY2K USA is the largest greyhound protection organization in the world, advocating to end the cruelty of dog racing and promote the rescue and adoption of greyhounds. www.grey2kusa.org

Cirque du Soleil has reinvented the modern circus with incredible, awe-inspiring, and animal-free shows performing around the world. www.cirquedusoleil.com

Chapter 19: Clean Conscience

Shop Smarter

Cruelty-Cutter is an app by the Beagle Freedom Project that allows you to search by name or product type or scan cosmetic, personal care, and household cleaning products to see if they're cruelty-free, with the added bonus of the Bite-Back feature that allows you to post on social media about products tested on animals to let your friends and the companies know you're disappointed. www.cruelty-cutter.org *App available for iOS and Android.*

Cruelty-Free Kitty is a beauty blog for animal lovers with guides to help you navigate specific stores and types of products for the best cruelty-free cosmetics. www.crueltyfreekitty.com

Good Guide is an online database and app that lets you search or scan personal care, household, food, and baby products to get science-based ratings on potential health concerns associated with the ingredients. www.goodguide.com *App available for iOS and Android.*

EarthEasy offers nontoxic solutions and product recommendations for all your household cleaning needs. www.eartheasy.com/live_nontoxic_solution.htm

Method cleaning products are Leaping Bunny certified and most of them have a Good Guide rating of 10/10, plus they're safe for use around companion animals and are packaged with waste reduction, recyclability, and environmental footprint in mind. www.methodhome.com

Chapter 20: What Not to Wear

Fur-Free Fashion

The HSUS Fur-Free Campaign advocates to end the killing of animals for fur and promotes compassionate fashion with an online list of companies with fur-free policies and resources to help you avoid any fur faux pas. www.humanesociety.org/issues/fur_fashion/tips/fur-free_shopping.html

Coats for Cubs is an annual fur drive by Buffalo Exchange to collect old fur coats to donate to wildlife rehabilitation centers to help injured and orphaned animals. www.coatsforcubs.com

Cruelty-Free Couture

PETA's Shopping Guide to Compassionate Clothing lets you search by company or product type, including sporting gear, to help you find clothing and accessories free from leather, wool, fur, down, and other animal products. www.peta.org/living/fashion/cruelty-free-clothing-guide/

Farm Sanctuary's Vegan Fashion Shopping List includes vegan designers, online retailers, and fashion blogs to keep animal lovers in style. www.farmsanctuary.org/vegan-fashion/

Unicorn Goods is the world's largest vegan store with clothing and accessories for men, women, and kids, including "lookbooks" for different styles, plus books, personal care products, and home goods for your animal-friendly lifestyle. www.unicorngoods.com

Reduce Your Clothing Footprint

SwapStyle is an online marketplace that lets you swap clothes and accessories, making it easy to try new styles without buying into fast fashion. www.swapstyle.com

The Story of Microfibers by the Story of Stuff Project provides a primer on the problem of microfibers and what needs to be done about it. storyofstuff.org/movies/story-of-microfibers/

Chapter 21: Old MacDonald Lost His Farm

Friends of Farm Animals

Farm Sanctuary is the largest farm animal rescue and protection organization in the United States with sanctuaries in New York and California where visitors are welcome. www.farmsanctuary.org

Compassion Over Killing advocates to end cruelty to animals in agriculture and to promote vegetarian eating through consumer campaigns, legal action, investigations, education, and outreach. www.cok.net

Esther the Wonder Pig is a 650-pound internet star who helps raise awareness about the amazing personalities of pigs and how people can help farm animals. www.estherthewonderpig.com *Follow Esther on Twitter @EstherThePig and on Facebook and Instagram @EstherTheWonderPig*

Good Food Institute works to advance clean meat and plant-based alternatives to animal products by supporting groundbreaking companies and innovators in the field, and promoting animal-friendly foods in the market. www.gfi.org

Discover Animal-Friendly Food

ChooseVeg is a user-friendly online kit by Mercy for Animals to help you transition to eating less meat and dairy with tools to build sample meals and a blog to keep you up-to-date on the latest vegan happenings. www.chooseveg.com

Physicians for Responsible Medicine has a vegetarian starter kit to help answer all your nutrition-related questions, plus the 21-Day Vegan Kickstart online program complete with meal plan, daily messages, and tips to help you take a plant-based diet for a test drive. www.pcrm.org/health/diets/vsk

Happy Cow is an app and online database of vegan, vegetarian, and veg-friendly restaurants and stores to help you find animal-friendly eats whether you're exploring close to home or on the road. www.happycow.net *App available for iOS and Android.*

VeganXpress is a guide to vegan menu options at fast-food and chain restaurants across the country to make it easy to eat for the animals when you're on the run. www.veganxpress.com *App available for iOS only.*

Vegetarian Society is the oldest vegetarian organization in the world, providing support to people who are considering or have already adopted a meat-free lifestyle, complete with a community forum to chat about all things veg-related. www.vegsoc.org

See chapter 15 for additional recipe links and information on sustainable seafood.

Chapter 22: Holiday Hangover

Holiday Planning

BringFido can help plan your trip when your holidays include travel with your four-legged family members, with recommendations for pet-friendly hotels, campgrounds, restaurants, and more. www.bringfido.com *App available for iOS. Similar app available for Android.*

Extinction-free BBQ has information and recipes to help you enjoy a barbecue season that's better for animals and the planet. www.extinctionfreebbq.com

ASPCA Animal Poison Control Center provides online information about plants, foods, and products that are toxic to animals plus a searchable app that shows level of toxicity, and twenty-four-hour hotline if you think your dog or cat may have ingested a poisonous substance. www.aspca.org/pet-care/animal-poison-control

Give and Receive

SoKind Registry lets you create an online wish list that can include experiences, skills, and donations to get what you really want, even if it doesn't fit in a box. www.sokindregistry.org

Etsy is an online marketplace where you can find creative, unique gifts that support artists as well as craft kits and customizable items to give personalized, meaningful presents. www.etsy.com

Chapter 23: Don't Get Catfished

Meet Your Match

The Shelter Pet Project is a collaboration between The Humane Society of the United States and Maddie's Fund to promote animal adoption that lets you search for rescue groups and shelters in your area, browse adoptable animals, and create your own shareable graphic to tell your adoption story. www.theshelterpetproject.org

Petfinder lets you scroll through adoptable animals online and on your smartphone; the website includes tips for choosing and caring for your new animal and the app includes resources to help you pick the perfect companion. www.petfinder.com *App available for iOS and Android.*

HeARTs Speak works to bring animal loving artists together with animal shelters to help increase the visibility of shelter pets. www.heartsspeak.org

Stop Puppy Mills

No Pet Store Puppies is the ASPCA's online hub to fight puppy mills, including the latest news on puppy mills and maps to search for which stores in your area do or don't sell puppies, to check out local ordinances that ban the sale of puppies in pet stores, and to see puppy mill laws by state. www .nopetstorepuppies.com

Best Friends Animal Society provides resources to help you take action to stop puppy mills with fifteen things you can do, plus tips on writing to your legislators or local newspapers, holding a pet store protest, and more. www.bestfriends.org/resources/stop-puppy-mills-15-things-you-can-do

Chapter 24: If You See Something, Say Something

Look Out and Speak Up

Animal Legal Defense Fund fights cruelty in court and provides information on prosecuting animal abuse and what you can do when you witness cruelty in pet stores, animal shelters, or your own neighborhood. www.aldf.org/resources/when-you-witness-animal-cruelty/

The Humane Society of the United States has the latest news on the fight against dogfighting, as well as tips to help you spot the signs, report suspicious activity, and take action to stop the cruelty. www.humanesociety.org/issues/dogfighting/

Sunbear Squad is dedicated to transforming animal lovers into animal defenders with information and resources to address common issues from severe weather to helping lost or injured animals, as well as a neighborhood watch plan to help you keep an eye out for your nonhuman neighbors. www.sunbearsquad.org

Unchain Your Dog provides resources to save dogs from life on a chain, including tips on how to talk to owners, build fences, and pass anti-tethering laws. www.unchainyourdog.org

My Dog Is Cool provides tips and resources for individuals, businesses, and government officials to help prevent dogs from dying in hot cars, including signs and posters to help spread the word. www.mydogiscool.com

Chapter 25: The Ambassador of Dogville

Good Dog Training

Positively is an online hub for positive dog training and behavior references and resources, created by Victoria Stilwell from Animal Planet's *It's Me or the Dog*. www.positively.com

Pooch is your personal dog trainer app that teaches you how to teach your dog and lets you track his progress as he learns new tricks. www.pooch.io *App available for iOS. Similar apps available for Android.*

The Association of Professional Dog Trainers website has resources on a range of dog training challenges and can help you find a certified trainer using positive, reward-based methods, whether you're looking for basic obedience or need to address serious behavior problems. www.apdt.com

Good Dog Laws

Best Friends Animal Society fights to give all dogs a chance, advocates for laws that outlaw dog breed discrimination, and provides resources on how to stop breed discrimination in your community. www.bestfriends.org/resources/dog-breed-discrimination-how-prevent-it-your-community

National Canine Research Council is a think tank that conducts research on dogs in human society to advocate for effective, science-based laws. www.nationalcanineresearchcouncil.com

Chapter 26: Unconditional Love

In Case of Emergency

Ready.gov has information to help you prepare your entire family for natural disasters and other emergencies. www.ready.gov/animals

ASPCA's Pet Safety App provides tips on preparing for disasters, plus the ability to store your animals' records in your phone and find assistance in searching for animals lost during emergencies. www.aspca.org/pet-care/general-pet-care/aspca-mobile-app *App available for iOS and Android.*

Pet First Aid by the American Red Cross provides step-by-step advice and videos for everyday veterinary emergencies, plus tips to help you be prepared. www.redcross.org/get-help/how-to-prepare-for-emergencies/mobile-apps *App available for iOS and Android.*

Keeping Families Together

RedRover is dedicated to helping families in crisis through emergency sheltering, disaster relief, financial assistance (including a directory of state, national, and other financial assistance programs), and education. www.redrover.org

Safe Place for Pets helps people find programs and safe housing for people and pets who need to escape domestic violence. www.safeplaceforpets.org

Beyond Breed is a New York–based organization that supports the bond between people and pets with local projects to provide pet care assistance and educational webinars to help others start similar programs in their communities. www.beyondbreed.com

Lotsa Helping Hands is a website to help you organize assistance for friends and family, so if someone in your life is recovering from surgery or facing other temporary setbacks that make it challenging for them to care for their animals (or themselves), you can easily coordinate meal delivery, rides to appointments, or dog walks. www.lotsahelpinghands.com

Pets of the Homeless is the only organization focused on ensuring that homeless families' pets receive food and vet care. www.petsofthehomeless.org

Chapter 27: Be the Change

Breathe and Relax

Moodtrack Diary graphs your moods to see how they're changing over time and identify any triggers that might signal that you need a break or extra support. www.moodtrack.com *App available for iOS and Android.*

Breathe2Relax walks you through breathing exercises to help decrease stress and anxiety. t2health.dcoe.mil/apps/breathe2relax *App available for iOS and Android.*

Headspace teaches you meditation and mindfulness, and how to apply them to everyday activities and different areas of your life that you'd like to improve. www.headspace.com *App available for iOS and Android.*

Get Organized

Evernote makes it easy to capture notes, checklists, attachments, and audio recordings on the go and across devices to help you get your life organized. www.evernote.com *App available for iOS and Android.*

SimpleMind is an easy-to-use mind mapping app to help you organize your thoughts, plan campaigns, and generate ideas for how you can help animals (or achieve whatever else you're going for). www.simplemind.eu *App available for iOS and Android.*

NOTES

Introduction

1 "Pets by the Numbers," Humane Society of the United States, accessed May 29, 2017, http://www
.humanesociety.org/issues/pet_overpopulation/facts/pet_ownership_statistics.html.

2 Toby G. Knowles, Steve C. Kestin, Susan M. Haslam, Steven N. Brown, Laura E. Green, Andrew
Butterworth, Stuart J. Pope, Dirk Pfeiffer, and Christine J. Nicol, "Leg Disorders in Broiler
Chickens: Prevalence, Risk Factors and Prevention," *PLoS ONE* 3, no. 2 (2008), doi:10.1371
/journal.pone.0001545.

Chapter 1: The Animals Need You

1 Natalie Angier, "Pigs Prove to Be Smart, If Not Vain," *New York Times*, November 9, 2009,
accessed May 21, 2017, http://www.nytimes.com/2009/11/10/science/10angier.html.

2 Julian Finn, Tom Tregenza, and Mark Norman, "Preparing the Perfect Cuttlefish Meal: Complex
Prey Handling by Dolphins," *PLoS ONE* 4, no. 1 (2009), doi:10.1371/journal.pone.0004217.

Chapter 2: Animal Advocacy 101

1 Julian K. Finn, Tom Tregenza, and Mark D. Norman, "Defensive Tool Use in a Coconut-Carrying
Octopus," *Current Biology* 19, no. 23 (2009), doi:10.1016/j.cub.2009.10.052.

2 Andrea Seabrook, "The Story of an Octopus Named Otto," *NPR, All Things Considered*,
November 2, 2008, accessed May 22, 2017, http://www.npr.org/templates/story/story.php?storyId
=96476905.

3 Dan Bilefsky, "Inky the Octopus Escapes From a New Zealand Aquarium," *New York Times*,
April 13, 2016, accessed May 22, 2017, https://www.nytimes.com/2016/04/14/world/asia/inky
-octopus-new-zealand-aquarium.html.

Chapter 3: Share the Love

1 G. Wegienka, C. C. Johnson, S. Havstad, D. R. Ownby, C. Nicholas, and E. M. Zoratti, "Lifetime
Dog and Cat Exposure and Dog- and Cat-Specific Sensitization at Age 18 Years," *Clinical &
Experimental Allergy* 41, no. 7 (2011): 979–86, doi:10.1111/j.1365-2222.2011.03747.x.

2 Goril Andreassen, Linda Catrine Stenvold, and Floyd W. Rudmin, "My Dog Is My Best Friend:
Health Benefits of Emotional Attachment to Pet Dog," *Psychology & Society* 5, no. 2 (2013):
6–23.

3 Karen Allen, Jim Blascovich, and Wendy B. Mendes, "Cardiovascular Reactivity and the Presence
of Pets, Friends, and Spouses: The Truth About Cats and Dogs," *Psychosomatic Medicine* 64, no. 5
(2002): 727–39, doi:10.1097/00006842-200209000-00005.

4 Christa L. Wilkin, Paul Fairlie, and Souha R. Ezzedeen, "Who Let the Dogs In?: A Look at
Pet-Friendly Workplaces," *International Journal of Workplace Health Management* 9, no. 1 (2016):
96–109, doi:10.1108/ijwhm-04-2015-0021.

5 "Part D. Chapter 2: Dietary Patterns, Foods and Nutrients, and Health Outcomes," *Scientific Report of the 2015 Dietary Guidelines Advisory Committee*, Office of Disease Prevention and Health Promotion, February 2015, https://health.gov/dietaryguidelines/2015-scientific-report/07 -chapter-2/.

Chapter 4: The Political Beast

1 "U.S. Endangered Species Act Protection Sought to Save Giraffes From Extinction," Center for Biological Diversity, April 19, 2017, accessed May 23, 2017, http://www.biologicaldiversity.org /news/press_releases/2017/giraffe-04-19-2017.php.

2 "White House Pets (1889–1953)," Presidential Pet Museum, January 25, 2017, accessed May 23, 2017, http://www.presidentialpetmuseum.com/whitehousepets-2/.

3 Ethan Trex, "White House Pets: Hippo, Gator and 'Satan,'" CNN, November 7, 2008, accessed May 23, 2017, http://www.cnn.com/2008/LIVING/wayoflife/11/07/mf.presidential.pets/index .html.

4 Jake Tapper, "Political Punch—'Dogs Against Romney'? Democrats Say Unleash the Hound!," ABC News, February 13, 2012, accessed May 23, 2017, http://abcnews.go.com/blogs/politics/2012 /02/political-punch-dogs-against-romney-democrats-say-unleash-the-hound/.

5 Jen Fifield, "Farmers Push Back Against Animal Welfare Laws," Pew Charitable Trusts, November 29, 2016, accessed May 23, 2017, http://www.pewtrusts.org/en/research-and-analysis /blogs/stateline/2016/11/29/farmers-push-back-against-animal-welfare-laws.

6 Lisa Held, "The Dairy Industry Takes on Alternative Milks," Civil Eats, March 1, 2017, accessed May 23, 2017, http://civileats.com/2017/02/13/the-dairy-industry-lashes-out-against-alternative -milks-with-dairy-pride-act/.

Chapter 5: Money Talks

1 Mindy Weisberger, "Saved by the Whale! Humpbacks Play Hero When Orcas Attack," Live Science, August 3, 2016, accessed May 22, 2017, http://www.livescience.com/55639-humpbacks -protect-when-killer-whales-attack.html.

2 Cliff Burrows, "Cochineal Extract Update," *Starbucks* (blog), April 12, 2012, http://blogs.starbucks .com/blogs/customer/archive/2012/04/19/cochineal-extract-update.aspx.

3 Gus Lubin, "McDonald's Twitter Campaign Goes Horribly Wrong #McDStories," *Business Insider*, January 24, 2012, accessed May 22, 2017, http://www.businessinsider.com/mcdonalds-twitter -campaign-goes-horribly-wrong-mcdstories-2012-1.

4 Katie Lobosco, "'Ask SeaWorld' Marketing Campaign Backfires," *CNN*, March 27, 2015, accessed May 22, 2017, http://money.cnn.com/2015/03/27/news/companies/ask-seaworld-twitter/.

Chapter 6: Compassion in the Classroom

1 Bradley E. Carlson and Tracy Langkilde, "Personality Traits Are Expressed in Bullfrog Tadpoles During Open-Field Trials," *Journal of Herpetology* 47, no. 2 (June 2013): 378–83, http://www .journalofherpetology.org/doi/abs/10.1670/12-061.

2 J. Akpan and J. Strayer, "Which Comes First the Use of Computer Simulation of Frog Dissection or Conventional Dissection as Academic Exercise?," *Journal of Computers in Mathematics and Science Teaching* 29, no. 2 (April 2010): 113–38.

3 James P. Lalley, Phillip S. Piotrowski, Barbara Battaglia, Keith Brophy, and Kevin Chugh, "A Comparison of V-Frog to Physical Frog Dissection," *International Journal of Environmental and Science Education* 5, no. 2 (April 2010): 189–200.

4 Darryl Fears, "One Last U.S. Medical School Still Killed Animals to Teach Surgery. But No More,"*Washington Post*, June 30, 2016, https://www.washingtonpost.com/news/animalia/ wp/2016/06/30/one-last-u-s-medical-school-still-killed-animals-to-teach-surgery-but -no-more/.

5 "Meatless Monday K-12," Meatless Monday, accessed May 24, 2017, http://www.meatlessmonday .com/meatless-monday-k-12/.

6 Joseph Price and David R. Just, "Lunch, Recess and Nutrition: Responding to Time Incentives in the Cafeteria," *Preventive Medicine* 71 (2015): 27–30, doi:10.1016/j.ypmed.2014.11.016.

Chapter 7: The Power of Words

1 "Research," Advocates for Snake Preservation, accessed May 23, 2017, https://www.snakes.ngo /research/.

2 Hugh Rawson, "Fowl Talk for Thanksgiving," *About Words* (blog), November 19, 2012, https://dictionaryblog.cambridge.org/2012/11/19/fowl-talk-for-thanksgiving/.

3 Brenna Ellison, Kathleen Brooks, and Taro Mieno, "Which Livestock Production Claims Matter Most to Consumers?," *Agriculture and Human Values* (2017): 1–13, doi:10.1007/s10460-017-9777-9.

4 Jonas R. Kunst and Sigrid M. Hohle, "Meat Eaters by Dissociation: How We Present, Prepare and Talk About Meat Increases Willingness to Eat Meat by Reducing Empathy and Disgust," *Appetite* 105 (2016): 758–74.

5 Uta Maria Jürgens and Paul M. W. Hackett, "The Big Bad Wolf: The Formation of a Stereotype," *Ecopsychology* 9, no. 1 (2017): 33–43, doi:10.1089/eco.2016.0037.

6 Carolyn L. Burke and Joby G. Copenhaver, "Animals as People in Children's Literature," *Language Arts* 81, no. 3 (January 2004): 205–13.

7 Marla Anderson and Antonia Henderson, "Pernicious Portrayals: The Impact of Children's Attachment to Animals of Fiction on Animals of Fact," *Society & Animals* 13, no. 4 (2005): 297–314, doi:10.1163/156853005774653645.

8 Sarah L. Stewart, "Best Vegetarian Restaurants in the U.S.," *Travel + Leisure,* accessed June 5, 2017, http://www.travelandleisure.com/slideshows/best-vegetarian-restaurants-in-the-us.

9 Helena Andrews-Dyer, "How Kanye West and Kim Kardashian West Ended Up at a Small Vegan Resto on Georgia Ave.," *Washington Post*, February 2, 2015, https://www.washingtonpost.com /news/reliable-source/wp/2015/02/02/how-kanye-west-and-kim-kardashian-west-ended-up-at-a -small-vegan-resto-on-georgia-ave/.

10 Alan Duke, "Pat Benatar, Beach Boys Join 'Blackfish' Cancellation List," *CNN*, January 16, 2014, http://www.cnn.com/2014/01/16/showbiz/blackfish-busch-gardens-cancellations/.

11 "Half of Americans Believe Celebrities Can Make a Positive Difference When They Support a Cause," Harris Poll, November 5, 2013, http://www.theharrispoll.com/health-and-life/Half_of _Americans_Believe_Celebrities_Can_Make_a_Positive_Difference_When_They_Support_a _Cause.html.

12 Valerie R. O'Regan, "The Celebrity Influence: Do People Really Care What They Think?," *Celebrity Studies* 5, no. 4 (2014): 469–83, doi:10.1080/19392397.2014.925408.

Chapter 8: Find Your Pack

1 C. N. Slobodchikoff, Andrea Paseka, and Jennifer L. Verdolin, "Prairie Dog Alarm Calls Encode Labels About Predator Colors," *Animal Cognition* 12, no. 3 (2009): 435–39.

Chapter 9: Green Is the New Black

1 "Countries Ranked by Ecological Footprint Per Capita (in Global Hectares)," Global Footprint Network, accessed May 26, 2017, http://www.footprintnetwork.org/content/documents/ecological _footprint_nations/ecological_per_capita.html.

2 C. P. Baldé, F. Wang, R. Kuehr, and J. Huisman, "The Global E-Waste Monitor," United Nations University, IAS—SCYCLE, Bonn, Germany, 2015.

3 "Pet Industry Market Size & Ownership Statistics," American Pet Products Association, accessed June 8, 2017, http://www.americanpetproducts.org/press_industrytrends.asp.

4 Jim Robbins, "Deadly Disease Is Suspected in Decline of Yellowstone Wolves," *New York Times*, January 15, 2006, http://www.nytimes.com/2006/01/15/us/deadly-disease-is-suspected-in-decline -of-yellowstone-wolves.html.

5 Kate Ravilious, "How Green Is Your Pet?" *New Scientist*, October 21, 2009, https://www .newscientist.com/article/mg20427311-600-how-green-is-your-pet/.

6 "Countries Ranked by Ecological Footprint Per Capita."

7 Phillippa Lally, Cornelia H. M. Van Jaarsveld, Henry W. W. Potts, and Jane Wardle, "How Are Habits Formed: Modelling Habit Formation in the Real World," *European Journal of Social Psychology* 40, no. 6 (2010): 998–1009.

Chapter 10: Conservation Uncaged

1 Campbell Robertson, "A Tiger, a Truck Stop, and a Pitched Legal Battle," *New York Times*, March 27, 2013, http://www.nytimes.com/2013/03/28/us/truck-stop-tiger-in-louisiana-stirs-legal -battle.html.

2 "Saving the California Condor," Center for Biological Diversity, accessed May 29, 2017, http://www.biologicaldiversity.org/species/birds/California_condor/index.html.

3 "Saving the Mexican Gray Wolf," Center for Biological Diversity, accessed May 29, 2017, http://www.biologicaldiversity.org/species/mammals/Mexican_gray_wolf/index.html.

4 Hugh McDiarmid Jr., "Detroit Zoo Elephants Going to a Refuge," *Detroit Free Press*, May 5, 2004, http://www.freep.com/story/news/local/michigan/oakland/2015/02/13/detroit-zoo-winky-wanda -refuge/23355697/.

5 *Poisoned Waters: How Cyanide Fishing and the Aquarium Trade Are Devastating Coral Reefs and Tropical Fish* (Tucson, AZ: Center for Biological Diversity, 2016).

Chapter 11: Neighborhood Bird-Watch

1 "So This Coyote Walks into a Quiznos . . . ," *Chicago Tribune*, April 4, 2007, http://articles .chicagotribune.com/2007-04-04/news/0704040747_1_coyote-anne-kent-bina-patel.

2 Scott R. Loss, Tom Will, and Peter P. Marra, "Corrigendum: The Impact of Free-ranging Domestic Cats on Wildlife of the United States," *Nature Communications* 4 (2013), doi:10.1038/ncomms3961.

3 "Saving the Monarch Butterfly," Center for Biological Diversity, accessed May 29, 2017, http://www.biologicaldiversity.org/species/invertebrates/monarch_butterfly/index.html.

4 Timothy Brown, Susan Kegley, and Lisa Archer, *Gardeners Beware: Bee-Toxic Pesticides Found in "Bee-Friendly" Plants Sold at Garden Centers Nationwide (Washington, D.C.: Friends of the Earth*, 2013), https://www.pesticideresearch.com/site/wp-content/uploads/2012/05/Gardeners-beware -report_8-13-13.pdf.

Chapter 12: Unplug Climate Change

1 Göran E. Nilsson, Danielle L. Dixson, Paolo Domenici, Mark I. McCormick, Christina Sørensen, Sue-Ann Watson, and Philip L. Munday, "Near-Future Carbon Dioxide Levels Alter Fish Behaviour by Interfering with Neurotransmitter Function," *Nature Climate Change* 2, no. 3 (2012): 201–04.

2 Chris D. Thomas, Alison Cameron, Rhys E. Green, Michel Bakkenes, Linda J. Beaumont, Yvonne C. Collingham, Barend F. N. Erasmus, Marinez Ferreira De Siqueira, Alan Grainger, Lee Hannah, Lesley Hughes, Brian Huntley, Albert S. Van Jaarsveld, Guy F. Midgley, Lera Miles, Miguel A. Ortega-Huerta, A. Townsend Peterson, Oliver L. Phillips, and Stephen E. Williams, "Extinction Risk from Climate Change," *Nature* 427, no. 6970 (2004): 145–48, doi:10.1038 /nature02121.

3 R. K. Pachauri and A. Reisinger, eds., *Climate Change 2007: Synthesis Report. Contribution of Working Groups I, II and III to the Fourth Assessment Report of the Intergovernmental Panel on Climate Change* (Geneva, Switzerland: IPCC, 2007).

4 Jhon Arbelaez, Shaye Wolf, and Andrew Grinberg, *On Shaky Ground: Fracking, Acidizing, and Increased Earthquake Risk in California* (Earthworks, Center for Biological Diversity, and Clean Water Action, 2014).

5 Galen L. Barbose and Naïm R. Darghouth, *Tracking the Sun IX: The Installed Price of Residential and Non-Residential Photovoltaic Systems in the United States*, report no. LBNL-1006036 (Berkeley, CA: Lawrence Berkeley National Laboratory, 2016).

6 Pierre Delforge, Lisa Schmidt, and Steve Schmidt, *Home Idle Load: Devices Wasting Huge Amounts of Electricity When Not in Active Use*, issue brief no. IP:15-03-A (New York: NRDC, 2015).

7 "Thermostats," Department of Energy, accessed May 28, 2017, https://energy.gov/energysaver /thermostats.

8 "Gas Mileage Tips," Fueleconomy.gov, accessed May 28, 2017, http://www.fueleconomy.gov/feg /drive.shtml.

Chapter 13: Plastic Detox

1 "Bottled Water and Energy Fact Sheet," Pacific Institute, February 2007, accessed May 28, 2017, http://pacinst.org/publication/bottled-water-and-energy-a-fact-sheet/.

2 World Economic Forum, Ellen MacArthur Foundation, and McKinsey & Company, *The New Plastics Economy: Rethinking the Future of Plastics* (Cowes, UK: Ellen MacArthur Foundation, 2016).

3 Chris Wilcox, Erik Van Sebille, and Britta Denise Hardesty, "Threat of Plastic Pollution to Seabirds Is Global, Pervasive, and Increasing," *Proceedings of the National Academy of Sciences* 112, no. 38 (2015): 11899–904, doi:10.1073/pnas.1502108112.

4 Oona M. Lönnstedt and Peter Eklöv, "Environmentally Relevant Concentrations of Microplastic Particles Influence Larval Fish Ecology," *Science* 352, no. 6290 (2016): 1213–16. doi:10.1126/ science.aad8828.

5 *Littering Behavior in America: Results of a National Study* (Stamford, CT: Keep America Beautiful, 2009).

6 "Global Plastic Production Rises, Recycling Lags," Worldwatch Institute, January 28, 2015, http://www.worldwatch.org/global-plastic-production-rises-recycling-lags-0.

7 "Products and the Environment," Hasbro, accessed May 29, 2017, https://csr.hasbro.com /sustainability/packaging-process.

8 Rebecca Smithers, "England's Plastic Bag Usage Drops 85% Since 5p Charge Introduced," *Guardian*, July 29, 2016, https://www.theguardian.com/environment/2016/jul/30/england-plastic -bag-usage-drops-85-per-cent-since-5p-charged-introduced.

9 Kate Bailey, "Be Straw Free Campaign, by Milo Cress," Eco-Cycle, accessed May 29, 2017, https://www.ecocycle.org/bestrawfree/.

10 "Results of the Bring Your Own Bag Ordinance," *San Jose City Hall*, accessed June 11, 2017, http://www.sanjoseca.gov/index.aspx?NID=5261.

11 Marisa Vasquez, Jen Carter, and Phil Valko, *Bottled Water Ban: Update 2015 (Saint Louis, MO: Washinton University)*, https://sustainability.wustl.edu/wp-content/uploads/2016/11/160118 _Bottle_Brief_Final.pdf.

Chapter 14: Down the Drain

1 Molly A. Maupin, Joan F. Kenny, Susan S. Hutson, John K. Lovelace, Nancy L. Barber, and Kristin S. Linsey, "Estimated Use of Water in the United States in 2010," *Circular*, 2014. doi:10.3133/cirl1405.

2 "What Is the Minimum Quantity of Water Needed?," World Health Organization, accessed May 29, 2017, http://www.who.int/water_sanitation_health/emergencies/qa/emergencies_qa5/en/.

3 "State Rainwater Harvesting Laws and Legislation," National Conference of State Legislatures, June 13, 2017, http://www.ncsl.org/research/environment-and-natural-resources/rainwater -harvesting.aspx.

4 M. M. Mekonnen and A. Y. Hoekstra, "Four Billion People Facing Severe Water Scarcity," *Science Advances* 2, no. 2 (2016), doi:10.1126/sciadv.1500323.

5 Benjamin I. Cook, Toby R. Ault, and Jason E. Smerdon, "Unprecedented 21st Century Drought Risk in the American Southwest and Central Plains," *Science Advances* 1, no. 1 (2015): e1400082.

6 "How We Use Water," EPA, March 24, 2017, https://www.epa.gov/watersense/how-we-use-water.

7 Howard Perlman, "Water Questions & Answers: How Much Water Does the Average Person Use at Home per Day?," USGS Water Science School, accessed May 29, 2017, https://water.usgs.gov/edu/qa -home-percapita.html.

8 Ibid.

9 *The Life Cycle of a Jean: Understanding the Environmental Impact of a Pair of Levi's 501 Jeans* (San Francisco, CA: Levi Strauss, 2015).

10 "Residential Toilets," EPA, April 19, 2017, https://www.epa.gov/watersense/residential-toilets.

11 "Repairing Your Leaking Toilets: Save Water and Stop Flushing Away Your Water Bill," New York City Department of Environmental Protection, accessed May 28, 2017, http://www.nyc.gov/html /dep/pdf/ways_to_save_water/toilet_brochure.pdf.

12 "Fix a Leak Week," EPA, April 12, 2017, https://www.epa.gov/watersense/fix-leak-week.

13 "Banish the Water Hog from Your Home," Don't Be a Drip, accessed June 1, 2017, http://dontbeadrip .org/.

14 "Bottled Water," International Bottled Water Association, accessed May 29, 2017, http://www .bottledwater.org/economics/bottled-water-market.

15 *Take Back the Tap: The Big Business Hustle of Bottled Water* (Washington, D.C.: Food & Water Watch, 2018).

16 Ibid.

17 *Michigan Citizens for Water Conservation vs. Nestlé Waters North America* (Court of Appeals of Michigan, November 29, 2005).

18 Daniel Ross, "6 Places Where Nestlé Is Threatening Local Communities with Its Bottled Water Plans," *Alternet*, December 13, 2016, http://www.alternet.org/environment/6-places-where-nestle -threatening-local-communities-its-bottled-water-plans.

19 A. Ertug Ercin, Maite M. Aldaya, and Arjen Y. Hoekstra, "The Water Footprint of Soy Milk and Soy Burger and Equivalent Animal Products," *Ecological Indicators* 18 (2012): 392–402.

Chapter 15: Take Extinction Off Your Plate

1 Henning Steinfeld, H. A. Mooney, F. Schneider, and L. E. Neville, "Livestock in a Changing Landscape," *Drivers, Consequences, and Responses* 1 (2010).

2 Henning Steinfeld, Pierre Gerber, Tom Wassenaar, Vincent Castel, Mauricio Rosales, and Cees De Haan, "Livestock's Long Shadow," in *Environmental Issues and Options (Rome: Food and Agriculture Organization of the United Nations*, 2006).

3 Cynthia Nickerson, Robert Ebel, Allison Borchers, and Fernando Carriazo, *Major Uses of Land in the United States, 2007* (Washington, D.C.: USDA Economic Research Service, 2011).

4 Jennifer Weeks, "Factory Farms," *CQ Researcher*, January 12, 2007, http://prairierivers.org/wp -content/uploads/2009/12/factory-farms.pdf.

5 John Robbins, *The Food Revolution* (San Francisco, CA: Conari, 2011), 238.

6 "2.7 Million Animals Killed by Federal Wildlife-destruction Program in 2016," Center for

Biological Diversity, March 14, 2017, https://www.biologicaldiversity.org/news/press_releases/2017/wildlife-services-03-14-2017.php.

7 Tracie McMillan, "The U.S. Doesn't Have Enough of the Vegetables We're Supposed to Eat," *NPR, Salt*, September 19, 2015, http://www.npr.org/sections/thesalt/2015/09/19/441494432/the-u-s-doesnt-have-enough-of-the-vegetables-were-supposed-to-eat.

8 Amy Harmon, "Retracting a Plug for Meatless Mondays," *New York Times*, July 25, 2012, http://www.nytimes.com/2012/07/26/us/usda-newsletter-retracts-a-meatless-mondays-plug.html.

9 Deena Shanker, "How Meat Producers Have Influenced Nutrition Guidelines for Decades," *Atlantic*, October 24, 2015, https://www.theatlantic.com/business/archive/2015/10/meat-industry-lobbying-political-nutrition/412243/.

10 "USDA Announces Plans to Purchase Surplus Cheese, Releases New Report Showing Trans-Pacific Partnership Would Create Growth for Dairy Industry," USDA, October 11, 2016, https://www.usda.gov/media/press-releases/2016/10/11/usda-announces-plans-purchase-surplus-cheese-releases-new-report.

11 USDI-BLM, USDA-Forest Service, *Rangeland Reform '94 Final Environmental Impact Statement* (Washington, D.C.: USDI-BLM, 1995).

12 FAO, *The State of World Fisheries and Aquaculture 2016: Contributing to Food Security and Nutrition for All* (Rome: Food and Agriculture Organization of the United Nations, 2016).

13 "Legal Petition Seeks Ban on Pacific Bluefin Tuna Fishing," April 9, 2014, Center for Biological Diversity, http://www.biologicaldiversity.org/news/press_releases/2014/pacific-bluefin-tuna-04-09-2014.html.

14 Amanda Keledjian, Gib Brogan, Beth Lowell, Jon Warrenchuck, Ben Enticknap, Greg Shester, Michael Hirshfield, and Dominique Cano-Stocco, *Wasted Catch: Unsolved Problems in U.S. Fisheries* (Washington, D.C.: Oceana, March 2014).

15 Center for Biological Diversity, "Genetically Engineered Seafood," accessed June 11, 2017, http://www.biologicaldiversity.org/campaigns/ge_seafood/index.html.

16 *A Roadmap to Reduce U.S. Food Waste by 20 Percent* (n.p.: ReFED, 2016).

17 Ibid.

18 *Food Wastage Footprint: Impacts on Natural Resources* (Rome: Food and Agriculture Organization of the United Nations, 2013).

19 Ibid.

20 *A Roadmap to Reduce U.S. Food Waste by 20 Percent.*

21 Ibid.

22 Ibid.

23 Christopher L. Weber and H. Scott Matthews, "Food-Miles and the Relative Climate Impacts of Food Choices in the United States," *Environmental Science & Technology* 42, no. 10 (2008): 3508–13, doi:10.1021/es702969f.

24 "Why We Need an Earth-friendly Diet," Take Extinction Off Your Plate, accessed May 28, 2017, http://www.takeextinctionoffyourplate.com/earth-friendly_diet.html.

Chapter 16: Let's Talk About Sex

1 *World Population Prospects: The 2015 Revision, Key Findings and Advance Tables*, working paper no. ESA/P/WP.241 (New York: United Nations, Department of Economic and Social Affairs, Population Division, 2015).

2 *Living Planet Report 2016: Risk and Resilience in a New Era* (Gland, Switzerland: WWF International, 2016).

3 E. Chivian and A. Bernstein, eds., *Sustaining Life: How Human Health Depends on Biodiversity* (New York: Oxford University Press, 2008).

4 Gilda Sedgh, Lori S. Ashford, and Rubina Hussain, *Unmet Need for Contraception in Developing Countries: Examining Women's Reasons for Not Using a Method (New York: Guttmacher Institute,* 2016), https://www.guttmacher.org/report/unmet-need-for-contraception-in-developing -countries.

5 Lindsay Abrams, "Alan Weisman: Just by Existing, We're Contributing to the Problem," *Salon,* September 24, 2013, http://www.salon.com/2013/09/24/alan_weisman_just_by_existing_were _contributing_to_the_problem/.

6 Lawrence B. Finer and Mia R. Zolna, "Declines in Unintended Pregnancy in the United States, 2008–2011," *New England Journal of Medicine* 374, no. 9 (2016): 843–52, doi:10.1056 /nejmsa1506575.

7 "The Human Foot Print—Journey of a Life Time," Greencontributor, accessed May 28, 2017, http://www.greencontributor.com/index.php/human-foot-print.html.

8 K. Kost and S. Henshaw, *U.S. Teenage Pregnancies, Births and Abortions, 2010: National and State Trends by Age, Race and Ethnicity* (New York: Guttmacher Institute, 2014).

9 Paul A. Murtaugh and Michael G. Schlax, "Reproduction and the Carbon Legacies of Individuals," *Global Environmental Change* 19, no. 1 (2009): 14–20, doi:10.1016/j.gloenvcha.2008.10.007.

Chapter 17: The Call of the Wild

1 *The Nielsen Total Audience Report: Q1 2016* (New York: Nielsen Company, 2016).

2 Neil E. Klepeis, William C. Nelson, Wayne R. Ott, John P. Robinson, Andy M. Tsang, Paul Switzer, Joseph V. Behar, Stephen C. Hern, and William H. Engelmann, "The National Human Activity Pattern Survey (NHAPS): A Resource for Assessing Exposure to Environmental Pollutants," *Journal of Exposure Science and Environmental Epidemiology* 11, no. 3 (2001): 231.

3 "2010 Census Urban and Rural Classification and Urban Area Criteria," U.S. Census Bureau, September 1, 2012, https://www.census.gov/geo/reference/ua/urban-rural-2010.html.

4 "Keep It in the Ground," Center for Biological Diversity, accessed May 29, 2017, http://www .biologicaldiversity.org/campaigns/keep_it_in_the_ground/index.html.

Chapter 18: The Animals Aren't Amused

1 "About Ric O'Barry," Ric O'Barry's Dolphin Project, accessed June 2, 2017, https://dolphinproject .net/about-us/about-ric-obarry/.

2 "Moving Ghost Town," ArtSlant, accessed June 2, 2017, https://www.artslant.com/ew/events/show /353307-moving-ghost-town.

3 "Aspen Art Museum Removes Live Tortoises from Controversial Exhibit," Center for Biological Diversity, August 26, 2014, http://www.biologicaldiversity.org/news/press_releases/2014/sulcata -tortoise-08-26-2014.html.

4 Gary Baum, "Animals Were Harmed: Hollywood's Nightmare of Death, Injury, and Secrecy Exposed," *Hollywood Reporter,* November 25, 2013, http://www.hollywoodreporter.com/feature/.

5 "American Humane Association Responds to the Hollywood Reporter," American Humane Association, November 25, 2013.

6 "Aspen Art Museum Removes Live Tortoises from Controversial Exhibit."

Chapter 19: Clean Conscience

1 Ben Vermaercke, Elsy Cop, Sam Willems, Rudi D'Hooge, and Hans P. Op De Beeck, "More Complex Brains Are Not Always Better: Rats Outperform Humans in Implicit Category-Based Generalization by Implementing a Similarity-Based Strategy," *Psychonomic Bulletin & Review* 21, no. 4 (2014): 1080–86, doi:10.3758/s13423-013-0579-9.

2 "About Cosmetics Animal Testing," Humane Society International, accessed June 1, 2017, http://www.hsi.org/issues/becrueltyfree/facts/about_cosmetics_animal_testing.html.

3 "Why This Matters—Cosmetics and Your Health," EWG's Skin Deep Cosmetics Database, accessed June 1, 2017, http://www.ewg.org/skindeep/2011/04/12/why-this-matters/.

4 Center for Food Safety and Applied Nutrition, "Product Testing-Animal Testing & Cosmetics," U.S. Food and Drug Administration, April 5, 2006, https://www.fda.gov/cosmetics /scienceresearch/producttesting/ucm072268.htm.

5 "Recommended Procedures Regarding the CPSC's Policy on Animal Testing," Consumer Product Safety Commission, November 26, 2012, https://www.cpsc.gov/Business—Manufacturing/Testing -Certification/Recommended-Procedures-Regarding-the-CPSCs-Policy-on-Animal-Testing/.

6 Cheryl Wischhover, "Why the U.S. Won't Ban Cosmetics Animal Testing Anytime Soon," *Fashionista*, January 30, 2015, https://fashionista.com/2015/01/us-cosmetics-animal-testing-ban.

7 Dana W. Kolpin, Edward T. Furlong, Michael T. Meyer, E. Michael Thurman, Steven D. Zaugg, Larry B. Barber, and Herbert T. Buxton, "Pharmaceuticals, Hormones, and Other Organic Wastewater Contaminants in U.S. Streams, 1999–2000: A National Reconnaissance," *Environmental Science & Technology* 36, no. 6 (2002): 1202–11, doi:10.1021/es011055j.

8 Chelsea M. Rochman, Sara M. Kross, Jonathan B. Armstrong, Michael T. Bogan, Emily S. Darling, Stephanie J. Green, Ashley R. Smyth, and Diogo Veríssimo, "Scientific Evidence Supports a Ban on Microbeads," *Environmental Science & Technology* 49, no. 18 (2015): 10759–61, doi:10.1021/acs .est.5b03909.

9 "Top 10 Pet Poisons," Pet Poison Helpline, accessed June 1, 2017, http://www.petpoisonhelpline .com/pet-owners/basics/top-10-pet-poisons/.

Chapter 20: What Not to Wear

1 J. Cerveny, S. Begall, P. Koubek, P. Novakova, and H. Burda, "Directional Preference May Enhance Hunting Accuracy in Foraging Foxes," *Biology Letters* 7, no. 3 (2011): 355–57, doi:10.1098/ rsbl.2010.1145.

2 Vlastimil Hart, Petra Nováková, Erich Pascal Malkemper, Sabine Begall, Vladimír Hanzal, Miloš Ježek, Tomáš Kušta, et al., "Dogs Are Sensitive to Small Variations of the Earth's Magnetic Field," *Frontiers in Zoology* 10, no. 1 (2013): 80.

3 Lauren Etter, "Slowing Economy Pelts the Global Fur Business," *Wall Street Journal*, February 12, 2009, https://www.wsj.com/articles/SB123439872449675207.

4 "World Production of Mink Drops," Kopenhagen Fur, June 15, 2016, http://www.kopenhagenfur .com/news/2016/june/world-production-of-mink-drops.

5 "Domestication and Natural Behaviour of the Farmed Mink," Fur Europe, September 23, 2015.

6 "HSUS to FTC: Take Action Against 17 Retailers That Sold Animal Fur as 'Faux Fur,'" Humane Society of the United States, August 9, 2016, http://www.humanesociety.org/news/press_releases /2016/08/hsus-ftc-action-against-fur-retailers-080916.html.

7 Alasdair Carmichael, "Man-Made Fibers Continue To Grow," *Textile World*, February 3, 2015, http://www.textileworld.com/textile-world/fiber-world/2015/02/man-made-fibers-continue-to-grow/.

8 Imogen E. Napper and Richard C. Thompson, "Release of Synthetic Microplastic Plastic Fibres from Domestic Washing Machines: Effects of Fabric Type and Washing Conditions." *Marine Pollution Bulletin* 112, nos. 1–2 (2016): 39–45, doi:10.1016/j.marpolbul.2016.09.025.

9 "The Story of Microfibers—FAQs," Story of Stuff Project, February 28, 2017, http://storyofstuff.org /uncategorized/the-story-of-microfibers-faqs/.

10 "The Facts About Textile Waste," Council for Textile Recycling, accessed June 2, 2017, http://www .weardonaterecycle.org/about/issue.html.

11 Doreen Cubie, "Cotton and Pesticides," National Wildlife Federation, February 1, 2006, https://www.nwf.org/News-and-Magazines/National-Wildlife/Green-Living/Archives/2006 /Cotton-and-Pesticides.aspx.

12 "The Facts About Textile Waste."

13 Lauren Indvik, "What Really Happens to Your Clothing Donations?," *Fashionista*, January 20, 2016, https://fashionista.com/2016/01/clothing-donation.

14 Elizabeth Cline, "Where Does Discarded Clothing Go?," *Atlantic*, July 18, 2014, https://www.theatlantic.com/business/archive/2014/07/where-does-discarded-clothing-go/374613/.

Chapter 21: Old MacDonald Lost His Farm

1 Maria Godoy, "Moo-d Music: Do Cows Really Prefer Slow Jams?," *NPR, Salt*, March 6, 2014, http://www.npr.org/sections/thesalt/2014/03/06/285314648/secret-life-of-cows-part-deux-milking-mood-music.

2 "How Many Adults in the U.S. Are Vegetarian and Vegan?," Vegetarian Resource Group, accessed June 1, 2017, http://www.vrg.org/nutshell/Polls/2016_adults_veg.htm.

3 W. J. Craig, "Position of the American Dietetic Association: Vegetarian Diets," *Journal of the American Dietetic Association* 109, no. 7 (2009): 1266–82, doi:10.1016/j.jada.2009.05.027.

4 Sean Carmody, "Factory Farming," Last Chance for Animals, accessed June 1, 2017, http://www.lcanimal.org/index.php/campaigns/other-issues/factory-farming.

5 Kat Hannaford, "Russian Cows Watch Samsung LED TV While You're Stuck With Your 32-Inch Coby," Gizmodo, March 23, 2010, http://gizmodo.com/5499955/russian-cows-watch-samsung-led-tv-while-youre-stuck-with-your-32-inch-coby.

6 "Grass Fed Marketing Claim Standard," USDA Agricultural Marketing Service, accessed June 1, 2017, https://www.ams.usda.gov/grades-standards/beef/grassfed.

7 Chase Purdy, "In Four Years, the Price of Lab-Grown 'Meat' Has Fallen by 96%. There's Still a Long Way to Go," *Quartz*, June 5, 2017, https://qz.com/997565/in-four-years-the-price-of-lab-grown-meat-has-fallen-by-96-theres-still-a-long-way-to-go/.

8 Sarah Marsh and *Guardian* Readers, "The Rise of Vegan Teenagers: 'More People Are into It Because of Instagram,'" *Guardian*, May 27, 2016, https://www.theguardian.com/lifeandstyle/2016/may/27/the-rise-of-vegan-teenagers-more-people-are-into-it-because-of-instagram.

9 "Compassion Over Killing Meatless Mondays Program," Compassion Over Killing, accessed June 1, 2017, http://cok.net/camp/meatless-mondays/.

Chapter 22: Holiday Hangover

1 Jimmy Stamp, "American Myths: Benjamin Franklin's Turkey and the Presidential Seal," *Smithsonian*, January 25, 2013, http://www.smithsonianmag.com/arts-culture/american-myths-benjamin-franklins-turkey-and-the-presidential-seal-6623414/.

2 "Turkey History & Trivia," National Turkey Federation, accessed June 2, 2017, http://www.eatturkey.com/why-turkey/history.

3 *Energy Savings Estimates of Light Emitting Diodes in Niche Lighting Applications* (Washington, D.C.: Department of Energy, 2008).

4 Dan Kedmey, "Should You Eat Turkey or Ham This Christmas?: An Analysis," *Time*, December 24, 2014, http://time.com/3646915/christmas-turkey-ham-dinner/.

5 "Consumption Stats," National Hot Dog and Sausage Council, accessed June 2, 2017, http://www.hot-dog.org/media/consumption-stats.

6 Pablo Paster, "Ask Pablo: Holiday Wrapping Paper," *Treehugger*, December 21, 2010, https://www.treehugger.com/culture/ask-pablo-holiday-wrapping-paper.html.

Chapter 23: Don't Get Catfished

1 "Pets by the Numbers," Humane Society of the United States, accessed May 29, 2017, http://www.humanesociety.org/issues/pet_overpopulation/facts/pet_ownership_statistics.html.

2 Ibid.

Chapter 24: If You See Something, Say Something

1 Amy Victoria Smith, Leanne Proops, Kate Grounds, Jennifer Wathan, and Karen McComb, "Functionally Relevant Responses to Human Facial Expressions of Emotion in the Domestic Horse," *Biology Letters* 12, no. 2 (2016), doi:10.1098/rsbl.2015.0907.

2 C. McLaren, "Heat Stress from Enclosed Vehicles: Moderate Ambient Temperatures Cause Significant Temperature Rise in Enclosed Vehicles," *Pediatrics* 116, no. 1 (2005), doi:10.1542/peds.2004-2368.

Chapter 25: The Ambassador of Dogville

1 Guo-Dong Wang, Weiwei Zhai, He-Chuan Yang, Ruo-Xi Fan, Xue Cao, Li Zhong, Lu Wang, Fei Liu, Hong Wu, Lu-Guang Cheng, Andrei D. Poyarkov, Nikolai A. Poyarkov Jr, Shu-Sheng Tang, Wen-Ming Zhao, Yun Gao, Xue-Mei Lv, David M. Irwin, Peter Savolainen, Chung-I Wu, and Ya-Ping Zhang, "The Genomics of Selection in Dogs and the Parallel Evolution between Dogs and Humans," *Nature Communications* 4 (2013): 1860, doi:10.1038/ncomms2814.

2 Gary J. Patronek, Jeffrey J. Sacks, Karen M. Delise, Donald V. Cleary, and Amy R. Marder, "Co-Occurrence of Potentially Preventable Factors in 256 Dog Bite-Related Fatalities in the United States (2000–2009)," *Journal of the American Veterinary Medical Association* 243, no. 12 (2013): 1726–36, doi:10.2460/javma.243.12.1726.

3 Ken Foster, *The Dogs Who Found Me: What I've Learned from Pets Who Were Left Behind* (Guilford, CT: Lyons Press, 2016).

Chapter 26: Unconditional Love

1 "FAQs," Pets of the Homeless, accessed June 2, 2017, https://www.petsofthehomeless.org/about-us/faqs/.

2 Barbara W. Boat and Juliette C. Knight, "Experiences and Needs of Adult Protective Services Case Managers When Assisting Clients Who Have Companion Animals," *Journal of Elder Abuse & Neglect* 12, nos. 3–4 (2001): 145–55.

3 Frank R. Ascione, Claudia V. Weber, and David S. Wood, "The Abuse of Animals and Domestic Violence: A National Survey of Shelters for Women Who Are Battered," *Society & Animals* 5, no. 3 (1997): 205–218.

4 Cheryl L. Currie, "Animal Cruelty by Children Exposed to Domestic Violence,"*Child Abuse & Neglect* 30, no. 4 (2006): 425–35.

5 Marita Mike, "Katrina's Animal Legacy: The PETS Act," *Journal of Animal Law & Ethics* 4 (2011): 133–205.

6 *Hurricane Katrina: Perceptions of the Affected* (San Francisco, CA: Fritz Institute, 2006), http://www.fritzinstitute.org/PDFs/findings/Hurricanekatrina_Perceptions.pdf.

7 Maryann Mott, "Katrina's Pet Legacy: Better Evacuation Plans, Bitter Custody Lawsuits," *National Geographic*, August 21, 2006, http://news.nationalgeographic.com/news/2006/08/060821-katrina-pets.html

8 Ibid.

INDEX